Publisher and wholesale inquiries: Storyteller Media, www.storyteller.media

This memoir reflects the author's present recollections of experiences over time. To adapt the author's recollections and the character interviews that corroborate the author's expressed experiences, some names and characteristics have been changed, some events have been compressed, locations have been altered, and dialogue has been recreated.

Storyteller Media and its logo are trademarks of Storyteller Media LLC, a joint venture with Gungnir Entertainment LLC, and the literary company of Curiosity Entertainment LLC

Cover design & Book layout design by Mohamed Samah

ISBN 9798999529954

Edited by Charles Allen

Publisher and wholesale enquiries:
www.storyteller.media

Distributed by macmillan

Printed in China

First Edition: 2025

CONTENT

AUTHORS' NOTE

What you're about to read is the most honest account I can give of the events that changed my life and helped shape a global market worth over $180 billion today.

This isn't an easy story to tell – not because the facts are unclear but because they're uncomfortable. Writing this book forced me to confront my own reflection: the decisions I made, the character flaws I carried, the behaviors I'm not proud of. As a young entrepreneur, I was bold and brash – at times, selfish and driven by avarice. In my pursuit of success, I often hurt the people I loved most without even knowing it.

This is me telling the story as it was, not as I wish it had been.

This book took me years to write because I was afraid, afraid to speak up, afraid of blowback from powerful people in high places – politicians, corporations, the machinery that holds them together – but I'm not here to make accusations or seek revenge. I'm here to tell my truth.

What you'll find is a look behind the curtain at how business, law, and politics operate in the shadows. Two public figures mentioned in this book have since resigned from office amid unrelated controversies. I make no claims about them beyond what I personally experienced.

For too long, my silence allowed others to control the narrative. Their version became the official story, but it never matched what really happened.

I wrote this book for my children so they would know the truth; for the employees who were affected by this situation and never understood what happened to them; for the thousands of people left scratching their heads – Wall Street bankers, insurance agents throughout the world, fellow YPO members, industry professionals who watched something they'd invested in simply vanish without explanation.

I'm not without flaws, and I have regrets, namely that I placed, at times, ambition, greed, and a competitive spirit ahead of my more noble intention: bringing dignity to people at the end of their lives.

This book is my way of giving those people the answers they deserve and reclaiming our narrative. It's time to set the record straight.

PROLOGUE

I rode in the passenger seat as the truck headlights cut through the pitch-dark morning, unsure whether I would ever see my family again. We said our goodbyes, but my wife's parents, Mr. and Mrs. Hull, still insisted on driving us to the airport.

The clock on the dash displayed a few minutes after five o'clock. Dick gripped the steering wheel of his red double-cabin dually truck with bloodless knuckles, silently driving us toward a faint light emanating from the private jet that waited for us on the otherwise empty tarmac. My wife, Tammy, rode in the back cabin of the truck. Our youngest daughter, Sydney, rode cradled in Tammy's arms, and Cole sat beside his grandmother, barely old enough to ride without a car seat. I tried to catch Tammy's attention as she stared out the window, but her thoughts were elsewhere. Judging from the worry lines that creased her brow, I assumed she was dreading our future and our kids' future. What will this new life be like for them?

My stomach tightened. The thought of what I was putting them through and the separation anxiety I already felt from leaving the rest of my family behind stabbed into me like knives, twisting deeper the closer we got to leaving our old lives behind.

Two pilots approached us from the Cessna Citation CJ2 jet, and I quickly stepped forward to meet them. I projected my voice out into the cold, crisp air of the morning with as much confidence as I could muster. "Hi, fellas. I'm Max." I said, giving them a fake name.

The lead pilot, a tall and lean man, responded, looking up from his clipboard like I'm just the next box to check on his pre-flight protocol, "We're making our final checks here. Do you have much luggage, Max?"

"Yes, sir. I gotta apologize upfront. We brought a lot of stuff,

mostly for the kids. We're going to be gone for a while. I hope I don't
throw off your maximum weight load," I responded, nervously looking back to the mound of suitcases filling the truck bed, soon to be
our only worldly possessions.

The pilot tightened his lip, exhaling his frustrations. "We'll try to
make it work."

The heavier the load, the more fuel we'd burn, and the pilots
and I both wanted to make sure we reached our refuel destination
near the Texas/Mexico border without incident. Tammy handed me
Sydney in her baby carriage. She looked up to me with her big blue
eyes, unaware of the danger we were in. I rocked her carriage side
to side, more to ease my own anxiety than hers, as the pilots loaded
our baggage into the fuselage. I had never seen so much luggage
loaded onto a small plane in all the days I had flown. We may have
to get some string to tie around that door, I think to myself. After the
pilot stuffed the last bag into the plane's nose, which at that point
looked like an overstuffed trunk of a car, the sweat-ridden lead pilot
approached me, wiping his forehead with his sleeve. "Is that the last
bag, Max?"

"Yes, sir. Are we okay?"

"We're at capacity," he admitted, and then with a hint of concern
he added, "should be able to make it...as long as the weather holds
up." Suddenly, he looked around, scanning the tarmac and asked,
"Where is Mr. Turak?"

"Oh, I almost forgot to tell you. He called me late last night to let
me know he can't make the trip with us. He said he'll catch up with
us in Mexico." The pilot looked perplexed. I became nervous that
this was going to become an insurmountable hurdle. I knew that a
flight plan had been called into the FAA, listing all the parties, including Jeff Turak, a family friend who booked the flight for me using his
passport because using mine was no longer an option. A ghostwriter
I hired a few months back had introduced me to an ex-CIA operative
who promised he could make me, Tammy, and the kids all disappear.
Based on his guidance, all of the names listed on the flight plan were
fake, except for Mr. Turak. I know the FAA office was closed at this

time of the morning, and if we couldn't leave as scheduled, we might never have made it out of the country.

The pilot stepped away to talk with his co-pilot, looking back in my direction. I held my breath in anticipation as I tried to swallow the lump forming in my throat. I could see it in his expression. He was going to say we can't take off until we get new clearance from the FAA. That was not a risk I could afford to take. The pilot ambled back toward me and said, "Max, we ..."

I interrupted him, saying, "We don't have time to waste. Look, I know this is unorthodox, but I've got something that'll make it worth your while." I reached in my pocket, pulled out an encased Mickey Mantle Rookie Card, and handed it to the pilot. "I'm certain this will cover any inconvenience we may be causing you," heavily insinuating that he defies protocol and get us into the air immediately.

The man observed the card, tensing his jaw while he considered my offer.

It's worth more than a lottery ticket in some states if he knows how to sell it, I thought, silently urging him to just take the card and get us the hell out of here. Money no longer had the same meaning to me that it once did. I had chosen money over my family too often in my past – not anymore. Things will be different now. I swear it will.

He looked me over, sucking his teeth. He glanced over my shoulder to Tammy and the kids. He clicked his tongue with finality and almost imperceptibly shook his head in agreement, digesting the whole event. As his head nod became more pronounced, he tucked the card away in his jacket pocket and said, "Alright, but we've gotta go now."

As the pilots climbed into the plane's cockpit, the tears started free flowing, uncontrollably, from my wife and me, the only ones on-board who understood the gravity of our exile flight. If the pilots had been paying attention, they would have found such behavior strange. I stood there, motionless, holding my baby girl in her carriage by the rubber-gripped handle. I didn't want to take another step toward the plane, but I was out of options. We had to get on this flight. My son, who had flown in the baby carriage many times before, stood beside me, looking to me for guidance. I grabbed his hand and approached the plane while Tammy hugged her parents one last time. Climbing up the small steps to board the aircraft, I was hit with the excruciating emotional pain of separating from our families. I loaded the kids into their seats on the small but well-appointed aircraft and forced myself not to look back as Jeff and Terri Sue waved to us from the tarmac. Tammy sat down next to me in the window seat, and we didn't even make eye contact, both mentally exhausted, with faces streaked with tears. I wanted to continue crying, but I didn't think I was capable of producing even one more tear.

The pilot closed the cabin door, and suddenly our problems seemed to be shut out with the door's latch. I'm not sure what awaited us next, though I was certain our quality of life would be better than what we were leaving behind.

The pilots initiated the plane's engine, and we began to speed down the runway, faster with each passing moment. The plane began to lift off, ascending from the runway. Tammy sat silently, staring out the plane's window as the Michigan landscape stretched out below us, sprawling and green. I reached out for Tammy's hand that dangled from her armrest beside me. I'm not great at expressing my emotions, so I squeezed her hand in mine, trying to let her know how much I loved her and reassure her that everything would be okay. She turned her head from the window, meeting my eyes while resting her head against the cushions of the leather seat. We both let out a long overdue sigh of relief. As we looked into each other's eyes, it became clear to me that she was my entire world at that moment and I was hers. From this point forward, we had to become a tighter team. If we didn't, it could cost us everything, everything that mattered anyway. I had never relied on another human being like I was about to with my wife. This was a time for renewed beginnings, for our lives and our relationship. As I looked into Tammy's cool, blue eyes, she looked at me in a way that reminded me of how she looked at me on our wedding day – full of hope, love, and a fair amount of uncertainty about our future.

As the plane rose higher, I suddenly felt like I was having an out-of-body experience. The stress and pressure from the past few years had been more than most people ever encounter in a lifetime. I don't wish that stress on even my worst enemies...well, maybe a few. The higher we rose in altitude, the more liberated from my past I began to feel. The aircraft peaked through the clouds, and the cabin filled with a brilliant light, as if the heavens parted to give us a glimpse of the incredible illumination people talk about seeing in the afterlife. As we rose above the clouds, the problems down below felt far behind us. For the first time in over three years, the weight of the world felt as if it was lifting from my shoulders.

The hypnotic hum of the engines quickly lulled Sydney fast asleep in her bassinet. Tammy reclined Cole's seat, wrapped him in a blanket, and secured him with the seatbelt.

"Gracias," Cole responds.

Tammy and I looked at each other, wide-eyed with disbelief, checking to see if we both heard the same thing. Some things in life can't be explained. Our four-year-old suddenly speaking Spanish was something I doubt I'll ever be able to explain.

Exhausted from the stress, Tammy and I began to fade off to sleep. After a much-needed three-hour nap, I awoke abruptly from the turbulence of the plane's landing flaps being deployed. As if someone stepped on the breaks, the plane grabbed the air, thrusting me forward. I had experienced this procedure hundreds of times in our small jet when in landing mode. I checked my watch. We were ahead of schedule. I looked out the window to a brown and barren landscape and assumed we were in Texas. Something didn't feel right.

The lead pilot turned in his seat in the cockpit to face us in the cabin and announced, "We're preparing to land. We've got to make a stop to refuel earlier than expected."

I started to worry. Is someone forcing him to land the plane early? Tammy noticed my concern, and I tried to reassure her with a quick smile. I swallowed the lump in my throat and asked the pilot, "What's the trouble?"

The lead pilot waved off my question with a reassuring hand gesture and responded, "The weather didn't hold up. Just hang tight, okay?"

Hang tight? If I hang any tighter, I might as well be preparing to parachute out of this fucking plane. I glanced out the window again and barely saw a cloud in the sky. Is he setting me up?

Tammy took my hand in hers and asked, "Everything okay?"

"Yeah. Uh huh. Shouldn't be a problem." I took a deep breath and tried to calm myself down. My knees started to bounce with jitters. I scanned the inside of the plane's cabin and started to feel claustrophobic, like I was in a flying cage. Are the Feds going to be waiting for me here?

The plane bounced with turbulence again, this time harder than before, waking our daughter. She began to cry, wailing loudly in the tiny space of the cabin. I assumed her ears hurt as the plane continued descending to the airport runway. I leaned over Tammy, toward the window, to better observe the airport, worried that unmarked cars with cheap hubcaps might be waiting for us to land. As we approached, I began to make out the airplane hangars along the runway and a few planes scattered across the tarmac and the airport plane lot. Cars filled the parking lot, just outside the airport grounds. A few cars sat parked beside our runway, and from this height, I couldn't tell whether the cars were black or dark blue. I suddenly became painfully aware of Sydney's shrill cries. They rang in my ears like a power drill cutting through concrete, intensifying my own anxiety.

I looked over to my son sitting in his seat. He was watching me intensely. I realized that I had been holding my breath and gripping Tammy's hand. I was squeezing it like a stress ball, way harder than I should have. I relaxed my grip, embarrassed, and said, "Sorry. Didn't realize what I was doing."

She continued holding my hand and tightened her grip. She looked into my eyes and said, "I know, Steve. We're in this together, remember?"

A sinking feeling dropped down from my chest into the pit of my stomach. How could I let it come to this? She doesn't deserve this; my kids don't deserve this. Hell, I've made plenty of mistakes, but I damn sure don't deserve it either.

I had only just left my in-laws that morning and my mom, dad, brother, sister, nieces, and nephews late the night before when we all stayed up together, sitting around a fire, sharing stories and memories and trying not to dread the future that awaited me, Tammy, and the kids. Sometimes it helps to look back at the past when we're afraid to move forward.

The plane hit a pocket of air, drifting us higher momentarily. I suddenly remembered the rush of the wind when I was a kid, running through the green hills of Appalachia around the property of my family's salvage yard in West Liberty, Kentucky, a town of only three thousand people. I thought of all the times I pushed my body and my mind to the breaking point to propel myself over the bar to become a state champion pole vaulter, the first person to ever win a state title in that small county. I applied the same relentless drive and competitive spirit to every aspect of my life, especially business. I built a billion-dollar company at the pinnacle of the multi-billion-dollar industry that I founded. I did it all with little more than sheer will and unwavering determination. The obstacles ahead of me didn't matter. If something or someone was in my way, then, by God, I would overcome it or crush it down to size because I wanted to be the best. I always had. I probably always will.

My memories provided me a much-needed boost of confidence. The plane descended lower, barely hovering above the runway. I scanned for the unmarked cars but couldn't find them anymore. Where are they?

Cole sat upright in his seat, still watching my every move. I sat back in my chair and tried to slow my racing heartrate. My face began to flush hot, and I could feel beads of sweat rising around the collar of my oxford shirt. My mouth was dry as I responded to Tammy, saying, "That's right. We're in this together now."

PART ONE
THE BUSINESS OF LIFE AND DEATH

A viatical settlement (from the Latin "viaticum") is the sale of a policy owner's existing life insurance policy to a third party for more than its cash surrender value but less than its net death benefit. Such a sale provides the policy owner with a lump sum.

KELLER:

In 1981, just as I prepared to enter college, scientists started to observe rampant cases of rare skin cancer, initially prevalent in gay men. As they probed the causes of cancer, they discovered a hideous new disease that compromised the immune system as it allowed cancer to take hold. Finally, as they discovered an expanding number of cases outside of the gay community, the Center for Disease Control knew they had a new and deadly virus on their hands: AIDS.

Just how AIDS came about, no one was exactly sure, but evidence showed that the virus made its way to America as early as 1969 through a single male who returned home after traveling to Haiti. By the early '80s, people lived in mortal fear of contracting this new disease, especially members within the gay community. Some gay friends of mine told me how the paranoia in the community destroyed friendships, broke up couples and caused a lifetime of pain as significant others died.

The thing was, AIDS was never just a "gay" disease, but early in discovery, the virus was labeled as such in the media. I was always amazed that the media portrayed itself as the most tolerant of all perspectives; however, in reality, American media contributed to the fear, paranoia, and alienation more than any other source. As we now know, AIDS was a virus able to be transferred through blood, so anyone could contract the new virus. Before there were tests, AIDS found its way into the blood supply and infected thousands of new patients, indiscriminately, across all populations and genders.

Despite the widespread and unbiased nature of the virus, our culture at the time viewed AIDS as a gay disease. Anyone who became HIV positive faced not only social out casting, but outright denial of fundamental human rights. During the crisis, multi-national insurance companies saw an opportunity to make money. That was their business, after all: to make money off of people's lives and deaths. That was, and still is to this day, their business model, and profiting on death is one of the most lucrative businesses in the history of mankind. Despite insurance company's best marketing efforts to convince clients "they are on their side," the entire industry profits on fear—selling the façade security. Health insurance companies often deny legitimate health claims when insurance holders are most in need. Auto insurance companies drop people for minor fender benders or hike rates beyond affordable coverage. The life insurance industry is even more callous in their calculated efforts to avoid paying death benefits.

Here is the brutal truth: life insurance companies don't care about you or your family. That isn't to say individual insurance salespeople or business executives don't want to help people. However, very few of those who actually care are empowered to make life-or-death decisions for their clients. Those with the real power are looking to the bottom line; it's why they exist. I know this information because I was once one of those high-level insurance industry executives. As CEO of a multi-national insurance firm, my approach to business was very different than most of my colleagues...but more on that in due time.

I can't tell you how many times I've sat across boardroom tables from insurance executives who actually laughed at denying people coverage. The stories told to me by insurance executives with the most pride were how they came up with creative ways to get around the law to deny contracted payouts to save their company money. Eventually, I made it my business to ensure every life insurance policy benefit was paid by the insurance companies – and paid in full. Such an idea made me popular with some people and hated by others.

When it came to the AIDS crisis, health insurance companies began to deny patients health claims, forcing sick patients to pay for the expensive medicine out of their pockets. As expected, the process and expense of attempting experimental drugs were soul crushing.

Many attempted a new drug that entered the market called AZT, and some may remember how quickly those patients passed away. Chemotherapy was implemented for those who contracted cancer, and hospice care drove people into bankruptcy. Desperate, AIDS patients tried to figure out what to do; there didn't seem to be any viable alternatives. Families, lovers, and friends mortgaged homes, sold possessions, and worked three jobs to pay the bills.

Finally, many of them hit on an idea of going around cancer patient circles; most of the successful AIDS patients bought life insurance policies before they got sick. Someone came up with the idea to treat life insurance policies like any other commodity. That is, they could sell the policy to a broker and get cash up front. When the people passed on, the broker would collect the money from the insurance companies. The people who sold the policies got money to pay their medical bills, and brokers made millions as the beneficiaries, or selling the rights, when the policies came due. It seemed like a win-win that solved everyone's problem.

THE BUSINESS OF LIFE AND DEATH

Gray surrounded me as I leaned back in an office chair, feeling suffocated inside my eight-by-eight gray fabric cubicle. I spent my working hours trying to finagle a deal over the phone as a stockbroker with Dean Witter in its Lexington, Kentucky office. I passed the downtime between trades and phone calls scraping together other business opportunities. *My time here is only temporary,* I reminded myself, nearly every few minutes each day. Between phone calls, I would click idly at the mouse and scroll through endless streams of stock quotes, thinking, *I will get out of here. I will start my own company someday. I will.*

A familiar face popped into sight above one of my four gray walls, the guy who worked in the neighboring cubicle, Chris Conway. His shaggy jet-black hair framed his tanned face as he peered down over the cubicle with a grim expression. His stern jawline and piercing eyes reminded me of Lou Diamond Phillip's character, Chavez, from the film Young Guns.

"Hey, Keller." He said.

"Yeah, what's up, Chavez?" I chided.

"Come on, Keller. Knock it off with the Chavez bit."

I found his discomfort funny and burst out laughing.

He shook his head, unamused, and said, "Listen, have you heard about this viatical stuff?"

"No, what is it?"

"You mean you haven't heard?! And here I thought you stayed up on the latest trends. The world is changing, my friend. This AIDS epidemic is shaking things up."

I shrugged, nodding my head, anxious for him to move on to another topic. Anything was better than talking about AIDS. "Okay," I said, "so what's the breaking news?"

Chris quickly looked over his shoulder to make sure our supervisor wasn't watching and then entered my cubicle. In a hushed tone, as if concerned that our co-workers might have overheard him, he said, "People are selling their life insurance policies to third-party brokers. A policyholder gets money upfront, then someone else cashes in when the policy comes due."

"You mean when the policyholder dies?"

"Yep." He said, raising his eyebrows with excitement as he sipped his coffee.

"So, wait, how does the broker get the money, and how is this even legal?"

"Well, as for legal, the laws are fuzzy enough or just plain nonexistent. No one has really thought about this concept before the AIDS stuff."

I nodded as the wheels in my mind began spinning...the possibilities... the numbers...the potential scope and scale of what a business based on the concept of buying and selling life insurance could become. I squeezed a stress ball with white knuckles, a habit I grew accustomed to when I needed to relieve excess anxiety. When I didn't, my nerves would race, tension would accumulate, and I would clench my jaw—or let out the stress in other, unhealthier ways.

Curious and excited, I pushed Chris for more details. "So, essentially, the person sells the beneficiary rights of their policy, right?"

"Correct. The seller simply adjusts who is to benefit from the policy when a patient dies."

"And they are doing this so they can pay their bills?"

Chris leaned against one of the cubicle walls, trying his best to look casual. He took a slow sip of his coffee and watched me over the rim of the cup, forcing me to wait with anticipation. "You got it," he finally said, "and that's the beauty of it, Keller. Life Insurance companies plan for about ninety percent of all policies to lapse due to lack of payment. People get old or sick or lose track of their expenses, and they miss a payment or two. Next thing they know, that policy they paid into for a lifetime gets canceled. That's the life insurance, business model."

"You got to be shitting me, Chris. You mean to tell me they do it on purpose?"

"A hundred-billion-dollar bottom line – why not? No law tells them they can't deny claims."

I shook my head in disbelief and repositioned my seat closer to Chris, anxious to hear what he would say next.

"With this AIDS outbreak, it's even worse. Health insurers are dropping coverage on AIDS patients left and right. People are mortgaging houses, and their family members are taking on extra jobs to help cover hospital bills, not to mention the cost of the drug treatments. Hell, that's a whole other story. The treatments cost thousands of dollars, and they might as well be a prescription for a quick death sentence."

"Chris, there's nothing right about any of this."

"Hey, that's the insurance business for you. What do you expect? They're in it for the money. Wouldn't you be?"

My jaw tensed. I began grinding my teeth as I considered, and then said, "Well, no, I don't think I would be."

Chris chuckled. "Easy to say when we're on the outside looking in."

I imagined what it looked like from the other side, from the top of the food chain looking down, from the vantage point of the big insurance companies, who owned thousands – tens of thousands of policies – or more; I saw numbers so big and so vast it was almost disorienting, like finding your way through hills that just had their tops blasted off by dynamite. *What if I could find a way?* I wondered.

I leaned closer to Chris and almost whispered in his ear for fear a co-worker might take my idea and run with it. "So, the broker, if they bought enough of these policies, could make a boatload of money."

"Yeah, seems like it." He responded.

"All the broker needs to do is come up with the upfront money to buy the policies, then make the premium payments on time to the insurance companies to stop the policies from lapsing, and then sit back while the money rolls in."

"When you say it like that, it sounds simple."

"Yeah! It's a no-brainer!" I said, laughing loudly with excitement. "And all a broker needs to do is make the insurance companies do what they should be doing in the first place! Chris, there's got to be a way!"

Chris raised his cup in cheers. "If you can figure that out, it sounds like poetic justice, my friend – profitable poetic justice."

HIGH HOPES

The following week, I took a day off from work. Rather than working the phones, hustling for deals inside my gray, four-walled hell, I packed a briefcase and hit the streets of downtown Lexington where the small city's flagship banks resided. When my supervisor asked why I needed the day off, I called it a personal day. I was packed with energy after I first talked with Chris about the life insurance market; my mind constantly reeled with endless streams of opportunities. I could barely sleep at night as new ideas and possibilities relentlessly filled my thoughts. I was obsessed. I knew there had to be a way to get into that market, and I wanted in.

I always felt I had an uncanny ability to recognize business opportunities, and I felt this could be my chance – my one big idea, that one big idea that everyone in business or with hopes to become an entrepreneur dreamed of. I researched, studied, and poured over every document I could get my hands on about the life insurance industry. Everything I found only confirmed my beliefs. This was my million-dollar idea – maybe even a billion-dollar idea.

I walked along Main Street that day, briefcase in hand, footsteps propelled by a dream. Inside my briefcase, I carried a proposal for a loan. After running the numbers dozens of times, I knew it was a sure sell. My idea was a no-brainer, and all I needed to do was what I did best: sell it.

I approached a tall, red-brick office building that towered nine stories above me, one of the tallest buildings in the town of roughly two hundred thousand people at the time. I noticed a sign at the top of the structure, *Fifth/Third Bank*. I entered through a glass doorway on the ground floor. A female bank teller smiled with forced effort and observed me through thick-rimmed eyeglasses.

I cleared my throat and flashed a toothy grin as I gritted my teeth, trying to reign in my nervousness. "Hi, there. Steve Keller to see Bob

Finley. I have an appointment."

"Yes, sir, his office is right over there."

I knocked my knuckles on the open doorway to a small corner office. I stepped inside the room, leading with a big smile. Bob Finley, a large, round-bodied, flush-faced man, stood from his swivel chair. He greeted me with a firm handshake from across his desk and offered me a seat.

"Well, Mr. Keller, I've had a chance to review your application." He announced.

I did my best to wait patiently, not wanting to seem too overzealous about landing the deal, but internally, my nerves were dancing like fireworks. I was thrilled to get the loan and rush into buying my first policies and then flip those policies into more policies. Usually, I'm pretty good at reading people, but Mr. Finley stared back at me stone-faced, like a ringer in the World Series of Poker.

Then he smirked. His lip curled like hot bacon in a frying pan. He then sucked his teeth, making a clicking noise with his mouth. "I will admit," he said bluntly, "the idea is highly original, to say the least."

"Oh, no, see, this is being done throughout the country. There just isn't a huge industry for it right now. I plan to create one with my company."

He smirked again and then outright laughed in my face. I felt my blood start to boil. I instinctively wanted to put a fist in his face, anything to make the laughter stop. I hated feeling made fun of or made to be the fool.

His laughter finally subsided, and he glared at me with condescending eyes. He said, "Young man, this bank doesn't just give out money for crazy schemes."

I scooted forward to the edge of my seat, eager to protest. "It's not crazy. The numbers are solid. Look what—"

He interrupted and raised a hand to shush me. "Son, this is the craziest and stupidest idea I've ever seen."

His words sliced through me to my core. My stomach clenched into a knot. I tried not to show the hurt in my eyes and the sting from his casual cruelty, but I stared at him incredulously, wondering how anyone could be so callous. A simple, no thank you would have sufficed.

He quickly grew impatient as I glowered at him, probably wondering why I was still sitting in his office. "Okay, then. Thank you for your time, Mr. Keller, and thank you for wasting ours."

I walked out of the building, defeated, and the world swirled around me. I suddenly felt so small, so powerless and belittled by this man's callous remarks. I found my way to a park bench across the street and stared up at the towering bank building above me as doubts gushed through me like a waterfall. *Am I wrong? Am I missing something? Is this loan officer, Bob Finley, with his fuckin' corner office right about how wrong I am and how stupid my business plan is? Maybe I should just go back to work tomorrow as a stockbroker and forget about my dreams of running my own business. Maybe he's right; maybe I'm not ready.* With the sting of rejection fresh on my face, I decided, *No, I will not be defeated, and I will not be defined by this rejection. No, the bank is wrong. He is wrong.*

I believed I had what it took to run my own business, and I didn't think they would know a good idea if it jumped up and bit them in the ass. I gritted my teeth and lifted my chin in defiance toward the height of the bank building that stood like a monolith before me. At that moment, I decided to transform my doubts and the pain from their rejection into a smoldering rage of defiant courage and will power to push harder and reach higher. A feeling burned inside of me that inspired me to prove him wrong. And more than that, I felt a deep-seated desire to prove myself right. I knew I was capable of more than what he thought of me. *I'll show you!* I thought.

I turned my back on the bank and ambled through downtown, vowing the bank and Mr. Bob Finley would hear from me again.

KELLER:

The promise sounded like an arrogant statement coming from a twenty-seven-year-old man with very little to eat in his own kitchen, most of which were canned foods. In hindsight, maybe it was, but the anger of the rejection fueled my resolve. I would make this idea work and drive it to success. I felt like I had to.

I've taken the time to think about rejection and what it does to us in the subsequent years. Many of us use it as an excuse to spiral into darkness, fueling our addictions and driving us into further failure. In reality, that is the easiest path and the one that, oddly, makes us feel the quickest sense of relief. We want to play the victim, nurse our own wounds, feel self-righteous and rise above our pain.

Fortunately, America has often allowed for those who fail in life to reinvent themselves, and for those truly determined to become a success. It is proudly a part of American culture. Most of us love a good underdog story because, at one point in time or another, we have had to struggle to overcome the odds. I took to heart that promise I made myself that day in the park, while I sat in the stinging pain of the banker's rejection. Back then, I saw only an enemy in the banker's red, arrogant face. I didn't yet know how his callous rejection would equip me. All I knew was that I didn't want my failure to define me, and I refused to give up on my idea.

CHECK

In the realm of big business, at least in the nineties, during the rise of entrepreneurialism and dot com startups, everyone scrambled for money to make things work and to keep pace with the growing demands. The ones who survived in big business secured bridge financing in the ninth hour, and to the rest of the world on the outside, business went on as usual, and no one was any wiser about how close a company actually was from tumbling over from the edge into financial ruin.

As a stockbroker, I got an insider's glimpse at some of those deals. I watched as publicly traded companies on the frontlines of industry scrambled to close deals and sell stock to acquire funding to stay afloat and meet quarterly deadlines. I watched it all from the sidelines, from within the confines of my gray cubicle.

I wanted off the sidelines and into the game. That required funding. That was my problem. Just like anyone else in business, I needed more capital. On my mission to acquire startup funding to launch my business idea, I had raised a total investment of zero dollars. The rejection from Fifth/Third Bank still stung my pride every time I thought about it. I assumed other banks were likely to give me and my business plan the same cold rejection, so I didn't want to waste my time submitting more loan applications; perhaps more accurately, I didn't want to subject myself to further humiliation from the Bob Finley's of the world. It pissed me off every time I recalled his parting words to me: "Thank you for your time, Mr. Keller, and thank you for wasting ours."

I often reminded myself that sometimes failure could be life's greatest teacher. The rejection inspired me to revamp my plans. I realized that if I could create a way to not only fulfill my need for capital but also help someone else achieve theirs in the process, I could raise money faster than by merely borrowing. I realized, the bigger the need another company had for money, the better it was for me. It just so happened that one of my clients, C'est Waters, a company with a cutting-edge water purification technology, oversold their stock earlier that quarter and desperately tried to raise the capital they needed to stay in business and prevent bankruptcy. I knew they needed funding, and fast. I had a plan, and I decided to bet my job on it.

I tapped my fingers against the surface of my Formica desk, then reached for the phone. I called the CEO of C'est Waters, Blake Goodman. As the phone rang, doubts gripped me tighter than my white-knuckled grip on the phone. I worried they wouldn't like my idea. I feared I would lose my credibility as their stockbroker and possibly them as one of my biggest clients. I imagined I would then lose my job with Dean Witter.

A firm voice greeted me on the other end of the line, "Hello?"

"Hey, Blake Goodman, this is Steve Keller at Dean Witter."

"Steve! How are you?" Blake said boisterously.

"Good, very good. Hey, I've been thinking over your lack of a capital problem."

"Oh yeah, what about it?" he barked.

I took a deep breath and gripped the phone like a flotation device at the end of a lifeline. "I think I've got the solution to help you."

I listened intently and only heard the slight buzz of the phone as they sat in silence.

After what felt like an eternity, Blake responded. "Gimme one sec."

I gnashed my teeth and considered placing the phone back into the receiver as if I never even made the call. As I waited in anticipation, I heard a noise on the other end of the line.

"Okay. Sorry, Steve. I wanted to close my door. Now, spill your idea."

I took a quick breath as if about to plunge underwater and then let my words fly. "I have a way for you to raise more capital. What if you were able to *guarantee* your investors their investment back? By purchasing insurance policies on terminally ill folks, you can guarantee it."

Silence. Then he awkwardly cleared his throat. "Uh, Steve? Tell you what. I'm going to patch you in for a conference call with the board. Hang on over there."

I stared like a horse with blinders into the gray fabric of my cubicle. I rocked back in my chair, loosened my tie, and swallowed hard as my hands jittered with nerves. The board at C'est Waters contained high-powered members who I knew could either make my career in an instant or crush me into insignificance and obscurity. My stomach tightened as I thought about all the big players who would be on the call in a matter of seconds. I knew Hank Warren would be there. *Hank Warren!* The Hank Warren! Hank Warren was a business icon and one of my idols. He was responsible for bringing the international sports drink, Gatorade, to market, and he became the youngest vice president in the history of Van Camp Stokley's. Then retired, he owned a minor league baseball team in Indianapolis. To me, it was the business-world equivalent to being an amateur basketball player with dreams to one day be in the NBA, and then suddenly, LeBron James steps out on the court. In addition to Hank, I knew the board contained other high-end finance guys from Pittsburgh who built large companies and knew the ins-and-outs of the finance world as well as anyone in the game.

I heard a click.

My heart skipped a few beats, and my stomach clenched like a pitcher gripping a fastball. *Do I announce my presence, or keep silent?* I waited. *It's now or never, Keller,* I reminded myself.

An excited voice cut through the silence on the line, nearly shouting, "Steve!"

"Yes, I'm here," I replied earnestly.

"Good, this is Blake Goodman. There for a minute I thought we had lost you."

A few voices chuckled on the line. My throat tightened as he continued, "Steve, I've patched us in here, and we're all anxious to hear more about your innovative idea. So, if you would, please take it from here."

My heart started racing like a Derby horse breaking from the starting gate. *What if they hate my idea? What if they laugh at me?* I tried to slow down for a split second and take a breath. I began speaking with slow, measured words, "Thank you all for allowing me a minute of your time.

Gentlemen, I have a revolutionary way to raise money for your company. Give me forty cents of every dollar you raise, and I will ensure your investor principal."

The response was only silence. Shit, I'm losing them. I better get to the point. I said, "I propose that you float money to purchase viatical life insurance policies as a way to ensure your investors' money and also guarantee a high rate of return."

A deep voice, one I hadn't heard yet on the line, said, "Mr. Keller, this is Hank Warren. Won't this be an added expense for the company?"

"Yes, Mr. Warren, it will, but acquisition cost is around thirty percent of the total benefit payout, which you receive in full upon a policy holder's death."

Dead air hung on the line, and before anyone could speak, I hustled to continue driving home my point. "With your upfront investment being backed by life insurance payouts, it will be much easier to raise more capital from your investors because you will now be able to offer a substantially higher return rate. Since you oversold your stock – let's face it – you don't have the assets to generate new investment using traditional methods. You need to get creative, and this new market is your chance at something that's going to be huge."

I started to feel more confident after I delivered my pitch and felt good about my delivery. I leaned forward in my cubicle chair and fought the temptation to babble on, trying to further convince them. I remind myself of a lesson my dad taught me early in life. I heard his voice in my head say, *Son, when making a sales pitch, give the facts, and then shut up. The first one who talks loses. Rambling causes your case to become less convincing, and people start wondering what you are trying to hide.*

I decided to deliver my closing statement. "That's my idea, Gentlemen."

And then I waited. The silence stretched on and felt suffocating.

I waited for someone to say something, anything, as cold sweat formed on my brow and at the back of my neck. My eyes drifted toward a small world map thumbtacked to the gray fabric lining my cubicle. While I waited for someone to respond, I searched the map for a friendly, small country where I could disappear. *Guam looks nice. No one knows me in Guam. Maybe Panama? At least it would be tropical. Did they mute me?*

Finally, I heard a click, then a voice. "Well, Mr. Keller, thank you for your call. Your idea, while certainly interesting, will require some time to review. Thank you for your time. Goodbye."

Click.

I felt like throwing up. I slowly put the phone back in its cradle. *What the heck just happened?* The feeling of defeat spread inside of me, and I dropped my head into my hands. I began considering alternative career options if I lost my job as a stockbroker. *Maybe my dad will allow me to join him in the family salvage business, back in West Liberty.* For all my hopes and big dreams to grow in business beyond where I was born, the thought of such a talk with my dad depressed me. I had a feeling he would turn me down anyways, seeing my request as an excuse not to pursue my own passions.

I saw my vision for the change needed in the insurance industry so clearly. I didn't understand how I could be so far off the mark. Every time I examined the details, over and over, it made sense – perfect business sense. It created a simple solution to an enormous need. People were dying – literally dying – impoverished and unable to obtain medical care to ease their suffering as the AIDS virus destroyed their immune systems. People needed money. If they paid into a life insurance policy throughout their lifetime, they should have been able to cash in their policy for value when their death approached and most needed help.

Everyone was a winner in every scenario I imagined. It just added up. Those suffering from AIDs would obviously benefit; the broker would benefit from substantial profit margins; and the investors would benefit too. It was a win-win scenario for everyone. At least, that was what I believed.

I looked back at the world map hanging in the corner of my cubicle. I really didn't want to move to Guam.

Suddenly, the phone rang.

I almost jumped out of my chair in shock. My thoughts came crashing back to earth and away from my sad daydream about exiling myself as I lunged for the phone.

"Hello, Steve, speaking."

"Mr. Keller! That was a powerful idea!"

The voice recognition region of my brain searched for a recollection of the voice. Nothing. I responded warily, "Pardon me, who is this?"

"I'm sorry; this is Mr. Rorrick. I'm on the board with Blake's company. I commend you for conceiving such a creative financial arrangement. In fact, I was so taken with this process that I want to purchase the policies from you, personally. Of course, only if it doesn't cause a problem with C'est Waters. I would also prefer that you keep such an arrangement between you and me. Is that doable, Mr. Keller?"

This must have been what it felt like to be drilling for oil and hitting a gusher. I leapt to my feet and began pacing within my cubicle, wanting to shout at the top of my lungs in triumph. I responded with my best attempt to maintain a calm voice, saying, "Mr. Rorrick, I will have to get back with you once I iron out something with Mr. Goodman. But yes, I do believe you, and I can work something out... separately."

"Thank you, Mr. Keller. This is my direct number. Call me here anytime."

"I will be in touch, Mr. Rorrick."

Click. I laid the receiver gently in the cradle, shocked at the sudden change in fortune.

Suddenly, the phone rang again. I answered and spoke with another board member who wanted to cut a similar deal to what Mr. Rorrick and I discussed. As soon as I hung up the phone, it rang again...and then again.

My business was officially up and running.

OFF TO THE RACES

I leaned back confidently in my cubicle swivel chair and made an interoffice call. No longer in the cubicle next door, I called Chris to reach his new office within the Dean Witter building. He answered on the second ring.

"Mr. Chavez, you and I need to talk."

"What's up, Keller?"

"Do you have anyone with you?"

"No, I'm clear."

"I'll come over now!"

I knocked on the open doorway to his new office. Chris raised his head as I entered the room like a thoroughbred charging ahead of a pack.

"Chris, you remember months ago you told me about people selling their life insurance policies?"

"Yeah, why?"

"Well, you know my client, C'est Waters? I talked with their board, and they're in!"

Chris squinted his dark eyes with recognition. "Okay, you've got my attention."

"Chris, this scenario is plug and play. They're going to finance the trades, and all we've got to do is broker the policies. It should be easy, and we can run this thing ourselves. Since you introduced me to the concept, and I don't know squat about insurance, how about you taking 30 percent stock of a company I form?"

Chris leaned back in his chair and threw his hands behind his head while he stared at the ceiling in contemplation. After a deep breath, he dropped his elbows onto his desk and leaned forward.

I remained silent.

A hint of a grin formed at the corner of his mouth, and then excitement flashed in his eyes.

"Okay, Steve. Let's do this. What are we going to call it?"

"I don't know. I haven't even thought that far. How about *Keller-Conway* or just *Kelco*?"

He spoke the name aloud as if taking in the sound of it.

"*Kelco*. Hmm. I like it. Okay, *Kelco* it is."

KELLER:

It's hard to believe that a company that would create a billion-dollar industry found its name because I threw two last names together. On the other hand, a lot of companies got their names just because the owners threw together two names. Again, I think it illustrates the point of simplicity in business. Think about Harley-Davidson and Hewlett-Packard. They've come to be such staples in American life that we don't think about the utter simplicity in their names.

Here's the brutal truth: the chances of making it big in business are comparable to those of an author getting a book published. Every day, small businesses fail in America at an alarming rate. The failure rate is in the ninety-percent range. Even if you succeed, your company's chance of becoming the next Google is narrower than a seam of coal.

Chris and I founded Kelco inside a virtual office that would answer the calls and forward the messages to our desks at Dean Witter. We cut costs and built our foundation, trying to appear larger than we genuinely were when, in actuality, we had more bills coming in than we had income.

Believe it or not, this is done all the time. Businesses often rely on similar sleight of hand tricks to create the illusion of being a big deal. Everyone wants to talk about the legitimacy of the supposed work world compared to other industries like Hollywood. The thing is, they are very much the same. Everyone has a plan, inflates their own credentials, and exaggerates their abilities. That is the way the game is played.

Still, after forming our own company, I couldn't bring myself to quit Dean Witter. We worked nights and weekends on Kelco, and I started telecommuting my work with Dean Witter to a new office space intended to grow Kelco. For all our effort, our first year amounted to a combined gross profit of twenty-five thousand dollars.

As much as we say we want to change our lives for the better, it can be scary to really cut the tether. Despite all my bragging and talking about doing my own thing, facing the prospect of actually doing it seemed frightening.

TO EACH HIS OWN

I approached Chris's open office door at the Dean Witter location. Dark circles hung heavy under my eyes and copious amounts of caffeine fueled my jittery energy. I peeked my head inside his office.

"Hey, Chris. What's up?"

He greeted me with a lukewarm expression. "Keller, shut the door."

My stomach clenched. These words never signal anything good. I approached his desk, and Chris didn't make eye contact with me. He looked down at the unfinished paperwork spread atop his desk as he spoke. "Steve, I got a job offer."

"Okay, where?"

"Bank of America merged their discount brokerage with us, so they're asking me to move to North Carolina to be their manager."

I looked down to the floor as I grasped his meaning. "So, no more Kelco for you."

"Yeah, bud, I'm afraid so. There isn't much more I can do. This position came up and it's just too good of an offer. I've got to take it."

My world began to swirl around me. I replayed all the lessons Chris taught me in the past year. I saw the dreams and visions I had of Conway and me on the cover of Forbes, telling crazy stories of the early days. I felt foolish forever considering such dreams and trusting that he would help me get there. I felt abandoned and betrayed by him, and my anger from the rejection rose to the surface, but I knew I couldn't blame him. He had a family. He needed to make the choice that was best for him and his family's future.

I stifled the simmering feelings inside of me, not wanting him to see my pain, stood and shook his hand from across the desk. "Good luck, Chris."

I turned my back and walked out of his office.

Now on my own, after a year of hard work, struggle, and sacrifice, I was back at square one.

A NEW DAY A NEW DEAL

I drove my twelve-year-old Ford Thunderbird into the parking lot of Kelco's new headquarters, the Office Suites located off the outer loop of New Circle Road in Lexington. I called the office the Heartbreak Hotel of business startups. It was the kind of office you might rent if you wanted to start a business but still had to sell moonshine on the side. Still, I felt a kindred spirit among my Office Suites neighbors. Their cars seemed as likely to fall apart at any minute as mine did. They didn't try to keep the "golden mean" by simply plugging along in a safe little life; they went big and faced the risk of failure every day.

Such determination inspired me. The occupants carried a passion and a burning torch for their dreams. The warmth of their small flames kindled the fire of my own dreams. We all wore clothes about three years out of style with gaunt, dream-like expressions in our eyes. Motivational and how-to-make-it-in-business books proudly adorned our bookshelves. We all talked an excellent game. Perhaps delusionally, we all believed one day we would live up to our own hype.

I walked through the front door to the Office Suites, where I passed through a small reception area. The secretary, Diane, idly flipped through a magazine on the counter of her desk with pink acrylic nails. Permed bangs hung over her forehead as she chewed bubblegum with a rhythmic clench of her jaw that would make a goat jealous. My footsteps echoed against the tile floors as I approached the reception desk. The echo reminded me of the sound one might hear if walking through a mortuary.

I greeted Diane with a big smile and a wave. "Morning, Diane! Let's make today count!"

The chewing gum motion stopped. Diane looked up from her magazine with a forced smile, then quickly returned to her casual reading material.

I opened the door to my tiny office. I sat behind my cheap desk in my cheap chair, and I felt a sense of pride. No more gray fabric cubicle for me. Four white walls and my own doorway. A space I paid for on my own. To start the workday, I thumbed through a thin Rolodex of contacts on my desk. I chose a number to a potential investor, then dialed.

No answer.

I flipped to another number in the Rolodex, then dialed again.

No answer.

I left a message.

"Uh, hi. This is Steve Keller. I'm calling to talk to you about a once in a lifetime opportunity. Please call me back. Thank you!"

I placed the phone back into the receiver and thumbed to the next number in the Rolodex, realizing I made a mistake.

"Ahh, shit! I forgot to leave my phone number!"

I shook my head in disbelief and dropped my hands away from the Rolodex. I rested my elbows on the desk and hung a heavy head onto a balled fist, like a demoralized version of Michelangelo's *The Thinker*.

I lifted the phone and dialed another number. I called my father on his business line.

My father didn't usually offer advice. He often told my older brother, sister, and me that he feared his direction might lead us to make the wrong choices for ourselves. He usually preferred to give general principles to live by, and taught us instead how to find our true selves, to learn to take our own risks, and to face our personal consequences. He always backed us up and supported our decisions, whatever we happened to choose.

The phone rang. My father answered. "Grassy Auto Parts. This is John."

"Hey, Dad, it's Steve."

"How are things, son? I heard you've got your own office now — brave move. How's it feel?"

"I feel great about it. I needed to get my own space and spread my wings, do my own thing...just like you."

He paused.

"That's great, Steve. So, how's the business going?"

"It's going. I'm still working with Dean Witter selling stocks. The work is steady. I'm telecommuting my work from there over in my new office, making phone calls, and taking meetings. There are some good leads in the hotel industry to pick up clients, and I've had some luck with the real estate guys too. I've taken on a consulting job on the side to help me stay afloat and cover the costs of the new office. I'm looking to expand that business too and help other companies go public. I'm still working on getting Kelco off the ground too. This first year has been tough. My partner left, so now it's just me, here in the office, trying to make the dream happen, you know? I'm mostly putting in hours at night and on the weekends."

I stopped talking and listened to the sound of his breathing on the other end of the phone. I could almost see his gentle smile through the phone as he finally spoke.

"That's a lot, Steve," he said softly.

His simple words struck a chord within me.

I quickly responded, wanting to prove myself, "Yeah, I guess so, but something will pan out." He paused again, slowing me down.

"Steve, no one human being is capable of doing everything you just described. What I suggest you do is pick one thing out of all those ideas you mentioned and simply become the best at what you pick. You do this, and you will never have anything to worry about."

His words hit pay dirt. I nodded my head in silence and allowed the meaning to sink in.

"Alright, son. I've got to get back to work. You hang in there."

"Thanks, Dad."

The phone call clicked and then silence. I was left holding the phone in my hand, reflecting on his words. I placed the phone in the receiver and stared at my Rolodex, feeling a new sense of inspiration – *one thing – just pick one thing and be the best at it.*

A loud voice jolted me from my thoughts. I recognized Diane's voice projecting from the reception desk and down the hall to my office.

"Mr. Keller, you have a visitor!"

My eyes widened in surprise.

"Really? Who is it?"

"Mr. Grant Sutherlin."

I heard Diane's footsteps walking toward my office. She peeked her head inside the room and dropped her voice down to a barely audible whisper.

"He looks like a high school kid."

"Oh, right, send him back."

Grant approached the doorway, behind Diane. He stood about six feet tall, skinny, with a thick, Harry Potter-style haircut parted to one side. He looked like a typical, clean-cut All-American kid, right out of "Typical American Kid" magazine.

He knocked on the open door with a shy but warm smile. "Mr. Keller?"

"Grant, come in. You can call me Steve. Love your parents. Glad they recommended you meet with me. So, are you a flyer like your dad?"

"Yeah, I've been flying planes since eleven. I love it."

"Excellent. I take it you're a licensed pilot now in your own right, huh?"

Grant nodded his shaggy black head of hair vigorously in agreement. "Yes, sir! I'm instrument rated. I can fly in any weather."

I nodded, finding myself taken in by his exuberance. "That must really be something. I've always wanted to fly too."

My words trailed off like a jet turning off course. I recalled early childhood dreams of one day piloting my own plane. I dreamed of the freedom to lift off from anywhere in the world and soar to outrageous heights among the clouds and then touch down in a completely different environment only hours later. I imagined flying to D.C. in the afternoon for a coffee and then flying to New York in the evening for dinner and drinks. *Now that's the life.*

The reverie faded, and I snapped back to the present moment where Grant sat before me. "So anyway, what can I do for you, Grant?" I asked, pointing toward a vacant chair across from my desk.

He sat with upright posture on the edge of the seat. "My grandmother left me some Merck stock. I want to have you to trade it for me."

"No problem. Should be pretty easy."

Grant leaned forward. "And there's something else. Do you buy baseball cards?"

I laughed. "Baseball cards? Well, not as a habit, but sure, I'll bite. I am an opportunist. What do you have in mind?"

Grant squinted his eyes and leaned over my desk as if letting me in on a secret. "I happen to have a Mickey Mantle rookie card here."

He passed the rare card, contained in protective plastic, across my desk. I knew when it came to commodities, condition was king. I held the card up to the light – no flaws, at least none that I could see. I cranked up the dial-up modem, initiating a series of beeps and hisses from the computer modem to access the internet. After signing in through the AOL web portal, I searched the current street price of the card. The average price was around three hundred and seventy-five dollars for mint condition.

I returned my attention to Grant and offered, "I'll give you three hundred dollars."

"Mr. Keller, I mean Steve. This is not an average mint condition card. It's rarer than that. It has been encased in that plastic longer than I've been on this earth. It's worth four hundred and fifty dollars, easy. I brought this to you as a gift."

The easiest person to sell in the world is a salesperson, and Grant made a compelling sales pitch. "Okay, Grant. I hear what you're saying. What about three fifty?"

"Mr. Keller – I mean Steve – you're not listening to me. I can get four-fifty for it right now at a card shop. I'm here because of the association with my family. Do you have four hundred dollars cash here?"

"As a matter of fact, I do."

"Okay, then it's yours."

I forked over the money and looked at the card in my hands. It was then that I realized what had happened. Grant was so convincing and so quick to close the deal it was over before I realized that he just sold me a baseball card for twenty-five dollars over street value, and I bought it with little to no questions. *This kid is a closer.*

I reached across the table and shook Grant's hand, sealing our agreement. I looked long and hard at Grant. He reminded me so much of myself at that age, the confidence mixed with just the right amount of cockiness. Then it hit me, I need this kid on my team. With Chris gone, my days were filled with loneliness, making cold calls on the phone in a silent, empty office, while Diane gave me cold looks from the reception desk. Some new life and energy inside the Office Suites would go a long way. I had a feeling that his youthful pilot's hubris could be the perfect addition to help Kelco lift off.

"Hey, Grant, what are you doing tomorrow?"

"Nothing much – it's the weekend – so no school. Why?"

"Do you want to fly me to McMinnville, Tennessee?"

Grant raised his dark eyebrows, intrigued, and a small smile formed at the corners of his mouth. "Yeah, I'd have to ask my dad if I could fly that far, but sure."

I leaned forward across my desk, mirroring his earlier tactic for closing me on the baseball card deal. "I know you came here about stocks, but I also run my own company, called Kelco. So, here's the deal: I took a chance on buying a life insurance policy a few months ago, and I'm meeting with an investor down in Tennessee about selling him this policy. The potential on this thing is huge, and I want you there with me."

A flash of excitement darted into Grant's eager eyes. "Okay, I'll get my dad to say yes. It's for business, so I know he'll be okay with it."

I stood from my office chair and passed him my business card from a small stack on the edge of my desk. "Okay, here's my cell number. Call me as soon as you find out."

Grant stuffed the business card into the pocket of his khaki pants in a hurry. "I'll call you as soon as I get home."

I extended a hand across my desk. Grant met my hand with a firm handshake, filled with exuberance. "Nice to have met you, Mr. Keller. I mean, Steve."

An excitement rises within me and uplifts my spirits. I beam from ear to ear with a smile, hoping this new energy leads to new life for Kelco and new life for my dreams of genuinely breaking out on my own and running my own business.

"You too, Grant. See you on the runway."

TAKING FLIGHT

I approached a single prop Cessna airplane on a nearly deserted tarmac. The Timex watch on my wrist read 7:30 A.M. Grant emerged from the two-seater cabin of the plane and greeted me with a big grin and a handshake.

"How is that baseball card working out for you, Steve?"

I chuckled. "It's my prized possession. I put it in my safe deposit box. You know, got to protect my overpaid investment."

Grant smiled knowingly. "Indeed, glad I could provide you with a great deal. You stole it from me, you know."

"Bullshit, kid, but I can't help but admire the way you did it.

He opened the door to the plane and handed me a headset. "All right, Steve, you ready? Let's load up!"

I climbed into the passenger seat, and Grant sat behind the controls of the small plane. Sitting inside the cockpit, I felt like a strong gust of wind could flip us over; it felt as if the plane was made from popsicle sticks. Grant flipped a few switches with expert precision, and the plane's engine roared to life. The propeller at the plane's nose churned, chopping the air, slow at first, and then spun beyond the ability of my eyes to follow.

Grant shouted into the headset over the loud roar of the plane. "Here we go! Clear!"

Grant drove the plane down the runway, and we quickly gained speed. The nose lifted; the wings caught a gust of air; and we rose into the sky. We left the ground beneath us, and everything below grew smaller and smaller as we climbed higher. *What a rush!*

We reached a cruising altitude for the small plane of around two thousand feet, and Grant eased back from the controls. "So how long have you known my parents?" He asked.

"They've been clients since I started at Dean Witter several years ago now."

My eyes drifted away from the conversation and out the window toward the ground below.

Grant noticed the shift in my attention. "How do you like it up here?"

"I love it! It sure puts things in perspective, doesn't it?"

"What do you mean, Steve?"

"Well, everything seems so big down there when we're on the ground; up here, it just shrinks down to nothing. What a way to grow up, kid, flying planes with your folks!"

"Yeah, it's pretty great. Anything I need to know about this meeting?"

I smiled. "You pulled a pretty good trick with that baseball card. You just do whatever comes naturally. I know you've got great instincts. Let's just hope I can do what you did with that card with this forty-thousand-dollar life insurance policy."

Grant grinned and looked at me from the side of his eyes. "I know you can."

WHEELING AND DEALING

The wheels of the plane touched down on the runway of McMinnville, Tennessee. Grant and I took a taxi to the small-town center and approached the offices of Matthews, Weinstein, and Curry. I waltzed through the office's entryway with the confidence of thousands of past cold calls and meetings under my belt as a stockbroker, but a feeling of nervousness bounced inside me, knowing this was one of only a handful of attempts at selling a life insurance policy in person. I also felt the pressure of Grant's watchful eyes on me, eager to learn from the way I conducted business, and looking for affirmation that I was someone worth learning from. I didn't want to disappoint him or myself.

A receptionist greeted us as we entered. "Good morning, how may I help you?"

I approached the counter and spoke in my best attempt at a bold and confident tone. "Yes, good morning to you too. Is Phil Blankenship, here?"

"Who may I say is here to see him?"

"This is Steve Keller, with Kelco," I said with a proud smile as I looked at Grant, who chose to hang back and watch my lead. I felt a confidence rise within me at the thought of how those words rolled off my tongue. It felt crisp and sharp using the name, Steve Keller, with Kelco. It just fit, like trying on a brand-new bespoke suit. I heard my father's advice, Find the one thing.

The receptionist pointed us to an office along a hallway. I stepped toward an open doorway with a knock.

"Hello, Phil. Steve Keller, with Kelco, and my associate, Grant Sutherlin."

"Come on in, gentlemen. So, what can I do for you, Mr. Keller?"

"I'll get right to the point, Phil. Kelco specializes in viaticals. The buying and selling of life insurance policies on terminally ill people.

"Interesting, I actually just read an article on your market, Steve. I've been trying to research how I could get involved – seems like everything is pretty new."

I turned to Grant with a hint of a smile, then refocused my attention on Phil.

"It is – brand-new, in fact, and Kelco is on the frontier's edge of creating this new industry, and if you're interested, you can be too. I've got a policy worth forty thousand dollars that I'd sell to you for what I bought it for. That's as good a deal as you'll find in this business. The way it works in this business is that each policy gains value every day because we're another day closer to the ultimate payout date."

He paused for a moment, looking uneasy.

"By payout date, you mean when somebody dies?" He asked.

I looked to Grant to catch the glassy-eyed expression on his face. I grinned at him and used the trick that Grant used on me only yesterday. I leaned over Phil's desk as if letting him in on a secret. "Phil, you ever heard the expression there are only two guarantees in life?"

Phil nodded his head in agreement.

"That's right. Of course, you have. Death and taxes – we both know the government controls taxes, so that only leaves us one guarantee to work with: death. It's not the prettiest business, but people die every day. And the truth is, most of these people who die, ninety percent of them in fact, let these policies lapse because they can't afford the premiums anymore. That's where we come in. We pay them upfront money so they can pay their bills, and yeah, sadly, nature takes its course, and eventually, those people die. But when they die, we make money. A lot of money."

Phil looked down at the policy he held in his hands, unsure of how to respond.

I responded for him. "That piece of paper that I'm selling to you for forty thousand five hundred dollars has a payout amount of one hundred thousand dollars."

Phil's eyes lit up with amazement.

I prodded ahead in agreement. "That's right. We don't wish ill on anyone, but that piece of paper could come due in a few years or a few days. So, you have to ask yourself, could you use an extra hundred thousand dollars, knowing it's only a matter of time until the payout date?

Phil smirked at the policy with a gleam in his eye.

"I think that I'd like to see your contracts and paperwork, Mr. Keller."

"Of course," I said, looking to Grant, who eagerly jumped into action to hand Phil a portfolio that contained the policy's documentation.

"Yes, sir," Grant said. "You'll find the ROI on this type of investment exceeds that of any other investment you're likely to find."

I read the excitement in Phil's eyes as he perused the details of the policy. He looked up from the portfolio with a greedy grin.

"I'll look this over today. If it all checks out, I'll put a check in the mail first thing tomorrow morning."

I extended a hand, and Phil locked in the deal with a firm handshake. "Deal. Thank you, Mr. Blankenship. I will be in touch as soon as I receive the contracts."

Grant and I walked out of Phil's office, grinning from ear to ear. I silently showed Grant a thumbs up, trying to contain my excitement as I thought to myself, *See, I can play this game too, boy.*

A heavy wind buffeted the side of the office building as we stepped out into the afternoon. Grant bounced with excitement and slapped me on the shoulder. "You were amazing! You were like Gordon Gecko in there!" Grant lowered his voice assuring his words wouldn't carry back into the office building behind us and then began an impersonation of my voice. "Death and taxes. It's the only guarantee in life. So how about you? Could you use an extra hundred thousand dollars?" Grant burst into laughter, and I couldn't help but be overwhelmed by his good-natured humored. I nearly doubled over laughing at my own words. We stepped into the waiting taxi at the curb, still smiling. The cab drove us back to the airport as storm clouds mounted on the horizon.

The sky grew darker as we hurried onto the tarmac. The wind gained intensity. Grant quickly readied the plane.

"Shouldn't be too bad – I think we'll get out ahead of it, but we need to hurry," He shouted over the noise of the wind.

I looked around, squinting through the wind. The storm looked ominous, intimidating. Perhaps, I was high from this first major sale, from the potential energy the sale gave me and Kelco. Perhaps, hubris and invincibility took hold of me for a moment when I told him, "All right, kid. I trust you. Let's go."

Wild, frontier behavior.

Grant wasted no time getting the plane in the air. Immediately turbulence threw the small plane up and dropped us down like a rollercoaster on the wind. The winds increased in speed and increased in fury. We climbed in altitude, rising higher and into stronger winds. Grant pulled back on the elevator, frantically trying to find the magic altitude to set us on a smoother path. The wind howled through the open slits in the windows. Even with the headphones covering our ears, the noise and the fury of the wind were all we could hear.

The color of the sky turned an ominous blackish green, a harbinger of bad to worse in tornado country. Clouds began to swirl in a violent clockwise funnel in the air ahead of us.

"Uh, Grant, does that look like a tornado to you?" I panicked.

His lips clamped into a tight line. His brow furrowed with determination and fear.

"Uh, huh." Was all he managed to respond.

A hole opened in the sky before us. Intense light broke through the clouds. The gap in the storm grew broader and brighter as the clouds of the funnel deepened with a dark gray, green, and black color.

A bolt of white-hot lightning cracked across the sky.

I clenched my entire body so tight I think my ass lifted the plane higher.

Rain began to fall, assaulting the thin metal skin of the plane as the wind tossed us from side to side like a rag doll in a laundry dryer.

Grant yelled at the top of his lungs, shouting to be heard over the rain pelting on the fuselage. "If we can make that hole of light before the clouds close off, I think we can make it out of here! If not, it's not going to be pretty!"

I grabbed Grant by the shoulder to get his attention and to hold him steady through the turbulence as he fought to maintain control of the plane. "Grant! Do you think we can make that tunnel?"

"Yes!" He screamed.

I looked at him – concentration, sense of survival all over his face – and believed him. I felt I could trust him with my life.

"Then go for it! I'm with you! Let's do it!" I yelled.

I watched in amazement as a new wave of confidence overtook him. He locked down several instruments and went all out on the throttle. I looked at his hands, steady with no visible shake.

The plane rumbled in protest against the fury and force of nature. Amid desperation, completely sobered after my intoxicating sale, I found myself thinking, *Damn I should have told Grant to turn the plane around.*

"Too late now!" I shouted aloud to myself as I gripped the edge of my seat with white knuckles. Down toward where I knew the ground should be, through all the black and green and gray clouds, I could only see darkness, until a bolt of lightning cracked across the sky. I struggled to breathe, and I couldn't move, suspended in the moment as the plane churned forward at the speed of my racing heart.

Grant screamed at his plane. "Come on, baby! Come on!"

He made another adjustment to the controls, and the plane careened toward the tiny opening in the sky with more speed. The light shined in the distance before us like a beacon, guiding us from disaster into safety. I gritted my teeth and looked through the rain-battered windshield as our plane fought the wind, inching forward toward our only glimmer of escape.

"Come on!" Grant yelled in desperation.

We approached the mouth of the tunnel. Our faces began to glow. The dark cockpit illuminated vibrantly as a brilliant light shined through a crack in the clouds. A perfect glimmer of sunlight shined on us. The light instantly grew more intense, blinding, as the plane broke through the opening in the clouds. The fury of the storm suddenly fell silent, giving way to smooth sailing and clear skies ahead.

I began laughing hysterically, once I realized I was still alive, like a man freed from death row.

"Uh, did we just take the portal to another world?" I asked with a goofy grin.

Grant smiled and steered the plane toward home.

"I don't know, but I can't believe what just happened."

We stared at each other for a moment. Grant's eyes were round; his face was still flush with adrenaline. Sweat rolled down both of our faces, and I knew I must have had the same starry-eyed expression on my face because he started to laugh.

"That was unbelievable! You look like a crazy person! Are you okay?"

"Yeah, are you?"

"I am now."

We both laughed in jubilation as we let out loud yells of sheer joy and slapped each other high fives. "Whew wee, yeah!"

Bonded through the life-or-death experience, Grant and I became instant friends. We faced the storm together, and Grant saved our lives through his incredible grit under pressure. I knew I could trust him. I knew from that point forward, we would both share an admiration for each other; we knew that we could count on each other's belief and encouragement when we needed it most.

"Hey, uh, just do me one favor, Steve," Grant said.

"What's that?"

"Don't tell my parents."

"Why not, you just pulled off an amazing feat! Own it! You deserve all the credit in the world!"

"Yeah, but I doubt they would let me fly by myself anymore. We took a bit of a risk – okay, a big risk. They're parents; it's what they do."

I thought about it for a moment and realized he was probably right. I didn't have kids, so I trusted his judgment for how his parents might view the situation and agreed to keep the secret between us.

The plane screeched to a halt in Lexington. Grant cut the power, and we jumped out of the plane, thankful to be on solid ground again. As we unloaded our belongings from the plane, Grant's parents, Bob and Carolyn, came out of their company sales office, eager to see how their son did on his first long flight.

Bob shook my hand enthusiastically and asked, "How was the trip?"

"Well, it got a little bumpy coming back, but your son did a marvelous job."

Grant coughed into his hand to conceal a laugh that threatened to break loose.

I interjected, gaining his parents' attention. "Listen, guys, I've had a chance to talk with Grant about this, but I want to take this opportunity to also tell you in person. I'm leaving Dean Witter immediately and going on my own. I'll no longer be a stockbroker. I'm running my own company now called Kelco."

Hearing myself speak, I felt the weight of the world leave my shoulders.

Carolyn and Bob looked to one another with surprise at my announcement that they would no longer be my clients. Carolyn shared a knowing glance with her husband.

"You see, Bob? I knew there was a lot that Grant could learn from Steve," Carolyn said, then fixed her southern charm in my direction. "Since you're going out on your own, Steve, maybe you could find a position in your new company for Grant?"

I looked to Grant in surprise at the idea, and he looked back at me eagerly. "Well, I hadn't thought about that," I lied. "He did bring me luck on closing a big deal."

Carolyn wrapped an arm around her son and leaned closer to me. "What do you say, Steve? He has extra time after school."

I looked to Grant, knowing what we just survived together, then addressed his parents.

"Okay, how about it, Grant? Do you want to come on as an intern for Kelco?"

HOPE AT THE HEARTBREAK HOTEL

On Monday morning I climbed the stairs to the second floor of the Office Suites, thrilled to get to my office and set up shop as the sole proprietor and owner of Kelco. I entered the reception area expecting to see Diane staring down into a magazine. Instead, I was greeted with a thick cloud of smoke and the vague impression of someone who was not my usual receptionist, Diane. I took a few cautious steps toward the entry desk, wondering, *who set the trashcan on fire?*

I inhaled the fumes and coughed out what was clearly cigarette smoke. Behind the desk I found the source of the fumes. A new receptionist pulled a long drag from a menthol, with an open pack at the ready by her side. As much as I liked having a secretary, I didn't know if my lungs could afford the luxury.

The woman greeted me with a small cough from her fog.

"You must be Mr. Keller. I'm Dianna," she spoke with a gruff voice smothered with well-intentioned southern charm.

I took a deep breath before entering the dense smoke, extending my hand to shake Dianna's.

"Nice to meet you," I offered.

"One of our tenants, Greg Elam, has told me a lot about you. Good to be on board," she said, expelling another puff of smoke from her pursed lips. Her southern drawl coupled well with the poise of hospitality with which she carried herself. Dianna's kindness was a welcome change from Diane. *Every day is a new surprise here at the Office Suites,* I thought.

"Ok, well, good to have you," I said with genuine appreciation for our new, friendlier, chain-smoking receptionist. "I'll be just in my office if you need me."

I hurried out from the fog and stepped into my office, closing the door behind me. I immediately sorted through the mail excitedly with hope that the check for the policy we sold arrived in the mail before I did. I sifted through a short stack of envelopes – no check from Tennessee. Now that Kelco's business felt more substantial, more permanent, I scanned the room with the intention to tidy up and make it my own.

I heard the front door to the office open, followed by Dianna's southern drawl greeting the guest warmly. "Hi, there. May I help you?"

"Yes, I'm Grant Sutherlin, here to see Steve Keller."

"Just a second, I'll buzz him." She said, then I heard her voice through the crackly intercom system on my desk, "Mr. Keller, Mr. Sutherlin is here to see you."

I passed through the smoke storm with my hand extended and greeted Grant in the reception area. "Hey, Grant, welcome to the Office Suites and the Kelco team. Dianna, this is Grant."

Dianna seemed apprehensive. "Yes, we've met."

"Grant is in high school and will be interning with me." I announced in my most professional tone.

Dianna smiled at Grant, and I took the cue to guide Grant down the hallway to my office.

"Here we are, Grant: The Offices of Kelco," I stated proudly.

Grant tucked his hands in his pockets and scanned the room.

"Great! So how should I start?" He asked.

I observed the room, unsure of how to answer his question. I already scanned the mail for the incoming check from Kelco's first sale. I approached a standing file cabinet beside the desk and opened one of the metal drawers.

"Here's what we're going to do, Grant. Anything that isn't Kelco related, toss it out."

I grabbed a file folder labeled Dean Witter and tossed it to the floor.

"And by the way, Grant, here's your first lesson as an entrepreneur: find one thing and be the best at it. That's what we at Kelco are here to do. Anything else, toss it out."

Grant joined me at the filing cabinet and scanned the contents. He found a file folder labeled business startup concepts. He withdrew the file and showed it to me.

"Like this?" He asked.

"Exactly. Toss it."

Grant's face beamed with pride. He dropped the file folder down onto the floor. He found another and tossed it down. We both grabbed file folders, one by one, and dropped them down to the floor. The pile grew as we grew in quickness and efficiency, tossing out more and more files. We worked well together and enjoyed the process, laughing as we became more creative in how we tossed files to the floor.

I grabbed a handful of files and slam-dunked them down onto the pile, letting them go.

Grant shot a hook shot like Kareem Abdul-Jabbar over the edge of my desk and papers flew out of the folder and floated onto the floor.

Together, Grant and I made this Heartbreak Hotel feel hopeful, and suddenly, work felt like having fun.

MAY I HAVE THE ENVELOPE PLEASE?

I arrived early at the office, unable to sleep from the anticipation that the check from Tennessee would arrive that day. I paced the office all morning, waiting for the mail. Hours into the day, the front door opened to the office building, and Dianna greeted someone, her conversation only partially audible. She laughed at some off-color remark, the type usually made by the mailman on our route who seemed to have a crush on Dianna. I could never tell when Dianna thought his jokes were funny or merely laughed because she felt uncomfortable. In either case, I chose not to interrupt what seemed to be an awkward situation between Dianna and someone in the lobby.

Finally, I heard the door open, and the flirty mailman left the building. I bolted out of my office and into the reception area, pushing through the smoke cloud to approach Dianna's desk.

Dianna sorted through a large stack of mail, filtering the envelopes into small piles for each Office Suites' tenant. She wrapped a rubber band around a stack of mail and presented it to me from across her desk. "Here you go, Mr. Keller; there's a thick stack today."

"I hope it's not all bills," I said, joking with her, but also half-serious.

Dianna laughed playfully, continuing with the joke. "If they are, I hope they're yours and not mine."

I took hold of the mail and noticed a large parcel at the bottom of the bundle, an overnight delivery package. I glanced at the postmark and saw the Tennessee return address.

A smile exploded across my face, and I quickly hurried back to my office. I tossed the pile of mail onto the desk and grabbed the overnight parcel. I rushed to open it but then stopped myself. *No, I decided. I'm going to wait for Grant. In fact, I'm going to let him open it.* I felt he had earned the right to be a part of our future at Kelco, and the kid deserved some good news early in his career. So, I waited.

I grabbed a cup of coffee and spent the morning talking with Dianna. She always wore a smile, but there was a sadness behind her eyes. To my surprise, she possessed a substantial amount of business knowledge, leading me to be intrigued by her background and how she arrived at the Office Suites as a receptionist. She didn't speak much about her past but alluded that she had fallen from greater heights in her career. Hearing her story further affirmed my belief about the Office Suites. The offices were a temporary home to an assortment of characters who were pursuing bigger dreams – or recovering from dreams that crashed and burned.

As much as I enjoyed talking with Dianna, I couldn't help but feel like I was paying the price for the conversation as I took in more second-hand smoke than one person should consume in a lifetime. The phone rang at the reception desk, and Dianna put on her headset and pressed a button on the switchboard. That was my signal to return to my office.

I watched from my office window as Grant pulled into the building parking lot in his compact, red Pontiac Lemans, which looked like the first version of a smart car. I kicked back in my desk chair and propped my feet on the desk and waited for him to enter. I plastered a smug smile on my face and a demeanor that screamed, I told you so. Salespeople called this behavior strutting, coined after a rooster strutting around the hens, feeling full of oneself.

Grant entered through the front door of the building.

"Hey, Dianna!" he said, quickly greeting her as his footsteps hurried down the hallway.

Grant stepped into the office to find me in a relaxed position, gazing out the large office window as if looking out over the world at large for the next venture to conquer.

"Well?" Grant demanded.

"Oh, hey there, Grant! You're here early." I said casually as I turned to strut barrel-chested to my desk.

"Yeah, I cut my class short today. All I could think about was whether the mail would come today. Did you get it?"

I grabbed the overnight parcel and slid it across the desk to him.

"You tell me."

Grant looked down at the overnight in disbelief.

He slowly reached for the package as if it contained a breakable object. He picked it up, examining every side.

"It's not opened?" he asked with a confused expression, bordering on disbelief.

It was worth the wait, I thought, before saying proudly, "Nope – not yet. I want you to open it."

Grant grabbed hold of the tear tab and ripped open the packaging. He pulled out the contracts that I faxed out to Phil only yesterday. Attached to the signed contracts was a paperclip holding a check. Grant grabbed the check and tossed the contracts onto my desk. With both hands on the check, Grant held it up high to the light as if examining it for forgery. A smile spread across his face.

"Forty thousand dollars!" He exclaimed.

I smiled and dropped the strutting persona as I jumped to my feet and clapped him on the back.

"Kelco lives, son! We're in business!"

PART TWO
AMERICAN AVARICE

GROWING PAINS

I sat behind my desk in the Office Suites, sifting through the Rolodex for the next call like a card shark shuffling a deck of playing cards. Grant barged in through the open doorway to my office, talking a mile a minute. "Steve, we're drowning. I've called all our brokers, and the flow of new policies is dried up. Any ideas, Wise Old Man?" he said with a smirk.

I felt the panic too, but I tried not to let him see my uncertainty. I needed to be a mentor and present a calm demeanor, at least on the outside. I knew Grant had never failed at anything in life, and I didn't want to let him down. On the other hand, I loved the feeling of living on the edge, teetering on the brink of outrageous success and utter destruction.

I attempted to derail his thought process. "How do you like your graduation present, Young Grasshopper?" I said, matching his wry smirk.

He ran his hand through his dark hair and then sat in a chair across from my desk. "You mean the office? I love it, but that's not helping us solve our acquisition problem. We're drowning over here! We need more policies to sell."

I leaned back in my chair to project an air of confidence, even though I didn't feel it. "Don't worry; I got an idea. The National Viatical Association is meeting in Dallas. Medical Escrow, the largest holder of policies in the country, will be there. I'm going to get their policy flow."

Grant chewed on his lip and said, "One problem – don't we have to be a member to go to the conference?"

"I'm a member of the board," I said, laughing.

"What?" he shouted.

"Back in my Dean Witter days, we were one of five companies who formed the association. Another broker with Dean Witter went to the meetings, an older guy with gray hair that I trained with in New York – which, by the way, Grant, it always helps to have a gray-hair on the team. Perception is everything in the business world. So, long story short, he got me on the board. Sooo, technically, Kelco is on the board too.”

Grant scratched his head, then ran a hand through his hair again. “Okay, but how the hell are we going to pay for it?”

“Plastic, my friend, the good ol’ fashion American way.”

Grant laughed and then leaned back in his chair, adopting a posture like mine. “What if you fail?” he asked.

“That’s not an option.” I lied, knowing that failure was always an option – an ever-present possibility, especially as a startup. *In fact, nearly all companies fail within the first three years of existence,* a thought I chose not to share with Grant.

Grant seemed to still be mulling over the likelihood of this idea panning out successfully. He broke the silence, asking, “So when is it?”

“This weekend.”

DALLAS BUYERS CLUB

I leaned against the check-in counter at a Dallas Marriott Hotel. My bags had long been stowed in my room. I waited patiently in the lobby, well, as patiently as I could manage while trying to appear casual. I checked my watch, 6:30 PM. Check-in for tomorrow's convention ended at 7:00 PM. I waved to the concierge behind the desk, a short dark-haired man with a touch of gray at his temples.

The man slowly looked up from his computer screen. "Yes, Mr. Keller? I notice you're still here in the lobby. Do you need help finding your room, sir?"

I knew the staff was starting to wonder about me lurking in the lobby for so long. *They've got to be here any minute now. Just a little bit longer,* I reminded myself. "No, that won't be necessary," I replied. "Can you arrange a limo to come to pick up me and a few friends?"

He reached for the phone within arm's length and removed the phone from the receiver. "Expecting someone, sir?" the man asked, his tone dripping with disbelief.

"Yes, as a matter of fact, I am," I responded, hoping to sound more confident in their arrival than I felt.

He smiled sympathetically. "Right. Of course, sir. What time would you like the car to arrive?"

"Now, thank you. Well, I mean, the sooner, the better."

The concierge dialed a number and placed the phone to his ear. He smiled at me over the phone with a big fake smile worthy of a picture frame stock photo. I took my cue to leave the counter and began pacing the marble-floored lobby again. I knew the National Viatical Association brought all the top viatical players in the industry to town each year. I had my sights set on arranging an impromptu meeting with the executives from one of the largest policy providing companies in the industry called Medical Escrow. They were listed to attend the hotel's convention tomorrow morning, and I knew they hadn't arrived yet. So, I paced.

A long black limousine drove into the valet area in front of the hotel.

I checked my watch at 7:06. *They're late.*

"Where the hell are those guys?" I remarked out loud to myself, drawing a strange look from the hotel concierge out of the corner of his eye as he pretended to look at the computer screen behind the counter.

Eight o'clock rolled around, and I took a seat on a low fabric couch. From my vantage point, a round wooden table with an enormous floral arrangement blocked my view of the reception desk. *What if they walk in and I can't see them?* The thought spurred me back to my feet, and I resumed vigil, pacing from side-to-side of the table.

The hotel security officer entered through the glass entrance doors. He noticed my sporadic behavior and looked to the concierge who only lifted his eyebrows and rolled his eyes. The security guard called out to me across the lobby, drawing extra unwanted attention from a few of the hotel guests.

"Sir, can we help you with something?"

"I'm waiting for a couple of business contacts," I replied.

"Okay, we're just curious as to why you seem to be lingering..."

Suddenly, our attention was diverted to a lady across the lobby. She called out to two men walking through the front entrance, shouting, "Hey, Rob! Jim!"

The men waved to the woman as they approached the check-in desk.

I turned to the security guard and concierge with a shit-eating grin across my face and stated, "Excuse me, fellas; my colleagues are here."

I approached the two guys standing at the check-in counter. One of the guys looked like a possible younger brother of Kurt Russell. He stood 5'11" with blond hair and a strong jawline. The other guy stood at least 6'2" with dark wavy hair. Both seemed very athletic, and surprisingly, both seemed young and around my age, late twenties, early thirties.

"Excuse me, fellas, are you with Medical Escrow?" I prompted.

Kurt Russell's look-alike turned around with a smile and announced, "Yes, I'm Rob Haynie."

"Steve Keller, with Kelco from Lexington, Kentucky," I said, shaking his hand with vigor.

"That's Jim Nutt, my partner," Rob said, gesturing toward the other guy who continued his conversation with a hotel clerk about their room.

"What are your plans tonight, Rob?"

"Our first plane was canceled today. We just got in. We're thinking about calling it a night early tonight."

I smiled and pointed toward the valet area outside the door. Rob followed with his eyes through the glass doors.

"You see that large stretch limo sitting outside the entranceway?" I asked.

"Yeah, I see it."

"Well, that's ours for the evening. It's headed to the best gentlemen's club in Dallas. Send your bags to your room, and let's get going."

Rob leaned over to Jim and tapped him on the arm. "Jim, this is Steve Keller from Kelco, located in Kentucky. Is that right?" he asked me quickly to ensure he had the facts straight and then continued saying to his colleague, "He wants to take us out to what he says is the best gentlemen's club in town, and he even has a limo waiting for us. What do you think? Are you up for it?"

Before he could speak, I took the initiative and said, "I hear this place is second to none, guys. If you don't like it, we can always cut the night short at any time."

"I'll leave this one up to you, pal," Jim replied.

Rob whistled for a bellman.

"Take these bags to our room. Here's the key." Rob slid a ten-dollar bill to the bellman then turned to me with a smile like a fox in a hen house. "I like your style, Keller. Let's go."

We piled into the limousine and arrived at the club. We sat at a low couch in the corner of a large dark room filled with scantily clad women. On stage, a woman spun topless around a pole as we ordered drinks and let the alcohol flow. While downing several rounds of drinks, the ladies of the night worked their magic to loosen their minds and open their wallets.

Even though I was the reason we were there, the sights, the sounds, the smell of it made me feel...gross. I suppose on a macro-level – in this case, perhaps even a microbial level – doing business in America can be gross. Our markets are obscene, exploitative, and almost everyone appears to be for sale. I suppose, at that moment in time, I lurked in that swamp too; I felt like I had to in order to survive in that shallow water.

So, of course, I alligatored straight at those Escrow boys., hoping to blur the line between business and pleasure.

"So, guys, let me tell you about Kelco," I shouted over the low bass rumble of the music and the women's distractions throughout the room. "We're currently the largest buyer in Kentucky." I lied. "What do you guys think about working together? Can you send some of your policy outflow our way? We pay top dollar."

I sat back in my chair and waited as Jim watched a waitress walk by our table wearing a thong. Rob snapped his head back in my direction and answered for them both. He said, "How many you want, Keller?"

I leaned forward and grinned with excitement. "As many as you've got."

A NEW DAY A NEW PROBLEM

Back in Lexington, I scaled the steps of the Office Suites two at a time, anxious to get to my office. I barged through the cloud of Dianna's cigarette smoke in the reception area with a quick wave to Dianna as she said, "Good morning, Steve," and her voice followed me down the hall.

I entered my office to find Grant standing behind my desk. "There you are! Steve, we've got a big problem," he said, running a hand through his hair with a stern expression.

His serious tone caught me off guard, cutting through my excitement. Before I could ask what the problem was, Grant hefted a box from the floor and dropped it on top of my desk. It looked like a large banker box.

"Grant, is that what I think it is?"

A smile lit up his face, and he lets out a big laugh, giving up the charade. "Yep, it's the fruits of your labor."

Grant opened the banker box like a chest of plundered buried treasure. He stepped aside for me to sit behind my desk. I sorted through the massive pile of policies, each policy a lengthy fifty to eighty pages, all of which needed to be processed, reviewed, copied, and sent to our potential buyer clients.

I flipped through the seemingly endless pile of policies and wondered aloud, "How are we going to do all this?"

Grant chuckled. "Yeah, I thought the same thing. I think the old copy machine here would explode."

I sighed. My eyes trailed into the hallway where the copy machine stood, bulky and ancient like an old truck on my dad's salvage yard. The copy machine looked like the prototype for the first copier ever made. I had a feeling the mountain of papers on my desk would be the death of that copier.

I gritted my teeth with determination and pronounced, "Grant, my friend, we need to expand."

KELLER:

As boring as this sounds, this is what startup companies deal with on a day to basis. First, we had a money problem. Then we developed a policy flow problem. Now, our infrastructure wouldn't work with our policy volume. These are issues they don't really tell you in business college; however, they are a very real part of doing business. Indeed, neglecting these little details is what kills most companies. That's why entrepreneurs must be careful about the team members they choose to help them in their venture. At this point, I knew I needed to bring on some new hires if I wanted to expand, and I did.

NEW HIRES

A woman strutted through the door to my office. She looked like Bonnie Raitt with long and wavy auburn hair and a sassy, rebel attitude to match. She approached the desk confidently, wearing a form-fitting dress that showed off her athletic physique. Grant and I both stood from our chairs to greet her with a handshake across the desk. I offered her a seat across from us. I felt a bit unsure of how to conduct a formal interview for hire, seeing as Grant was my first and only employee up to that point.

"Thanks for coming in, Cynthia," I said to get the conversation rolling.

"So let me get this straight," she said, wasting no time. "You're giving people cash for their policies, which then allows folks to utilize their own life insurance money as a form of health care when they get sick?"

"Yeah, that pretty much sums it up," I said with a nod.

She dropped a hand onto her seated hip and said, "So you're forcing the insurance companies to do what they're supposed to do – pay out death proceeds! At least that's what they claim, but they sure don't practice what they preach!"

I smiled, unsure of where the weight of experiences behind her angry insinuations came from, but I knew I liked her fire.

"Yeah, that's about the size of it," I replied.

"I used to work for an insurance company, you know?" she said as a mischievous smile slowly spread over her face.

"Yeah?"

"And I couldn't stand the fact that insurance companies always fought us on paying out legitimate claims! It's in their policy manuals; did you know that?"

I nodded, and she stared down at the table for a moment. Her eyes darted across the desk, and with a grin, she said, "So when do I start?"

"Now." I blurted.

She pursed her lips and tilted her head toward me in confusion. I laughed, realizing how strange that must have sounded...and how novice. I tried to reframe my answer more in line with what I envisioned to be a typical employer's response. "Sorry," I said, "We really need the help, and we see you as a perfect fit for our lead underwriter. How about you start tomorrow?"

"I'll see you tomorrow." She said as she stood to shake my hand with a firm grip.

Cynthia strutted out of the office, and I turned to Grant, who wore a big grin on his face. He flashed a thumbs up as he nodded his head in approval. "I like her," he said, blushing.

"No kidding, she's a force of nature!"

The intercom on my desk buzzed. I pressed a button to hear Dianna's voice from the reception desk. She said, "Mr. Keller, your next appointment is here: a Mr. Keith Drach. Should I send him back?"

"Yes, thank you, Dianna," I said and then quickly turned to Grant. "This next guy has a ton of experience. He ran a big pharma company."

"How much is he going to cost us?" Grant exclaimed with wide eyes.

"More than you and I make together," I said with a smile.

"What? Steve, we can't afford that."

"It doesn't matter if we can afford it. It matters if you want to be driving a Mercedes in a year."

Grant rocked back in his chair, and I could see him struggling with the concept.

"You're the boss," he said.

"We need him on board with us, Grant, so get ready. You know the drill."

Grant smiled and shot a pointed finger in my direction, saying proudly, "Fake it 'til you make it."

Before I could respond, Keith was standing in the doorway. My face flushed bright red with embarrassment. I rushed to stand.

"Come on in. Hi, I'm Steve, and this is Grant."

Keith stood stoically in the doorway wearing brown slacks, a white button-down shirt, and a blue blazer. He looked like a version of Superman's alter ego, Clark Kent, only with blond hair and a touch of gray peppering his temples. He noticed my embarrassment and cut through the ice with a jovial smile.

"Keith Drach." He said as he pressed a pair of thick round frame glasses against the brim of his nose.

He extended a hand in greeting. For some reason, I felt an immediate connection with Keith. I stepped around the desk to greet him with a handshake and offered him a chair.

"Mr. Drach, great to meet you. I understand your last company had a hundred-million-dollar market cap. Tell us a little about yourself," I said, reclaiming my seat behind the desk.

"I'm going to be upfront with you both. In my last position, I was a partner for a pharmaceutical company. Unfortunately, a change in federal regulations took away our tax breaks and eventually forced us into bankruptcy. To be honest, the law change destroyed our startup and forced me into personal bankruptcy too. But the experience only made me more resilient. My family and I have fought back and are doing very well. I'm now looking for a company to grow with, which brings me here to you."

Out of the corner of my eye, I saw Grant giving me a sideways glare.

Bankruptcy, I thought to myself. I watched him as I considered what to say next. He sat across from me, calm and composed with a determined resolve about his demeanor.

"Mr. Drach, I'm sorry to hear about your last company. I don't know how familiar you are with the viatical settlements industry, but it's kinda' a wild west right now. We're running into new regulations and rule changes in our sector too. Your experience just might be a good fit for this evolving market. As long as that doesn't scare you off."

Keith looked to me with a steely-eyed, Clark-Kent-like resolve through his glasses. "Not anymore," he professed.

"Well, thank you, Mr. Drach. I'll call you soon with more news," I announced, placing my hands down on the desk with finality.

We all stood from our seats and shook hands. Keith held his shoulders back, and his head high as he exited the office.

Grant clapped me on the back and whispered, "So when are you gonna hire him?"

"It shows, does it?" I relented with a smile.

"Come on, Keller. He's a risk-taker, competent as hell, and what about the whole 'gray-haired' thing you were telling me about? What more do you need to see?"

He's asking for a six-figure salary. How the hell am I going to make this work? I scratched my head, suddenly aware of the rapidly thinning hair atop my scalp. I clamped down on my teeth, masking my nervousness with a confident grin. "Yeah, you're right. We kinda' clicked, didn't we?" I said with an awkward chuckle.

"Yeah, plus, I like him. Let's do it," Grant said, ribbing me with an elbow.

"Well, let's hope he'll take a serious pay-cut." I sighed, pressing the intercom button to call the reception desk. "Dianna, is Mr. Drach still in the building?"

"Yes, sir. He's just leaving now." Dianna replied, her charming southern drawl rolling through the intercom.

"Dianna, can you ask him to come back in? Thank you."

Keith returned to the office with a curious expression. I greeted him at the door.

"Keith, we'd like to offer you the job," I said proudly.

Keith's face lit up like an out-of-season Christmas tree, and he smiled. He had kind eyes and infectious joviality. We vigorously shook hands, both excited for the journey ahead of us.

"But wait, Keith, only on one condition. Let me first show you our current accounting methods."

"Of course, where are the books?" He asked.

I reached into my back pocket with a big grin and pulled out my checkbook. "Here you go!" I said, almost embarrassed.

I dropped my checkbook into his hand as he laughed, unsure and uneasy about how to respond. Finally, he said, "Okay, you guys are funny; you know that? Really, where are your books?"

Grant and I looked at each other and shrugged.

"It's no joke," Grant said.

"We've been running a million-dollar company out of my back pocket," I said earnestly.

Keith opened the checkbook and realized the truth of the situation. "How the heck did you guys even make it this far?" He chuckled.

I clapped Keith on the back and said, "God only knows, my friend. Just think of it this way: you get to build the books from scratch. I know you'll do a fine job. Welcome to Kelco."

NEW HORIZONS

With the new hires in place and our policy volume in full stride, thanks to the Good Ol' Boys at Medical Escrow, our small company was moving at an incredible speed. To my shock and proud delight, Kelco was quickly setting the pace to become one of the fastest-growing private companies in the country. I approached the entrance to our latest expenditure, the new Kelco offices. I may have only stood five-feet-eight inches tall, but I felt like a giant as I pushed open the tall double-glass doors to our new office space. Steve Keller, with Kelco, I thought proudly.

Stepping into the tile-floored lobby of the new office reminded me of the tsunami of changes that Kelco had undergone in recent months to stay afloat; our aspirations were a hard tide to hold back. I was immediately greeted by a new face behind the reception desk, a strikingly beautiful young lady with blond hair and bright blue eyes. She said, "Hi, welcome to Kelco," as I approached the reception desk, my eyes wide with surprise at the attractive unfamiliar face.

"Hi, who are you?" I said, almost stumbling over my words.

She looked down at the phone close at hand and touched her collarbone. "I'm Staci. I'm the new girl. I'm sorry, who are you?"

"I'm the new guy too," I said, smiling big and wide.

The phone at the reception desk rang, and Staci quickly placed a headset over her ears. She smiled shyly and turned her attention toward the phone, giving me my cue to leave. I walked away from the reception desk, thinking to myself, Wow, what a tsunami, indeed.

I entered an open room that housed nearly a dozen cubicles. A small group of newly hired employees worked within their respective stations. As I walked by, I was reminded of my own days inside a gray, four-walled cubicle for Dean Witter, still recent history. I hurried toward my corner office, unlocked the door, and closed the door behind me, excited to start the day. I sat behind a large walnut desk and examined the stacks of viatical policies on the desktop, awaiting my signature for approval.

I called out to Grant from behind my desk, "Hey, Grant?"

"Yeah?" Grant's voice answered.

I stood from my office chair and approached a crude hole knocked in the wall between our two offices, where we built a dummy window with a wood panel that we could open and close. One might guess that a whiteboard hid behind that closed panel. In reality, it was an opening into Grant's office to keep our communication flowing as our company grew. Through the hole, I saw Grant stand from his desk and come meet me at our do-it-yourself intercom system.

I spoke in a hushed, conspiratorial tone through the opening in the wall, "Did you hire that new girl at the front desk?"

Grant scratched his chin. "Wasn't me. I wish I could take credit for it — must have been Keith."

"I told you hiring Keith was a good idea."

We both laughed, and Grant said, "Wasn't it me who said you should hire him?"

"Speaking of Keith, did you swap out the chairs?"

"Yep, I can't wait to see the look on his face," Grant chuckled, "No sign of him yet. Listen, Steve, did you give any more thought to letting me run with the purchasing department we talked about."

I sighed heavily, feeling a sense of responsibility toward my young protege and best friend. "I have. Don't you want to go to college, Grant?"

"Are you kidding me?" he blurted, "Why would I go to college when I'm already making more here than I ever would in an entry-level position somewhere else after I get out of school? Plus, I'm gaining more practical experience than I ever could in a classroom. I want more responsibility, Steve. You know I can handle it."

"I know you can. Hell, you can outbid anyone in this industry, but look, Grant, here's the deal. I'm okay moving forward with the purchasing department like you want, but I insist on another buyer handling incoming purchases."

"I don't understand, I can handle the workload." he protested, crinkling his face in disgust.

"It's not that. Every department is already at least two people deep. Even I'm backed up. If I'm stepping out of the buying arena, I need this department to possess a depth of capable people."

Grant frowned and relented, saying, "Have you got anybody in mind?"

"Yes, Missy Fannin."

"Steve, come on! My *assistant*, Missy?"

Grant glared at me in shock.

"She already understands the buying from handling your transaction paperwork, and she's competent as hell," I said with an even tone, trying to reassure him.

He thought for a moment then said, "Will I still be in charge of the department?"

I walked away from the hole in the wall and returned to my seat behind my desk as I responded, "Yeah, but I need you to train Missy."

"Oh, come on, Keller!" Grant's face disappeared from the hole in the wall, and I heard his footsteps stomping out of his office. He stormed through the doorway to sit in one of the two plush leather chairs across from my desk. He pushed aside the frustration on his brow with a quick run of his hand through his hair, and he composed himself. He said, "Listen, I'm not saying Missy can't do it. I'm just saying this is a crucial time for Kelco, and we need buyers with experience."

I formed a power-tent with my fingers, my elbows resting on top of my desk. In my new office space, I felt a new sense of power. I said confidently, "That's why you're going to train her."

Grant sighed heavily, grappling for the right words, then said, "We've got a problem here, Steve. I've been going back and forth in my head about how best to tell you this, but I'm just going to come right out and say it: our largest supplier, Medical Escrow, is screwing us. I think they're backing out of the deal."

My fingers tightened, nearly snapping the tent formed with my hands. "I noticed they haven't sent us a new policy in weeks. What'd you find out?"

Grant leaned forward in his chair. He looked over his shoulder and spoke in a hushed tone to ensure no one in the cubicles could hear us through the open doorway to my office.

"You know my vacation this weekend, down at Treasure Island in Florida?" he asked.

I nodded eagerly, prodding him to continue. Grant looked down to the floor, suddenly bashful.

"I went with Courtney," he admitted.

"Medical Escrow's secretary!" I shouted, nearly jumping out of my chair. I stepped around the desk and gently closed the door to my office. "Alright, spill it. What's the scoop?"

Grant nodded. "Yep, that's the one, and long story short, you can just say I got to the bottom of it." Grant's face flushed red, and he shook his head. "To our problem, I mean. She said they're selling policies directly to our buyers now. Completely cutting us out of the loop!"

"Bastards!" I said as I paced through my office, unable to sit down. "I trusted those guys. It's my fault. I let them know too much about our business. They're probably using our same model now. Hell, I'd bet they're using our same contracts!"

Suddenly, we heard a loud crash.

"*What the heck?*" A voice screeched from another office.

Keith just found the prank we planted, I thought. Grant and I looked at each other and busted out laughing. Moments later, Keith swung open the door to my office, red-faced and flushed, pressing his glasses against the bridge of his nose.

"Okay, guys, hilarious, you got me," he barked.

Grant and I continued laughing as I said, "What's the matter, Keith? You look like you just took a spill!"

Keith's frustration turned to laughter as he joined in on our amusement. He brushed the joke aside, saying, "Grant, I see your old broken chair found its way into my office. Thank you for that. Funny one, guys."

"Keith, how about that new hire behind the reception desk? Was that you?" I asked quietly.

"You said, since we moved into this new office, you wanted to hire up, right?" Keith admitted, smiling shyly.

Grant chuckled along, still laughing at Keith's spill from the chair we planted. I found her very serious about her job and makes a great first impression as you enter the lobby.

Keith replies with a coy Shrug, well she's not only smart, she was a Nike model."

"I can see that," I acknowledged, redirecting their attention to a more serious matter. "Keith. Grant and I were just talking. We're going to expand the purchasing department and employ some new tactics. We need more policies."

Keith blustered, quick to interrupt me, "We're growing fast enough as it is. We've added ten people to the payroll in the past two months."

"We're just getting started, Keith, and thanks to Grant's recent reconnaissance work," I turned to Grant, and he blushed, "We now know why our policy flow from Medical Escrow dried up. They cut us out of the loop."

Keith's mouth dropped as he scoffed at the betrayal. His nostrils flared open wide as he inhaled sharply through his nose. He said with disbelief, "They're selling to our buyers?"

I nodded slowly, admitting, "Yep. That's about the size of it, so we have to go bigger. We need more sources for policies. We're expanding the buying department, and Grant's going to head up the department and train Missy to take over his previous role."

Grant nodded his head in determined agreement.

I rested my elbows on the desktop. I said, "You have to grow the department, and I can't have you focused on individual policies. We need your talents in other areas, like the espionage department."

He smiled, "And how do you propose I do that?"

"Well, maybe they have single receptionists," I suggested. "As you know, they are the industry's gatekeepers."

Keith turned to Grant with a puzzled expression as Grant's face brightened red.

I clasped my hands above my desk in excitement. "That's why, my young friend, James Bond and I are going on an espionage mission next week."

Keith squinted in confusion. "Dare I ask, or is it top secret?"

"There's an industry conference in Florida next week, and Grant and I will be there."

KELLER:

In the early days, the viatical industry was like the "wild west," and borrowing a metaphor from my favorite Clint Eastwood western, law barely existed; criminals masqueraded as the good guys; large corporations tried to bully everyone; and sometimes companies lived or died by way of a bloody shootout.

Kelco's biggest problem still revolved around trying to find policies and cut out our competition. Keith, Grant and I tried to come up with ideas to find new policies as our cash flow started to slow down. We couldn't just go to the corner stockbroker and buy it like any normal commodity. Also, we battled several new startup companies who looked to encroach on our territory. On top of that, no significant federal or state laws yet governed the buying and selling of life insurance policies. Therefore, everyone made up their own rules as the industry rushed forward. All three of us wanted to act ethically and within the law. The problem came when we ran into significant gray areas. I'll be the first to admit; we exploited those gray areas aggressively.

THE WILD WEST

Grant and I stood close to one another, resting our drinks on a tall cocktail table. We scanned the hotel conference room where the who's who of the viatical and insurance industries mingled around cocktail tables and drinks. Grant leaned his weight against the table with one leg casually crossed in his stance. I smirked, assuming the James Bond comment went to his head. I leaned across the table with a smile.

"Looking sharp, Double O Seven," I commented.

"Thanks," Grant replied, observing his dark blue blazer and khaki slacks. "Do you see Courtney? She said she'd be here."

I took a sip of whiskey and sloshed the ice around the glass as I said, "See if you can find out from her exactly which of our clients Medical Escrow is selling to now."

"I'll try my best. You think we can undercut them and win our clients back?"

"Wouldn't that be poetic justice?" I said with a smile, raising my glass to Grant.

Grant, not yet of legal drinking age, raised a glass of soda water in cheers. We both drank deeply, and then I pressed on, saying, "They really screwed us, you know it? They're the biggest player in this market right now, and I'd bet they're trying to take us out, keep us small. That way, we don't threaten their growth by winning more of the market share. Keith went over the numbers with me before we left. It'll take ten smaller policy providers to make up for the flow we lost from Medical Escrow. We need to connect with new sellers, and since they're now dealing directly with our buyers and cutting us out, we need to bring in new buyers too. We gotta raise the stakes."

"I'll find out what I can from Courtney," Grant said with a smirk and a wink. "I'll work all the back channels too, see if I can steer more buyers our way."

"Don't be afraid to pour on the charm there, James," I said with a laugh. I tightened the tuck of my white oxford shirt into my gray suit pants and adjusted the collar of my sports coat, quickly surveying the room. "I gotta bring some of these people together, or your girlfriend's company is going to bankrupt us all."

Grant blushed, always eager to rise to a new challenge as he asked, "Split up then?"

"Yep, let's circle back in an hour or two and hit the bars.

I nodded to Grant and took my drink with me as I stepped away from the table. I strode slowly and purposefully through the huddles of industry people gathered around cocktail tables throughout the conference room. I scanned the groups, searching for a familiar face to make my entrance. I made eye contact with a tall, athletically built black man with a shaved head. He seemed to recognize me somehow. He was speaking animatedly to a group gathered around a table. When he noticed me, he quickly concluded his conversation and approached me with a jovial smile.

"George Nichols," he said with a booming voice. "You're Keller; am I right?"

I shook his hand firmly and looked him in the eye, trying to assess how he might know me. "Hi, George," I said, "yes, Steve Keller, of Kelco."

"Kelco – that's what I thought. That name has come across my desk more times than a few."

I held a tentative smile on my face, unsure of how to respond. George took the cue and continued to fill in the blanks for me. He said, "I'm the Insurance commissioner for the state of Kentucky."

The tension dropped from my shoulders. I responded, "Ah, yes, it's good to see a friendly face from back home; these Floridians are wild-eyed. Pleasure to finally meet you. You're also the chairman of the national association of insurance commissioners, right?"

George nodded thoughtfully. "Right you are, Mr. Kelco. You've been making some big waves lately."

I laughed, pushing the comment aside. We locked eyes, and I nodded thoughtfully in response. "We're just getting started. Hopefully, you and I can work together along the way."

"I'd like that." George reached a mighty hand into his pocket and fished out a business card. "Give me a call sometime and let's see what we can work out."

We shook hands and parted ways. I walked forward, feeling a sense of accomplishment at finally shaking hands with Kentucky's Insurance Commissioner. *I need people like George in my corner. One stroke of the pen from him could clear a path to success straight to the top of the food chain...or he could just as easily, with a single bill of legislation, devour me and my hopes for Kelco. I need to stay on his good side,* I reminded myself, storing away a mental note.

I noticed the empty space at the table where George stood only moments before we spoke, and I veered toward the vacancy within the huddled crowd. A group of four unfamiliar faces huddled around the tall cocktail table sipping on their drinks. I sidled up to the table and claimed the open space and offered, "Hey there, Steve Keller of Kelco, based in Kentucky."

A heavyset balding man in his late forties nodded in my direction and said, "Hiya, Steve, Bruce Lundy. I'm here in town from Georgia. Good to meet you." He gestured with a half-empty glass of his white Russian cocktail toward a tall, slim man with gray hair. "We were just talking about the forecast in D.C. Mark here thinks we're in for some changes and some rough weather. How's it looking your way in Kentucky?"

"Well, Bruce, Mark, I hate to break it to you; I see nothing but blue skies!" I said, laughing and raising my glass to them to spark a good-natured, competitive spirit.

Bruce joined me for a laugh, but Mark remained stone-faced and stern.

Mark sighed heavily, "The big insurance companies are screaming bloody murder on Capitol Hill. They haven't figured out a way to take over our industry yet. Who can blame 'em? Instead of changing their business to accommodate the changing landscape, they're threatening to shut down the whole operation! They have a powerful presence in D.C. too. Just this month, as a matter of fact, they're trying to pass a bill that prevents the sale of policies outright. They want to shut us down and go back to the days of lapsing policies and more money on their balance sheets."

"I'm with you, Mark," I said, sipping my whiskey. "There's some turbulence out there, but there's some good legislation circulating in D.C. too. Jim Bunning, a senator out of Kentucky, is trying to pass the 'Tax-Free' Bill. That could blow the doors wide open on this industry. It's all changing. We are in the wild west, my friend." I glanced at each of the faces around the table. "Anybody here happen to be with Medical Escrow?"

Mark cleared his throat and responded, "I spoke with a man by the name of Jeff earlier, said he's able to price match any offer I can make to a buyer and beat me to the punch."

Bruce laughed heartily, "Yeah, I talked to him too. He's a cocky sumbitch!"

I glanced around the table, gaining the attention of the other two industry insiders, a pudgy young man with short blond hair, and a short man with glasses and a thinning comb-over. "Yep," I agreed, "they completely cut me out too, and then went behind my back and stole my buyers!"

The men around the cocktail table shook their heads, and we all shared a collective groan. I wrapped my arms around the shoulders of Mark and Bruce conspiratorially to lean in closer to the group. "Here's the deal. You guys want to know how we beat them?"

The four men around the table leaned in, waiting to hear my next words.

I patted Bruce and Mark on the back and leaned back to hold my space in the conversation now that I had their attention. "We team up," I suggested. "We all work together and beat them at their own game. We undercut them and beat them to the buyers!"

Mark, the gray-hair of the bunch, scoffed and ruffled his eyebrows with a stern expression. "Well, I don't see how we're going to do that. That'll ruin our margins! We can't do that!"

I responded quickly without missing a beat, expecting an adverse reaction from at least one person at the table. "Mark, if you want blue skies, you have to fly through the clouds! Right, guys?" I gestured around the table to see Bruce nod knowingly as I continued, "These are David and Goliath battles here, guys, and those giants are not going down without a fight. Same with the big insurance companies. We gotta bring the fight to them. They're going big; that just means we gotta go bigger!"

Bruce laughed and shook his head with doubt and an inkling of optimism. "It sounds all well and good, but how do you propose we do that, Steve?"

"Sell me all of your policies," I stated bluntly.

The four men gathered around the table all burst out laughing.

"Now, why would we do that, Steve?" Mark chided.

"You want to win, don't you?" I said, angling toward a close. "If we don't do something, we're all going to be out of business by next year. You're worried about your margins, I get it. But those days are over, Mark. This is about survival. Sure, your margins might drop from a thirty percent markup down to twenty percent, but they're dropping anyways up against Medical Escrow! Let me handle all the work of selling to buyers on the backend, and you focus all your efforts on upping your volume. Think about how much you'll save in payroll and overhead by eliminating your sales team. I'll buy all your policies at a twenty percent margin. You double your intake, cut your costs in half, and we all double our profits!"

Bruce slapped me on the back with gusto as his face lit up with a smile. He said, "hell, Steve, you're a ballsy sumbitch, but I like the way you think!"

Mark nodded his gray-haired head, seeming to relent, saying, "That's actually not a bad idea."

Bruce raised his cocktail glass. "Here's to a couple of David's teaming up to sucker punch Goliath right in the mouth!"

I raised my glass in cheers to Bruce as Mark slowly raised his glass. Mark said, "It's going to take me some time to reposition, but I'm open to it."

The four men at the table all raised their cocktail glasses in solidarity against our common enemy. A smile stretched across my face like a plane streaking across the sky. I toasted the group and our future together, fighting against the Goliaths of the industry, against the odds. I addressed our new alliance, saying, "To poetic justice!"

KELLER:

The lack of regulation in the early days of the viatical market allowed anyone with a bit of money to hang out a shingle and start buying policies. As can be expected, this left the industry-wide open to shysters, hucksters, and just plain thieves. These criminals would take advantage of the sick, elderly, and infirm at their greatest time of need and take them for all their hard-earned money. Corruption ran rampant throughout the industry, and we tried to be careful. Grant, Keith and I worked hard to sort through the various shady characters who came calling, looking to slide under the radar without acquiring a brokerage license, or even forging a fraudulent license while conducting business within the industry. Therefore, when a little-known company called United Benefits from South Florida called, we all put up our guard; we could see and smell the scum hanging off these swamp crocs.

I don't know what it is about Florida. Personally, I love visiting and vacationing in the state. The beaches are beautiful, the weather during the winter is perfection; and the lifestyle is comfortable. However, for some reason, the state attracts some of the business-world's slimiest shallow water reptiles.

CHARACTERS AND CON ARTISTS

I wrapped my knuckles on the doorway to Keith's office as I stepped inside to find Keith behind his desk, his tall stature rounded forward, eyes pouring over paperwork piled in front of him. He slowly lifted his gaze from his work and adjusted his glasses. He greeted me with a smile and said, "You're back."

I stood behind one of the two office chairs in front of his desk, using the chairback to lift my posture upright. My eyes felt heavy and tired. "Yep, got in late last night. Grant and I were out crawling around Florida this weekend. You ready for the meeting?"

"Long weekend, huh?" he asked, looking at me like he could smell the swamp on my clothes. "You look worn out. How was the conference? Did you guys dig up any new leads?"

I pushed my tiredness aside, stepping in front of the chair. My eyes widened with excitement to match my smile. I said, "You're going to see a new wave of policies hit the books soon. You ready for this meeting?"

Keith looked at me without saying anything. He took a deep inhale through his nose, then exhaled with his whole body. He nodded and stood from his chair.

"Steve, you ever think about settling down?" he asked.

"Settling down? I'm having too much fun!"

Keith stepped around his desk as we both turned to leave his office, but he stopped me short, saying, "I don't know how you keep up this pace, Steve. I admire your drive, but you're really burning the candle at both ends. The pastor gave a great sermon at church yesterday. He talked about how relationships are what keep us grounded in what's most important in life – you know, meet a good girl, slow things down a little bit. There's this girl that you really should meet. Her name is Tammy."

I patted him on the back. "Keith, I'm not into blind dates, and you should know by now that I've got two speeds: full throttle and over-drive. I'm fine, Keith. Today's Monday. What do you say we leave church for Sundays and focus on closing this next deal?"

Keith and I entered the conference room to find Grant sitting in one of the chairs behind the long, rectangular glass-top table. Grant greeted us with a subtle nod of his head and a casual smile. I sat in the chair to the left of Grant, and Keith sat beside me.

"I heard you two had a good weekend," Keith said conspiratorially, smiling at Grant.

"Good is an understatement," Grant said, laughing in my direction as he scratched the back of his head.

Keith alternated glances between Grant and me, trying to decipher what more happened on our trip. I laughed openly and let Keith linger in the unknown.

The conference room door swung open, and Kelco's secretary, Staci, entered the room. Her face was clouded with a confused expression. She announced, "Your eight o'clock meeting is here – I think."

"Did they say they're from United Benefits?" I asked.

"Yes."

"Thanks, Staci, yes, please send them back."

Moments later, five men strutted through the doorway to the conference room, looking like a confluence of South Florida leach lines. One of the men wore an assortment of gaudy jewelry, complete with thick, rope-chain gold necklaces, swollen rings, and a gold Rolex with diamonds all around the face. Two of the guys looked more like big burly construction workers than Corporate America executives, complete with scraggly beards, and rolled-up shirt sleeves, revealing hairy forearms and calloused hands. One of the other men wore a white linen suit contrasting against his bronze tan. The fifth man of the group wore a burly beard, flannel shirt, and baggy jeans.

After formal introductions, the bearded guy who sat across the table on my right assumed the role of spokesperson for the group. As he began by saying, "Thank you for having us here, Mr. Keller. My name is Rick," my eyes drifted down to the tattoos on his wrists beyond the cuffs of his flannel shirt.

"No problem, Rick. What's on your mind?"

"Well, we've put together a good company to buy policies, and our operation is really picking up steam. The bottom line is we need policies. Word on the street is Kelco's becoming one of the biggest players in the game."

I leaned forward on the glass table, already knowing the answer to my next question. I said, "So, Rick, I have to ask; are you licensed in Florida?"

Rick placed his open palm down on the table, exposing more black ink above his wrist. He said in a firm tone, "We have our application in the Department of Insurance ready to be signed. The Insurance Commissioner, Bill Nelson, he's in our hip pocket, as the expression goes. Trust me, it won't be a problem."

I maintained a placid expression, attempting to mask how uneasy this guy made me feel. *Something doesn't feel right,* I thought to myself as the hair on the back of my neck began to crawl. *If what he says is true, then why isn't he licensed yet?* After a long moment of silence, I looked over the top of my fingertips toward the burly man sitting across from me. I broke the silence and said, "Gentlemen, right now, we are covered up with buyers, and I'm not looking for any additional sources. We can't supply the ones that we have." I lied.

Rick's open palm on the table suddenly balled tightly into a fist. "Look, Steve, we really need your help," he said, forcing a feigned laugh. Then he released the grip with his fist to open his palm on the table again. "How can I say this? Steve, I own two of the biggest Harley dealerships in South Florida. What's it gonna take to make a deal with you?"

I looked nervously to Keith and Grant before saying, "I'll tell you what. Throw in a Fat Boy Harley, and we'll talk." I instantly felt relieved as everyone in the crowded conference room laughed, easing the tension. "Seriously, guys," I said, redirecting everyone's attention, "I can't do business with you until you get licensed."

Rick stared into my eyes, unflinching. He finally broke the silence. He stood suddenly from his chair and said, "I understand." The four men who flanked him all rose from their respective seats. Rick reached his hand across the table as if it pained him to have to be cordial with me now. I shook his hand. He smiled through his teeth and said, "We will get the license pronto, boss. Don't you worry. Steve, it was a pleasure. Thanks for your time. We will be in touch."

Grant, Keith, and I watched them leave the office. As soon as they stepped through the glass door and the door closed behind them, we all breathed easier.

"What the hell was that about?" Grant exclaimed.

"Shady, Steve, really shady," Keith said, shaking his head.

"Yeah, I know. Grant, no dealings with them until I see the actual paper to prove these guys are licensed, and I don't anticipate that is ever going to happen. I feel slimy just talking to them."

Keith nodded and said, "Yeah, I think I need a shower now."

Staci cautiously opened the door to the conference room. She peeked her head inside and said, "Your next appointment is already waiting in the lobby. Should I send them back, or do you want me to stall them until eight-thirty?"

"Is Trish Sills waiting?" I asked.

"Yes."

"Ask her to come back first. Thanks, Staci."

Grant walked to the coffee machine, saying, "I'm glad that's over. I thought that guy was going to jump over the table at you, Steve."

I laughed, feeling a twinge of truth behind Grant's words and then confessed, "I have to warn you two; this next guy coming in is a bit of a character."

Keith tilted his head in my direction. "Hopefully, not as interesting as the last group, Steve."

Staci entered the room and behind her walked Trish Sills, a young woman full of exuberant energy. Her brown hair hung in bangs over her forehead and draped down onto the shoulders of her blue suit jacket.

"Hi, Trish," I said warmly as I greeted her. "So, Trish, can you tell Grant and Keith about the character that we are about to meet?"

Trish flattened her dress skirt as she joined us at the table. She bubbled with excitement as if about to let us in on a juicy bit of office gossip. In her thick southern accent, she said, "Well, guys, for as long as I've managed Genesis brokerage, I have never met anyone quite so unique as this character." Trish laughed. Her laugh sounded like a quick, flitter of joy. She said, "Okay, Steve, put me on the spot, why don't you? Well, I'll do my best to sum this guy up." Trish folded her hands in front of her on the table as if to hold back her excitement. "Chuck's story is that he started out in the Billy Graham crusades as an evangelist with the church. He was heavily involved, well, that is, until they found out he was gay. Billy Graham exiled him from the megachurch community. Chuck still calls himself a reverend. Now he's relocated to California."

"An openly gay reverend – does he have a church?" Grant asked.

"He says he does. He claims it's enormous, some seven thousand members." Trish replied.

"Well, he is in San Francisco," Grant agreed, turning to Keith and me.

I heard a loud knock against the glass door. The four of us at the table looked up, expecting to see Staci. Instead, we saw the massive bulk that was the good reverend standing red-faced behind the door, wearing a brown leather jacket and blue jeans. He knocked again with a heavy hand on the door.

"I'll get it," Trish said.

She swung open the door, and Chuck entered the conference room like a wrecking ball. His body mass seemed to take up half of the room. He clutched a two-liter bottle of 7-Up in one hand, breathing heavily as he introduced himself, "Good to meet you. I'm Chuck. Trish, I didn't want you to get started without me."

Grant looked at me and tried not to smile.

We all shook hands, then returned to our seats, and Chuck placed his two-liter of 7-Up on the table in front of him. Chuck rocked in his swivel chair.

"Thanks for having me here," Chuck said, addressing the room. It's a pleasure to finally meet the team behind Kelco. Trish says you're looking for more policies."

I couldn't resist feeling a sense of amusement at Chuck's unusual presence.

"I understand you came all the way from California today and that you are a reverend?" I said, unable to hide my baffled smile.

Chuck nodded gravely and unscrewed the cap to his two-liter. He took a gulp of soda and quickly screwed the lid back on the bottle as if nothing happened. When he spoke, he spoke passionately, waving his hands over the conference table for emphasis. "That I am, Mr. Keller," he stated emphatically. "The good Lord calls us all in unique ways, and today he's called me to Lexington, Kentucky to enter into the field of viatical insurance sales."

I held a smile on my face, trying to prevent myself from laughing out loud as I looked to Chuck and then to his two-liter on top of the conference table.

"Guess this is a bit unusual, eh?" he said, smiling at me.

I couldn't help myself any longer. I finally laughed and replied, "Yeah, just a little bit, Reverend."

"Well, I usually carry one of these around all day long. A friend turned me onto this diet using caffeinated drinks to charge my metabolism and flush out my system. I used to weigh over four-hundred pounds. I'm now down to two hundred and ninety-two by drinking seven of these a day."

I nodded my head and shot a sideways glance in Grant's direction. "Seven a day?" I asked, barely able to hold a straight face. "How long have you been doing this?"

"Over a year now, I think."

"That is a lot of 7-Ups!" Grant exclaimed,

"Whatever works, right?" Chuck responded quickly. "Gentlemen... and lady. If you don't mind, may I, um, use your restroom?"

"Down the hallway, on the right," I replied.

Chuck stood from his chair with effort and swiped his two-liter bottle from the table as he hurried out of the room. Several minutes later, Chuck re-entered as if he never left. Boisterous and reinvigorated with a fresh wave of caffeine-infused energy, he said, "Where were we?" He then plopped back down into a chair and positioned his 7-Up in front of him.

"Okay, Chuck, here's what we can do," I offered. "We are looking to expand our market share by bringing in new policies direct from insured policyholders, in addition to our other policy flow streams. We don't have a presence in California yet, and from meeting you today, I know you have quite a presence."

Grant bit down on his lip, restraining his laughter.

I continued, "We're going to connect you with a law firm we use in Pittsburgh to help shore up any of the gray areas in the new policy acquisition space. You run everything through them to make sure we maintain a clean business reputation. If you can agree to that, then we can authorize you to broker policies in San Francisco."

Chuck suddenly became deathly serious. He nodded his head solemnly in silent appreciation. He then clasped his hands in prayer in front of his massive girth and bowed his head. I stood from the table, not wanting to disrupt the man's ritual. Chuck then opened his eyes and shook my hand, eager to seal the deal. Chuck grabbed his two-liter bottle from the table with gusto and chugged deeply in celebration. He screwed the cap on as he walked out of the conference room.

The door closed behind him. And with the closing of the door, Grant let out a pent up burst of laughter.

"Well, that was a bit unusual," Grant sputtered between breaths of laughter.

"Just a bit." I agreed, chuckling along with him. "Trish, thank you for the introduction...I think. We'll give him a shot. Let's see how this goes."

CHANGING OF THE SEASONS

Soft white lights lined the long autumn-leaf-covered driveway that led to Merrick Inn. Tall ash trees towered above the pathway as the engine of my brand-new Porsche 911 purred with raw power. I slowed to a stop at the valet stand near the brick-paved entrance. The valet opened the driver's side door for me and said, "Welcome, Mr. Keller, good to see you."

"Hi, thanks," I said as I stepped out of the driver's seat and into the night. I approached the canopied restaurant entrance and almost stopped in my tracks at the sight of a woman standing beneath the awning. High heels accentuated her long slender legs. The hem of her fall dress flirted playfully in the wind. An overcoat hung casually over her shoulders; her arms not wrapped within the sleeves but draped down by her sides. She wore her dark brown hair pinned up in chopsticks and seemingly no makeup on her stunningly beautiful face. She suddenly smiled in the direction of my Porsche.

She said, "I like your car."

I eagerly stepped closer to her with my most charming smile. She blushed and looked to me with a hint of intrigue in her eye.

"Well, aren't you bold?" she flirted.

My smile doubled, and I pushed my luck by stepping closer again. "I'm Steve."

A flash of recognition danced across the delicate features of her face; then quickly she resumed her casual demeanor and smiled. "Nice to meet you, Steve."

"What brings you here tonight? Do you want to have a drink with me?" I replied.

She playfully looked in my direction and then looked away as if waiting for something.

"My friends set me up on a blind date," she admitted.

"Lucky guy...You've never met him; why not come have dinner with me instead?" I offered.

She looked into my eyes, longer than an ordinary exchange. A smile lifted the corners of her red lips. "Tempting," she said, "I'm not usually into blind dates, but I have a good feeling about this one."

I held her gaze. "That's too bad. My friends tried to set me up on a blind date too. If I imagined she had your sort of gravitational pull, I would have taken them up on their offer and fallen straight to earth."

She suddenly broke eye contact with me to look toward the parking lot, presumably waiting for her date. "Enjoy your night, Steve," she said with finality.

There's something special about this woman, I thought. A rush of excitement ran through me. I smiled, saying, "Pleasure to meet you. If your date falls through, you'll know where to find me."

I stepped away from her, feeling disappointed. I approached the soft-lit entryway where a hostess held open the door. A second hostess greeted me and guided me through the dining area. Paintings of thoroughbred Derby winners adorned the walls near dimly lit sconces. Candlelight danced on top of each white-linen-covered table. She led me down a short set of stairs, and we passed a woodgrain bar-top lined with a seemingly endless variety of bourbon and whiskey. I saw a group of fifteen friends and business associates gathered around a large table in the back near the fireplace.

Grant was the first to notice me. He jumped from his chair and greeted me with a bear hug, followed quickly by a handshake. "Keller! You made it." He turned to everyone sitting around the table. "The guest of honor is here...well, sort of," he chided loudly as he jabbed an elbow to my ribs.

Grant and I both laughed, and the friends seated around the table joined in the laughter. I greeted everyone at the table quickly, shaking hands with Keith and hugging his wife, Susan. I said hello to our office manager, Cynthia, several other employees, and the president of Genesis Group, Trish Sills. As I took my seat at the sprawling table, I noticed everyone casually stealing glances toward the doorway. Grant noticed me see the strange looks. He projected his voice to redirect everyone's attention, shouting, "Guys, listen up! I have to tell you all about how I first met Steve. Has anyone heard this story?"

Everyone at the table turned their attention toward Grant to hear the story, but as he talked, I still noticed a few friends glancing over their shoulders at the door.

Grant, unperturbed, continued, "I was a senior in high school at the time."

Keith interjected with a dry-humored joke through a fit of chuckles, "Not that you're so much older now."

Grant took the comment in good-humored stride, continuing, "Our waitress can vouch for me. I'm twenty-one now, thank you very much!" Grant raised a glass of bourbon to his lips and sipped the drink. "Ah! The privilege of old age!"

"Old age! Sit down!" Keith rebuked. "I have shoes older than you!"

Everyone at the table gushed with laughter.

"Anyways," Grant continued, "Steve was working out of this tiny office space called the Office Suites. Just awful."

I interrupted his story. "Hold on now, Grant. You told me you loved that office."

"What's not to love?" Grant said sarcastically. "The smoke cloud in the lobby and that printer that should have been put out to pasture years ago. Anyways, I digress. So, my parents sent me in to talk to this guy about opening a stock account..."

Keith glanced over his shoulder toward the door, and my gaze followed. A woman walked down the short staircase wearing an eclectic form-fitting fall dress, and I recognized the woman from the valet. Most of the women I met in Lexington would try to wear their hair sprayed into position, with every hair in its perfect place, and their makeup painted on their faces as if they were composing a temporary mural. This woman though, she seemed to scorn Lexington's sense of fashion. She strode forward into the room with confidence.

Grant nudged me with an elbow. "Right, Steve?" he prompted.

I caught myself still staring at the woman as she walked closer. I shook my head and snapped my attention back to Grant. "Yeah," I responded, not really knowing what he was talking about.

"The Mickey Mantle – what did you say about it after I sold it to you?" He asked.

I turned my attention back to watch the woman approaching. Keith stood suddenly from the table, and his wife, Susan, stepped forward to greet her as she approaches the table. Susan hugged the woman quickly and turned to address us. She said, "For everyone who doesn't already know, this is Tammy Hull. Tammy, this is Steve Keller."

Keith and Grant laughed as Keith said, "Steve, this is who we've been trying to introduce you to, but you said you weren't into blind dates!"

My face turned bright red. I held an awkward smile and spoke through nearly clenched teeth, "Hi, Tammy, nice to meet you," I said, frozen with embarrassment, "and you were all in on this?"

Everyone seated around the table laughed heartily in amusement at my red-faced embarrassment. Grant offered Tammy his seat beside me and found another place on the other side of the table, taking his drink with him. I instant felt the chemistry between Tammy and me as she sat down beside me.

"You got me!" I whispered.

"I couldn't resist," she whispered back. Tammy then slid her chair closer to the table and closer to me. A few long strands of silky hair fell across her face from where they were held back with chopsticks. She casually tucked the stray strands of hair behind her ear as she smiled.

I smiled, feeling the charm she possessed about her. I detected a quick wit and a sharp sense of wry humor. The night carried on, and the drinks flowed freely, raising the bar to new heights of bizarre activity, even for the Kelco crew. While I attempted to play it cool and treat Tammy like any other short-term acquaintance, something was different about her. I couldn't get a pulse on it.

The rowdy crowd at the table grew louder throughout the night, causing Tammy and me to only lean closer to be able to hear each other. I found myself intoxicated by her, allured by her personality, and undeniably attracted by her figure in her fall dress. At one point, I couldn't help myself from saying, "That dress looks beautiful on you."

"Oh, this?" she asked, looking down at her dress in mock surprise.

"You seem incredibly athletic. I'm sure you work out. Maybe we could go together sometime."

Tammy smirked and said, "The only time I work out is if you count running late as an exercise."

We both burst into easy, effortless laughter. I fell for her at that moment, and I fell hard. In the blink of an eye, our laughter quieted to a hushed silence on the air, electricity thick between us. We found ourselves very close and staring each other in the eyes. Before I knew it, we were kissing. What I did know, at that moment, was that I was falling off a cliff toward her.

AN UNWELCOME SURPRISE

"No, Gary, we agreed on the price. Hell, we shook hands on it," I said through gritted teeth into the phone.

The intercom buzzed on my desk. I ignored it.

"We don't have any room to maneuver, Gary. We're holding up our end of the deal. I expect you to do the same," I stated.

The intercom buzzed again. In exasperation, I placed my phone call with Gary on hold, a backend policy buyer from New Hampshire, and answered Staci's dedicated line from the receptionist desk.

"Stacy, what's going on? I'm trying to close this deal," I said.

"Steve, I'm so sorry, but I need you to come to the front," she said, her voice thick with panic and fear.

The sound of her voice made my stomach clench.

"What's going on? Is there a shooter in the office or something?" I asked in fear.

"No, well, no, not exactly," she whispered. "There's a guy here to see you. He looks a bit, uh, scraggly and rough, and he's insisting to see you."

"What does he want?"

"He says he has something for you," she whispered.

Who did I piss off today? I asked myself. Is someone here to attack me? I had no defense there, no guns, not even security. Yet I knew I didn't want such a guy around the staff. *Where is Keith?* I wondered. *He's a good-sized fellow. Maybe he can back me up.*

"Staci, I'll be right there," I stated.

I unmuted the phone and returned to the call as Gary said, "Keller, are you there? Hello?"

"Gary, we have an emergency I have to deal with. I expect payment in the mail by Thursday – at the latest. Thanks, Gary, take care," I tersely replied.

As I lowered the phone toward the receiver, I heard Gary's response of protest fade away into silence. I left my office and hurried down the hallway toward Keith's office.

I heard Staci's voice yell, "Sir! Sir! You can't go back there!"

The man rounded the corner from the lobby and entered the office with Staci following in pursuit. He stood about six foot two or three and wore a cutoff t-shirt covered with a leather vest. Sewn patches of a wide variety accentuated the black leather vest. I noticed a litany of tattoos covering both of his arms and his neck. A chain hanging from his belt rattled as he approached. Grease stains covered his black jeans and dust-covered his well-worn black leather boots. He wore a black bandanna tied around his tangled salt and pepper hair. A thick black beard, peppered with streaks of white, obscured his face and hung down to the middle of his chest. He pointed a finger in my direction.

"Hey, you Keller?" the man asked in a gruff voice, striding purposefully past the cubicles toward me. "You! Are you Keller?" he asked again.

If this gets ugly, maybe I can lock my door. I thought as I took a few steps backward toward my office.

"Who wants to know?" I asked.

"Listen, somebody sent me to deliver you a message. I need you to come out front with me," the man demanded with a grim expression on his face.

Everyone stood within their cubicles, watching me with panic-stricken expressions. I noticed Keith step into the doorway of his office. I motioned gently with my hands for everyone in the office to calm down. The man stood in front of me, his massive frame towering above me, urging me to come with him.

"Fair enough, my friend," I said reassuringly, hoping to avoid conflict, especially in front of the entire staff, "let's go."

I followed as this guy led me through the office, the lobby, and then out of the building. I glanced over my shoulder as I walked through the exit doors, hoping to see Keith trailing behind us. In the parking lot, I noticed a huge black truck parked near the entrance. Hitched behind the truck was a black trailer with a giant Harley Davidson sign displayed on the side. The man stomped in his leather boots directly to the trailer and unlocked the doors. He lifted the back gate of the trailer as I stood at a distance.

"Come here," the man yelled over his shoulder.

I approached the open liftgate as the man extended a ramp from the tail of the trailer.

"Help me back this bad boy out!" the man demanded.

I peered into the trailer. I was shocked by an impressive sight—a solid black, chromed-out, Harley-Davidson Fat Boy motorcycle.

"What the hell?" I said with a laugh. "I don't believe this!"

I helped the man back the huge bike out of the trailer onto the parking lot's flat surface. The man showed me a toothy crocodile grin and said, "Man, I've been driving two solid days, straight from Fort Lauderdale to get this to you."

"This is a beautiful bike," I replied, almost at a loss for words.

"You ever rode one?"

"Not this big. Mostly just dirt bikes."

"Let me show you how this works. Get on it."

I sat in the black leather saddle of the massive bike, and he instructed me about the gears, the kill switch, the clutch, and other basic pointers to get me started.

"This here is the ignition," he said. "Go ahead and crank her up."

I revved the engine, and a deep rumble roared to life. The feeling of unbridled power within my grasp was intoxicating. I wanted more. I cranked the throttle, and the engine rumbled like a thundercloud beneath me.

The man smiled and clapped me on the back. He said, "That's how I felt with my first Harley too." He then handed me a folder filled with papers. "Here's the title and sales information. If you need anything, call Rick Sikes. He wants me to tell you this is a gift from United Benefits. I've got to get back to Fort Lauderdale. Enjoy the bike!"

"Thank you. I really appreciate your effort," I said, grinning atop the bike.

The man closed the trailer and locked the doors. He jumped into the driver's seat of the truck, flashed me a peace sign, and drove away.

I noticed Keith, Staci, and several other office staff standing near the doorway watching me. Keith exclaimed, "What was that all about, and where did you get this from?"

"Well, Keith, do you remember the characters that came up here from Florida?"

He frowned, saying, "You have got to be kidding me! You let them come back?"

"The guy said it's a message from Rick Sikes," I said with a shrug.

"What if it's stolen?" Keith asked.

I gestured to the folder in my hands. "Well, here's the title and bill of sale."

"You cannot keep this bike, Steve. There are strings all over this bike, you know that. Don't you remember those guys?"

I looked at the bike longingly and brushed the black and chrome finish with the back of my hand. I really wanted to keep it, but I couldn't deny that Keith had a point.

"You can't accept something like this," Keith continued. "This is not good. I'm telling you, Steve. You really need to be more careful! I can't believe you let him drop this off – and here at the office of all places!"

"Okay, okay, calm down. I'll call him right now and see about paying him for it," I offered.

I killed the engine to the bike, along with my motorcycle riding dreams, and rolled it into a parking space. I returned to rny office and called Rick Sikes of United Benefits.

"Rick, Steve Keller here."

"Did you get something today?" Rick asked in a gruff voice.

"Oh, yea, I couldn't believe it, Rick! It's a beautiful bike."

Rick laughed. "Glad you like it."

"I really do. But look; here's the deal: I still can't do business with you unless you're licensed."

"That's okay. I'm working on that." He reassured me.

"Your guy gave me the bill of sale on this bike. Why don't I just send you a check for that amount? Is that fair?" I asked.

Silence hung on the line as he didn't respond. I got the sense that

I offended him. Finally, he answered and said, "That's a gift from me to you, Steve."

"Rick, I appreciate the gesture, but I can't accept such an expensive gift. It represents a serious conflict of interest for me. And believe me; the bike won't change things between us. I'm not able to do any business together until you're licensed."

"Don't worry about it. Just enjoy the bike. Let me take care of my end, and I'll call you when I get the license. If I can't get the license, you're under no obligation to me. I just wanted to do something for you."

"Are you sure you won't let me pay you for it?" I asked. *I hope he doesn't,* I thought as I waited to hear his response.

"I won't hear of it. Enjoy the bike, and I will call you again when I have my license," Rick replied with finality.

I placed the phone on the receiver, and my open-mouthed surprise stretched into a nervous smile. *I just accepted a motorcycle.*

RALLY THE TROOPS

"Shut the door. I want to talk about some things."

Keith and Grant looked at each other, knowing I never asked them to shut the door unless it was about something serious.

"What's up, Keller?" Keith asked.

"Guys, we're doing great – more than great, actually – but we've got some problems. You know that, right?"

Grant responded with a nod, "The big insurance companies are breathing fire and threatening anyone associated with them. They don't want anyone dealing with us."

Keith chuckled. "Of course...we're putting a serious dent in their profit tables."

Grant smirked, saying, "I think I'm number one on their hit list for all my James Bond work: wine, women, and policy information."

We all burst out laughing, imagining Grant on his corporate reconnaissance missions, gathering important intel from our competitors' attractive secretaries. It was amazing what he could uncover by spending time with their front desk staff.

I redirected the conversation and said, "Every time our staff calls one of the insurers to process paperwork, the insurers hang up the phone! They're really stooping to new levels here, trying to avoid paying out the policies that come due. Another one of their new tricks is mysteriously losing our paperwork. More and more insurance companies are deliberately blackballing any association with the viatical companies and particularly Kelco. We can't let them get away with this. We have to fight back."

"So, what do you have in mind?" Keith asked.

"First, we clean up this industry," I said, holding a finger in the air. "I'm tired of taking meetings with people like United Benefits. Anyone with extra money thinks they can put up a shingle in front of their office and start trading policies. We need to petition politicians for stronger laws."

They both looked at me with surprise, and Keith seemed to love the idea. He nods, saying, "I'm with you on that."

Grant interjected with a laugh, and replied, "It can't be all bad, Keller. You got a brand-new Harley out of the deal."

"Hey, I offered to pay them for it," I said with a chuckle and a shrug while still holding a finger in the air. I paused for effect, then put a second finger in the air. "Second, we're running up against the big boys now. These guys have multi-billion-dollar market caps, and they want to shut us down. So, here's what we do: we take an end-run around them, appeal to a larger market, contact huge banks, and grow past just the AIDS community. We know that, before we came along, ninety-nine percent of all life insurance policies lapsed before payout, but most people don't know this. We need to educate the market! We have to go bigger."

No one spoke.

I wanted to make money, sure; I also took a great deal of satisfaction from poking these massive companies in the eye. In my opinion, they represented the very worst of capitalistic corruption and greed. Not only did they not want competition, but they actively sought to destroy it through dirty tactics and by using their power to lobby the government.

"Yeah, I can see that," Grant said, "but what about the AIDS market? It's still our biggest customer."

"I don't want to rely on just that. I think other people deserve to know what they can do with their life insurance policies; don't you?" I asked, imploring them to see my vision. "Not just the AIDS market but the entire market."

They both nodded.

"Besides, we just got a big boost on the Federal level; didn't you hear?"

"Yeah, Jim Bunning, our senator from Kentucky got that tax-free bill passed yesterday," Keith replied.

Grant raised his eyebrows. "You mean, people now get to sell their policies and not pay taxes on it?"

A smile stretched across my face. "Bingo – the market is now wide open. All we need to do is find the customers."

"So how do we tap the broader market?" Grant said, squinting his eyes with excitement. "Wait, are you thinking about tapping the overseas market too?"

"I am," I said as I widened my eyes and expanded my hands in front of me. "I'm thinking about tapping every market we can. We take Kelco global."

Grant and Keith watched me with wide-eyed expressions. Keith finally asked, "How?"

"A commercial."

Keith's eyebrows bunched above his glasses. "This worries me, Steve. I don't know if we're ready for that."

"It's the only way, Keith. We're not here to settle or go small. If we do, the big guys will snuff us right out of the industry. We have to go bigger."

Keith sighed. He nodded his head slowly while Grant and I waited with anticipation. Keith finally relented, "It worries me, but you know...it makes sense. This plan just might work."

SHOWTIME

I sat behind my desk, feeling like a captain at the helm of my ship. I rocked forward in my high-backed chair and picked up the phone to contact Bruce Gabbard, my ad agent.

"Bruce, Steve Keller, how are you?" I asked.

"Good, good – doing well, Steve. So, I hear you want to do a commercial? You want to secure a few slots for local TV?" he asked.

"No – bigger – I don't want some cheese-ball ambulance-chaser ads."

"Okay, so what are you thinking?" He asked. His curiosity edged on excitement.

"A full-on, three-minute commercial that will educate people about our services. A mini-infomercial."

I could almost hear Bruce's raised eyebrows over the phone. "Okay, go on. What do you have in mind?"

"Do we keep fighting these doctors' offices about telling their patients about our services. So, let's tell them through the commercial. We've got a few physicians willing to go to bat for us against the insurance companies and go on air to educate the public. And I want network time, not local time; got it?" I said, loving the newfound authority in my voice.

He laughed. "Not asking for much, are we? It's gonna cost a bundle, especially if you hit your big markets: New York, Chicago, Florida, Arizona, and California. Those are not going to come cheap...at all. What's your budget here?"

"Whatever it costs."

He sighed heavily through the phone. "I'm being serious, Steve."

"So am I."

If Keith hears me talk like this, he might develop an ulcer overnight, I considered. We talked about doing a commercial, but I didn't tell them what I had in mind. I knew I had to find the cash from somewhere on my own to finance the project. I was staking the company's life, people's livelihoods, and my own future on this one idea. Still, I didn't see any other choice. The insurance companies were stonewalling us; our magazine ads didn't bring in enough business; and we could go bankrupt in a year if we didn't do something drastic.

"Steve, you there?" Bruce asked.

"Sorry, when can you get all the pricing information, filming budgets, etc. for me?"

"Might take a few days. Give me some time."

"No problem, just let me know," I said and hung up the phone.

Several weeks later, after hundreds of hours of research and negotiations, Bruce arrived at our office. Keith and Grant sat on either side of me in the conference room as Bruce sat across the table. Bruce began the conversation, saying, "Gentlemen, we have some decisions to make. It's going to take a lot of moving parts coming together for us to accomplish this thing, but I think we can get there. It's not cheap, but you will have the potential to reach millions of viewers."

I smiled. The thought of Super Bowl ads flashed through my mind. I couldn't believe the colossal effort it took to make a three-minute commercial. I tried not to think of all the work that went into making a major Hollywood production. "So, Bruce, which markets offer the most exposure and biggest bang for our dollar?" I questioned.

"Well, you asked me to concentrate on the biggest markets. I've narrowed it down to three – California, Arizona, and New York.

These three states have time slots available during the late afternoon: that's your prime time viewing audience. I've got verbal commitments for our commercial to run for one month in each state, starting in New York for one month, traveling to Arizona for the following month, and then the third month in California."

"That's a long run. What's the cost?" Keith asked.

"To produce the commercial and air it six to eight times a day will run you close to a million dollars."

The blood drained from Keith's face as he stared blankly ahead, ghostly white.

Even Grant balked at the number. He shook his head and said,

"What if we just run it in one state?"

"You can do that, but the quote for the three states is considered a special deal. One state could cost you half this. I've crunched every deal available, and right now, this package is the best value."

"What will be the volume and demographics reached?" Keith asked.

"You're going to hit numbers of ten to twenty million on certain programs. You will be aired in New York on the evening news segment. This is the big leagues, gentlemen." He clasped his hands in front of him on the conference room table.

This is the big leagues, I thought, letting Bruce's words hit home. The commercial could be a blazing banner to the world that Kelco existed. I quickly ran a few mental calculations, assessing Kelco's infrastructure. I knew we weren't big enough – not yet. We wouldn't be able to handle the possible influx of customers. I knew we couldn't just do the commercial, tell millions of people about our services, and then not be able to handle the volume. When it came to business, such details were a matter of life and death for a company. A simple miscalculation could bring down the whole thing, no matter how successful the advertisement.

"Steve?" Bruce said as he looked at me with concern.

"Sorry, I was just thinking about some things."

"As I was saying, for me to get this three-state deal, I need to let the network agents know within three days, so we need an answer, ASAP."

"So, we need a million dollars to pull this off, right?" I asked, as if, of course, we have a million dollars lying around to spend on this campaign.

"Yep, that's about the size of it," Bruce confirmed.

"Okay, thanks, Bruce. I'll let you know in three days." I sighed.

The truth was, we didn't have a million dollars to throw around. After Bruce left, Grant and Keith avoided asking me where we would get the money for the campaign. I'm glad they didn't because even I didn't know where the money would come from. We didn't have any capital that we could afford to spend, other than the value in the life insurance policies we carried.

KELLER:

I never wanted to make an offer that might come in too low and fall short of seeing my dream come to life. All dreams come with a cost, it seems. As I was on the precipice of seeing this dream through to the next level, I learned what my dream would cost – or what I thought it would cost me: one million dollars. That was the price he quoted to make my dreams come true. I saw the amount as merely an obstacle standing between me and my dream. It was a new goal that I had to conquer. Let me know the price, and I would find a way. I always have. I believe in the six degrees of separation. It's the idea that everyone in the world is only six connections, or fewer, away from each other. In my mind, the obstacle of raising one million dollars was only six of the right phone calls away.

A FRIEND OF A FRIEND

I rushed out of the conference room without saying a word and hurried to my office. I stood in front of my desk and reach for the phone, urgently calling my biggest buyer, Tom, a guy who owned a firm in Grand Rapids, Michigan, that bought insurance policies.

"Keller! You have more policies for me?" Tom said, greeting me with an excitable voice that always sounded like he was speaking with a cigar on his lip.

"Well, sort of. We've been having trouble finding policies. You know how it goes, Tom; insurance companies are playing hardball."

"Bastards," he concurred.

"Yeah, so I've come up with a huge solution."

Tom waited in silence for me to continue.

"So, hear me out here, Tom. We got a package deal to run this commercial in New York, Arizona, and California for one month each, in consecutive order. This ad will reach millions of potential policy owners. If we only receive one percent of the viewers' business, we can pay for the commercial and break even. Anything above that is all profit, and then I'll be sending a lot more policies your way."

"How much is the commercial?" Tom said. His voice gave nothing about his position away.

"To produce the commercial, with airtime included, it will cost us one million dollars," I said, cringing as I waited for a response.

"I'm listening," Tom replied.

"Here's what I propose. I'm going to place one and a half million dollars in face value of policies into a trust. You will loan me the one million dollars against the policies. If all goes well, I will pay your money back from the commercial. If not, you can take the policies."

"How long do you think it will take to pay it back?"

"If this works out, a few days after the ads air."

I waited for his reaction for what felt like a minute...stretched into an hour. Tom, come on, say something, I thought, not wanting to break my rule and be the first to speak after making my pitch.

Finally, he said, "Steve, when do you need this money?"

I closed my eyes and gritted my teeth. "I have to give the guy a commitment in three days."

"What the hell?" Tom blurted into the phone, "Three days! Are you crazy, Keller?"

"I don't need the money in three days. I just need to give the networks a verbal commitment and probably sign a contract. I need a commitment from you that you will do this deal."

"Do you have the policies?"

"I have some, but I can find more to fill the pool."

"Guess I have no choice, Keller; I need more of what you got. Send me the paperwork. Let's hope for both our sakes we can find what you need."

Grant walked into my office as I hung up the phone.

"So, how goes it? Are we shooting a commercial or what?" he asked with a cheesy grin.

I grinned, and with my best Hollywood director impersonation, I said, "Lights, camera, action!"

ACTION

The day of the commercial dawned cold and damp. Mounds of snow from a recent winter storm were piled alongside the nearly deserted downtown Lexington streets. I arrived at the location of the commercial shoot early, not wanting to miss anything. A large truck pulled into a parking space within the lot, and Bruce leaped out of the driver seat. He approached my car, and I rolled down the window.

Bruce said, "Didn't take you to be such a morning person, Keller. Let's get out of this cold and get inside. The hospital is being fantastic. They're ready to accommodate us in every way they can. It's going to be perfect. We even had a few of the hospital staff agree to be extras." Bruce smiled and added, "For free, of course. No extra cost to you."

We shared a laugh and walked through the sliding glass doors to the hospital. Warm air rushed at us as we stepped inside the building and out of the cold. Bruce led me down a long corridor where the commercial production was prepared to shoot for the day. He quickly introduced me to the crew and the actors on set. Standing in the hospital hallway among all of the lights, camera rigs, dollies, makeup artists, wardrobes, cast, and crew felt like what I imagined it must be like on a Hollywood film set. I found it exciting to see how it all worked behind the scenes.

"Quiet on the set," the director yelled. "Sound."

"Speed," responded an audio engineer.

"Rolling," confirmed the camera operator.

"Action!" yelled the director.

Two actors playing female nurses, one black and one white, walked down the hallway. The white nurse said, "You know, my dad is worried about his medical bills. Health insurance companies are denying him coverage."

The black nurse shook her head and replied, "Yeah, it's a crying shame. What are people going to do?"

A look-alike for stereotypical doctor, complete with gray hair to imply years of experience, approached the nurse's station as if he happened to overhear their conversation. The doctor looked at the nurses over the top of his clipboard and dramatically asked, "Have you heard about Kelco?"

"Cut!" yelled the director.

The actors then returned to their original marks and then repeated the same lines from different angles while the director and camera crew recorded their every move.

I leaned toward Bruce's ear and whispered, "Bruce, do they ever get sick of the same lines?"

He smiled and whispered, "Nah, they're all pros. This is how it goes. Takes away some of the glamour, doesn't it?"

For a million-dollar price tag, I mused to myself, *this production better end up with some glamour.*

The director again yelled, "Quiet on the set!"

I leaned away from Bruce and watched in silence. Seeing the process behind the scenes gave me a greater appreciation for people who work in the entertainment industry. I had no idea how grueling and tedious their work could be.

After a twelve-hour day of shooting, the director finally seemed satisfied, and we all went home exhausted, including me after only watching them work. The commercial production event through the editing phase the following week. A week later, Bruce played a rough cut for me in his office. At the end of the commercial, the director chose to add a voice-over that, in a severe tone, stated, "If you or a loved one is suffering from a terminal illness and own life insurance, call Kelco to see if you qualify for the money you need – today."

THE BIG DAY

Keith, Grant, Cynthia, Staci, and nearly twenty more members of the Kelco team gathered in front of the cubicles in the open area of the Kelco office. As I scanned the faces before me, I felt a sense of pride swell within me. I knew the decisions I made impacted each and every one of their lives. The risk of the commercial and the responsibility I carried weighed heavily on my thoughts as I prepared to address them all.

The excitement and the jitters of anticipation constricted my lungs before I spoke. I cleared my throat coarsely and addressed the crowded office, saying, "As you all know, we go live with the commercial in less than an hour."

Grant cheered like an enthusiastic fan at a concert. His enthusiasm inspired laughs and cheers that echoed from the team. I smiled, letting my excitement stretch wide across my face. "Today is a big day!" I cheered. "By the end of today, Kelco will be in millions of homes."

I paused, allowing the insinuations to sink in. "We created Kelco to improve people's lives," I continued, "to improve the lives of people who are vulnerable, preyed upon by those insurance company buzzards; to improve your lives, to concentrate your lives at work on something worthwhile and give you and your children hopes for more prosperous lives. I take great pride in Kelco and in you; we do our jobs better than anyone else out there. Even though we like to have fun – I don't know about you guys, but I've had a lot of it" – we all shared a laugh, "it doesn't change the fact that what we are doing is important and necessary. This commercial broadcasts us and what we are doing here, showcases the impact we hope to have in this industry and on people's lives, out to the world. Over ninety percent of all life insurance policies lapse due to lack of payment and lack of understanding from the consumer. The big insurance companies want it that way, and today, we are changing that."

I paused and looked at the crowd of people who comprised the Kelco team.

"There are, what, twenty of us now?" I asked.

"Twenty-two!" Keith chimed in.

Everyone laughed, and I blustered with a laugh at my miscalculation as I said, "We're taking a huge risk today. I'm not going to lie. When these commercial airs, millions will know the truth about our industry. The insurance companies already don't like us. You guys have experienced it firsthand when they slow-play our orders or just downright avoid our calls or hang up the phone!"

Heads nodded among the group.

"After this, the big insurance companies are really going to hate us! They want to keep us small or try to shut us down completely, and I'll bet you they think we don't belong in the big leagues with them! But you know what we're going to do?"

I paused for dramatic effect, scanning the faces of the employees before me.

I broke the silence, excitedly sharing, "We're just going to go bigger! We're not going to be bullied or silenced by the big companies that try to take advantage of people for a profit – no, not us! What we are going to do is empower those same people – educate them! When medical bills start to rise and those premiums become too high to cover, that's where Kelco comes in. That's where we come in. We're letting people know they have a choice! And this commercial is broadcasting that to the world. We are going bigger, so get ready for the ride because this little company in Lexington, Kentucky, is about to revolutionize this industry!"

Grant whistled through his fingers and cheered. Other voices cheered with excitement, and Keith clapped loudly. I cheered along with them, my smile brimming from ear to ear. I held my hands up to quiet them.

"If this thing goes well, the phones will be ringing off the hook," I added. I then laughed nervously, unsure if my words would prove to be true. "This kinda' attention puts us in the big leagues now. We're going to have some extra help fielding the calls. I brought on a professional call service to help with any overflow, so let's stay focused and offer the best service we can to each person who calls looking for our help. If we all buckle down and see this thing through, we may even be able to take Kelco public someday." I looked to Keith, who raised his eyebrows in shock at my ambitious declaration. I heard murmurs of surprise from the staff. I continued sharing my vision and announced, "That means stock options for everyone, p, pension plans...you name it! The sky's the limit! Now let's go watch this commercial...and pray it goes well!"

I laughed, and the employees cheered with elation at the possibilities for the future. "Wooo!" I shouted, thrusting my fist in the air. I stepped to the side of the group, laughing nervously after my outburst. My face was flushed with the rush of excitement from their energy and my own anxiety about the commercial. We crammed into my office, and I turned on a television set. The commercial was set to air at 4 PM in New York. I checked my watch. 3:58.

The time arrived. 4:00. The television program switched to commercial break. The first commercial to air was a laundry detergent ad. The commercial ended and then a fake medical professional, a doctor wearing a white overcoat, addressed us on screen.

My teeth clenched as I watched with a mixture of pride and fear. Our hired actor in the white overcoat discussed his patient's needs and the former lack of options to overcome the rising medical expenses. He then described how Kelco offered his patients a better alternative. The Kelco logo appeared on the screen. And just like that, the commercial ended and the television cut to another local advertisement.

Wow, I thought to myself. I just spent a million dollars on that. I looked around my office at the faces huddled around the television screen. No one seemed to breathe, and the room was filled with silence.

Cynthia, the fiery office manager, spoke first. She said, "Well, I like it!"

Grant agreed and said, "Makes me want to go out and buy a policy just so I can sell it back to Kelco!"

Grant's comment inspired a few laughs from the group. We all knew the next hour would decide if our gamble worked. If it didn't, we could all be out of a job. *Will people call? Will they take a chance on an unknown company?* I could almost feel everyone holding their breath.

"All right, folks, everybody back to their stations. Now we wait for the phones to ring," I said, addressing our group.

Everyone shuffled out of my office and returned to their desks. Keith lingered in my office after everyone cleared out. He scratched his chin and adjusted his glasses with a concerned expression. I smiled at him with my best attempt at confidence.

"We just have to have faith," he said as he patted me on the back. He then stepped out of the room.

My mind drifted to the days when I first dreamed of Kelco. *We've grown faster than I ever expected – a million-dollar ad placement. I wonder what my dad will think when I tell him about it. Well, let's see if I'm still in business by the time I talk to him again.* I hunkered down behind my desk, letting my thoughts drift in the silence. *Shoot, maybe it didn't work.*

Suddenly, a phone rang. Then more phones rang, filling the office with digital tones. Everyone scrambled to answer the ringing phones. I hurried to the purchasing department floor to eavesdrop on a call. I overheard a woman named Janet ease through the conversation with our predetermined script, saying in a pleasant tone, "And how did you hear about our company?"

I scanned the office floor of phone attendants fielding calls, and several employees made eye contact with me, giving me a smile and a thumbs up in salute. According to a list that our media producer, Bruce Gabbard gave me, I knew the next airing of the commercial would be at 4:30, during the Oprah Winfrey show, followed by the local news, and then several times during the evening news with Tom Brokaw. According to Bruce's marketing studies, any company that advertised or ran a promotion alongside the Oprah show tended to take off in a big way. Oprah stood for so much more than just a brand name. She was a one-woman marketing force. I was bristling with anticipation to see the impact she would have on our newfound influx of business.

The initial calls from the first commercial slowed down, and the employees shifted their focus to chat with one another about the quick turnaround of results from the first airing of the commercial. I announced, "Everyone, the Oprah commercial will be airing any minute now. Get ready for the next big wave!"

Minutes later, the phones rang like a chorus of wind chimes. I rushed to my desk and placed a call to the call center that was fielding our overflow of calls. I announced myself and asked to speak to our account manager. A man answered on the other end, saying, "Mr. Keller, I'm sorry; our phones are jammed. I've never seen anything like this. We're at capacity right now, but don't worry. We're scrambling to bring in more operators to handle the overflow."

I hung up the receiver, not bothering to respond. I sat back in my office chair. My eyes drifted to the distant vision of a future growing brighter with each new ringing phone line. My ears savored the sound of ringing phones and the enthusiastic conversations from the purchasing department. *I just hope we can handle the new volume of customers.*

KELLER:

Every day that the commercials aired, the call volume kept crashing the phone lines. To top it off, a reporter from NBC did a follow-up piece after our commercial and interviewed me alongside a real-life customer who had sold us his life insurance policy. We were hit with a massive wave of new business as policies came flooding in. We immediately tripled our office staff. The commercial was a big deal for us but not necessarily how we anticipated. Local insurance companies who weren't beholden to the more prominent companies noticed as well. They started to call and make deals with us. We had thousands of incoming calls, but the percent of actual deals that were able to be purchased in short order and resell for a profit afforded us to pay back the million-dollar loan after all the smoke cleared. The most significant benefit from the marketing exposure wasn't profit, but from educating the insurance industry about our Life Settlements product. We amassed some thirty thousand agents that had been excited by the commercial and the new opportunities within the life insurance industry. Not only was it a windfall for the consumer, but the agents also saw this as a huge income opportunity. Kelco now had the most significant sales force in the entire industry.

Keith, Grant, and I didn't realize what it would mean to gouge these ogres, these multinational insurance companies, in their giant, greed-centered eyes. We went from an annoying horsefly buzzing around their hindquarters to a sharp-slinging shepherd slamming a stone of barium sulfate straight into their corneas. I saw us as a David taking aim at a Goliath who was taking advantage of an unknown marketplace, that guaranteed people's benefits, rather than policies simply lapsing or going unpaid. I felt justified and righteous in our cause to go after them and take away their profits. Pardon the mixing of metaphors, but I also felt like a Robin Hood of sorts. When this commercial aired, it was as if we'd reached into the pockets of the multi-national insurance conglomerates and yanked out their wallets. All of a sudden, they'd be legally forced to pay out their consumers on policies that they counted on to expire.

I knew we couldn't meet the funding needs required to absorb the policy flow. The amount of money that the industry was raising was like a drop of water in a large sponge compared to the funding needed for our new Life Settlement product. The market's response to the new product had come at us like a tsunami, moving full force and relentlessly with the new demand. Over the next few months, we began working with one of the largest actuary firms in the world, William Mercer, to refine the Life Settlement product, which made it possible for anyone to sell their life insurance policy, going beyond the original scope of the viatical market, which mostly served those suffering from terminal illnesses such as AIDS. It took a year to build the Life Settlement product in a way that was ready to be packaged for all markets.

In 1998, we simply added a tag line to our existing running commercial stating, if you or a loved one are 65 years or older and want to sell your life insurance policy call Kelco. It was the first introduction of the Life Settlements product to the world. The tsunami of new business that came in was beyond our wildest dreams. Within two months, we had six billion dollars in face value of policies flowed into Kelco.

In business, there are two kinds of possible failures: one is straight-up failing to hit the mark; the second is failing to handle the success. The first scenario can be fixed; a business can adjust and often increase sales. The second, in my book, is the worst scenario. If you advertise that you handle widgets and then receive so many widgets that you can't handle all of them, the reputational damage from customers' word-of-mouth can be unrecoverable. The market is unforgiving, and the term "second chance" is almost never spoken when it comes to business because of the inherent risk. We were teetering on the latter scenario. We needed more money to fund our growth and handle the massive inflow of business. If I didn't do something fast, Kelco was going to implode. I knew there was only one place for me to go.

NEW YORK, NEW YORK

A bartender mixed cocktails in a dark lobby bar of the New York Hilton. Grant sipped on a beer in the seat on my right, and Tammy sat on my left, sipping a club soda. Business executives lounged in the bar, wearing suits and ties. Women wearing dark colors, urbane fashion, and makeup straight off a Vogue magazine cover page lingered around the bar. I flagged down the bartender with a finger in the air.

"Another bourbon on the rocks – and make it a double," I ordered.

Grant turned to me with a grin, excited to be in the big city. He said, "All right, boss, here we are. We've conquered the small screen; what now?"

The bartender placed the drink on the woodgrain bar before me. I acknowledged him with a quick nod. "Thank you, my good man," I said, turning to Grant with my glass raised. "Welcome to Wall Street!" We tapped glasses, and I downed my bourbon in one gulp. "Keith should be here any minute," I added.

Tammy stood from the bar and flattened her sleek red gown. She said, "I guess that's my cue."

Grant looked to Tammy with a puzzled expression. "Tammy, don't run off. Won't you at least have a drink with us – at least one for good luck?!"

Tammy reflexively lifted a soft hand to rest on her belly. She coyly shifted her gaze in my direction. My face turned beet red. Grant looked to me in shock as he began to realize the unspoken news.

"Yep," I confirmed as a proud smile widened across my face, "we're going to have a baby!"

Grant's jaw dropped open. "I can't believe it! Congrats, you two!" Grant flagged down the bartender with a wave of his arm. "Another round, please! We're celebrating!"

I laughed with a mixture of nervous energy and joy. I instinctively wrapped an arm around Tammy. As the bartender prepared our drinks, I stuffed a hand in my suit pocket beneath a long gray overcoat to withdraw a wad of cash thick enough to asphyxiate a horse. I peeled off five one-hundred-dollar bills and slipped them into Tammy's open palm. I said, "Here, honey, we won't be long."

Tammy and I kissed, sharing a quick moment of intimacy.

"I love you. Go get 'em, guys," Tammy said sweetly.

Tammy left gracefully, and I watched her walk away, enjoying the way her body glided through the lounge. Businessmen eyed her greedily as she sauntered past their tables and out the door. The bartender slid two cocktail glasses across the bar. I clapped Grant on the back with one hand as I raised my glass with the other.

"To new beginnings!" I cheered.

Grant tapped my glass and said, "To new beginnings...and to landing this fucking deal!"

We slugged back the drinks with gusto. I dropped cash onto the bar, and together we exited the Hilton lobby. We stepped onto the busy downtown Manhattan sidewalk toting our briefcases in hand, wearing our suits and long overcoats like New York Mad Men from the golden era. All I could hear in my head was Frank Sinatra's words: *"I'll make a brand-new start of it. In old New York! If I can make it there, I'll make it anywhere! It's up to you. New York, New York!"*

I lived and breathed for moments of outrageous opportunity like what we were approaching. I felt like a rookie that signed on with the majors, stepping out for my debut game. Nervous wasn't the word for it – excited, thrilled, and, admittedly, intimidated. Another phrase quickly entered my mind: *it can all change in a New York minute.*

A yellow cab rolled into the valet area. Keith lumbered out of the backseat and welcomed Grant and me with open arms. We all then shuffled into the cab together, and Keith directed the Middle Eastern cabby to our destination, "Wall Street, please."

The cabbie glared at us through the reflection in the rearview mirror. He mumbled something in response, and the car rolled into the slow-moving stream of traffic. We drove for several blocks, going over our notes for the upcoming meeting. As we talked, Keith sat behind the driver and looked up to the massive buildings surrounding us. He recognized one of the buildings. "Wouldn't you know it?" Keith pondered. He pointed a finger against the glass toward a building. "Talk about reminding me of a lifetime ago. That's my old office, Paco Pharmaceuticals."

Grant brushed the comment aside. He remarked, "The one that went under while you were CFO?"

Keith frowned. "No, that was after I left Paco to go at it on my own. And to be clear, Grant, the government changed the regulations, and we did well to stay in business as long as we did."

We entered a construction zone on our route, and traffic slowed to a halt. A cacophony of blaring car horns filled the six lanes of traffic around us like a thousand air-raid sirens going off at the same time.

Grant shook his head in annoyance. He said, "Why'd you have to bring that up? Look, now we're going to be late."

"Keep it together, guys!" I yelled over the deafening noise of car horns.

"We need to hoof it!" Keith yelled in response.

Grant impatiently checked his watch. He rolled down his window to shout at the traffic in front of us, "Let's go people! Some of us have places to be!"

Keith made eye contact with me as he said, "Come on. There's no time to wait. Besides, this cab driver is on the wrong side of the road dividers. We have to make a break for it."

No time for pleasantries, I threw a wad of small bills toward the front seat to pay the cabbie. We opened the door and stepped into the traffic-filled street. We shuffled between honking cars like three Wall Street regulars, each carrying briefcases and huddling inside our suits and long overcoats to fight the cold winds whipping between the buildings. We maneuvered through six lanes of cars and climbed over a concrete barrier, weaving through a barrage of oncoming traffic. Dodging rageful taxi drivers and ER-visits, we leaped onto the sidewalk. We all looked to one another amidst our rush, communicating silently, *We have eight blocks to go within ten minutes. We don't have a choice. Let's go for it!*

We picked up the pace and hit the ground running, literally. We didn't even have time to stop and catch our breath. Our hearts were pounding as we finally reached a panel of tall glass doors. We pushed open the doors and scurried into the building. The behemoth of an entrance lobby was lined with marble from floor to ceiling. The grandiosity stopped us in our tracks. The lobby bustled with activity as people hustled in every direction, everyone in a rush to get wherever they were going.

I clapped Grant and Keith both on their backs. "See, Positive thinking – we made it," I cheered between gasps for breath.

Keith attempted to respond but thought better of it. He instead used his wheezing breaths to fill his lungs. Grant pointed toward a bank of escalators. "There," he huffed.

We each breathed heavily to calm our heart rate on the otherwise silent escalator ride to the second floor. We approached an attractive brunette woman seated behind the long counter of a reception desk.

"May I help you?" she asked.

Keith breathed heavily and composed himself. He responded, "Yes, we're here to see Paul Houston with Lehman Brothers."

"Mr. Houston, your ten o'clock is here," she said into her intercom system as she smiled in our direction. "He'll be right down."

We all breathed more comfortably, knowing we arrived on time. Thoughts of excitement raced through my mind. This is *our first meeting with an investment bank, and what a meeting we landed!* We also spoke with AON by phone and planned to meet with them the next day. I used both banks as leverage against each other, casually dropping the information that I would be meeting with the other bank while in New York. Both firms had expressed interest in acting as our agent to help us arrange meetings and secure lines of additional financing to grow our portfolio of policies.

One of the elevator doors opened. In his early thirties, a man with neatly combed and heavily gelled dark hair extended a hand in greeting. "Gentlemen, I am Paul Houston," he said.

After brief introductions, he whisked us away to the forty-seventh floor of Lehman Brothers. From Paul's casual yet confident composure, I sensed he was versed in finance and street smart, with years of experience. He gave me the impression that he wasn't likely to be thrown off target by any curveballs that I may throw his way.

We exited the elevator together. Paul led us down a corridor where one glass wall encased a glass shrine. I paused to stare into the display case. A bright light beamed down on miniature cars and toy corporate symbols that stood proudly on platforms. I recognized most symbols or logos on the toys as common household names: Coca-Cola, JIF, Monsanto...

Paul noticed my intrigue. "Steve, Lehman Brothers is one of the oldest investment banking firms in the country. All of these companies you see before you have been taken public by Lehman. One day, Kelco will be in that case," Paul stated, with firm intent in his voice.

A chill ran down my spine. It felt so surreal, but here we were. It was as if my whole life's dreams stood on display in front of me, memorialized behind that glass. From my childhood onward, this type of success was what I had always wanted. I watched my dad run his own salvage yard business and become successful in the small town of West Liberty. I admired him and wanted to create my own version of success, but I dreamed of something bigger that could positively impact more lives across the country, and maybe someday, around the world. Seeing the names memorialized behind the glass gave me a new goal to strive for. They had won the game. A game I had only begun. But I knew I wanted Kelco to be in that case. My dreams were so close to becoming reality and that was a reality I carried on my shoulders as a promise to our employees. I wanted to take Kelco public to expand our capability and to pay back our employees for their hard work helping us reach these new heights. My thoughts began to drift... *Kelco goes public. Kelco revolutionizes the insurance industry. Steve Keller, the first billionaire businessman from West Liberty, Kentucky, goes down in his hometown's history books as a man who helped hundreds of thousands of people live in comfort during the most painful and frightening times of their lives. Kelco employees become millionaires overnight.*

"Steve... Steve?" Paul spoke sharply. His voice brought me back to reality as I realized I had been lost in the moment, mesmerized.

"What?" I said, shaking my head to lose the daydreams. I leaned closer to Paul with a mischievous grin as if he caught me with my hand in the cookie jar.

"Before you get in that glass case, Mr. Keller," Paul said with an amused chuckle, "we have a little meeting to attend with a lot of anxious investment bankers waiting on us. Shall we?"

Paul turned abruptly, and we all picked up the pace, scurrying down the long-carpeted hallway lined with mahogany wood paneling. We reached a nondescript door that Paul seemed to frequent. He swung open the door, and we all stepped inside a small room, the exact opposite of the grand space I expected after walking through the grandiose lobby and corridors.

A large oval table nearly filled the entire room. Huddled around the room stood five guys, mostly in their mid-thirties or forties, except for one older gentleman, whom I recognized as the vice president of Paul's division, who was in charge of new asset securitizations. We all extended brief introductions and took seats around the table. One of the young Lehman representatives smiled bashfully and joined Keith, Grant, and me on our side of the oval.

Once the coffee was passed around the table, we dove headfirst into the discussions regarding the new Kelco product, Life Settlements. Questions were fired at us across the table in quick succession with pointed precision about our business's inner workings.

"What is Kelco's acquisition cost per policy?"

"What is your float rate?"

"Tell us about your staffing and infrastructure."

Keith, Grant, and I fielded the questions, and outwardly, to me, we sounded like a polished debate team, all working in unison to collaborate and drive home our points. Internally, I knew we were flying by the seat of our pants. Staffers from Lehman Brothers listened intently, furiously populating notepads as we continued volleying questions and answers across the table.

Grant began describing Kelco's bidding process. Abruptly, Paul jumped to his feet. He made pointed eye contact with me and said,

"Steve, can I see you for one minute outside, please?"

Paul and I stepped outside. His face held the strained look of someone struggling to restrain his anger with a pleasant expression. He quickly grabbed the door handle, just short of slamming the door behind us. "Steve!" he nearly shouted, though somehow still in a whisper, "how many people have you got here representing Kelco?"

"Just the two that came with me, Grant and Keith, why?" I respond, looking to him in confusion.

"So, you're saying the fourth gentleman on your side of the table isn't with you?" Paul replied.

"No, I thought he was with Lehman," I said, suddenly feeling concerned.

"We've got an imposter on our hands!" he claimed.

"An imposter?" I wondered aloud in confusion.

Paul burst through the door and stormed into the room. I hovered close to Paul and looked over his shoulder to witness the event. Paul interrupted the meeting and raised his voice. With authority, he announced, "Gentlemen, I do not want any further conversations regarding Kelco until each one of us announces who he is and what company he represents."

"Keith Drach with Kelco."

"Bill Horton with Lehman Brothers."

"Mike Lomax, with AON capital markets," said the young man sitting beside Keith. He suddenly began to gather his belongings. He looked down at his gear with a smug smile and said, "Yeah, I guess the gig is up."

Paul glared at him and shouted, "Sir, I am going to have to ask you to leave this meeting at once!"

"Okay, okay, I understand, gentlemen. I bid you a good day," he said, snapping shut his briefcase. He squeezed out of his chair and made his way to the door as quickly as possible.

"Well, that certainly was unexpected," Paul said, once the man exited the room.

"That takes some balls!" I said, voicing my thoughts.

Paul chuckled. "Oh, that's not the first for us. It's rare, but up here, it happens."

Grant leaned over the table and looked back in my direction to make eye contact with me. There was a gleam in his eye that only Keith and I could see. Paul, de-escalating the raw tension in the room, stated, "Looks like we need to expand our corporate espionage department."

I smiled at Grant, then turned to the flustered Lehman Brothers representatives sitting across from us. *That does it. I know we have them.* I sat back in my chair, unconcerned about the rest of the meeting. I glanced out of the forty-seventh window and marveled at the New York skyline and the blue skies beyond. I envisioned the future and my dreams of Kelco's helicopter flight to heights such as these.

KELLER:

We couldn't have staged a better stunt or paid for a better marketing campaign than what that act of corporate espionage did for Kelco's reputation. Word spread throughout the investment banking industry of the stunt that Mike Lomax of AON pulled. Other investment banks assumed it must be a hot deal if AON sent a spy to cabbage the deal. Kelco became like a piece of meat dropped in a piranha tank that created a feeding frenzy on Wall Street. The bidding war that ensued morphed the small company in Lexington, Kentucky, into a Wall Street darling. We arranged, from some eighty-five banks and insurance companies, more than three billion dollars in funding, with our total goal being thirteen billion. It was a lofty goal that seemed ridiculous quickly became a reality.

Over the next two years, we were in New York an average of three days each week. The meetings were always with the top of the food chain. We dealt with the CEOs of major banks and insurance companies or the operations officers who reported to the CEOs. By the end of 1999, Kelco had four thousand senior life insurance policies enter the company, a face amount of six billion dollars in insurance. In comparison, just 1.3 billion worth of viatical policies had been bought since the start of the industry. On a broader scale, this meant we had invented an entirely new form of security, one that was in open competition with those already existing and also with the products of the insurance companies. We had found a way to leverage the asset they created, in a way they had never contemplated, and we had prevented them from directly or effectively competing with us in the marketplace. I couldn't seem to dream big enough or fast enough to keep pace with the growth of the company. Kelco was moving like a dot com on steroids.

A FRACTION OF A BANK

I stood at the cornerstone of a beautiful nine-story red-brick and gray-stone structure in downtown Lexington. Built in 1905 and named the LCBN by the turn-of-the-20th-century architects Richards, McCarty, and Bulford, the building stood the test of time as one of the country's premier bank buildings. The beautiful old building overlooked a grim part of Lexington's history. The plaza beneath the structure once held the local slave auctions centuries during a far uglier time in our history. In modern times, the square hosted free concerts on the weekends. The symbol for 5/3 Bank stood boldly emblazoned above the doorway as I entered the building's glass doors.

A female bank teller looked at me kindly through thick-rimmed eyeglasses as I approached the counter with a big grin. I announced, "Hi, Steve Keller of Kelco; I'm here to see Bob Finley."

"Yes, sir, his office is right over there." She smiled warmly and pointed to the doorway of a cozy corner office that I recognized.

I wrapped my knuckles on the door to the office and stepped inside the room with a smile. Bob Finley stood from his swivel chair, heavyset and flush-faced. He greeted me with a firm handshake from across his desk and offered me a seat. He adjusted his tie then sat across from me as his chair groaned in protest.

"So, Mr. Keller, what can I do you for?"

I smiled with a big, shit-eating grin and said, "Well, Bob, you must not remember me."

A puzzled expression clouded his face, and then he shook his head, no. He said, "Wait, I know who you are – Kelco, right? but I don't think we've ever had the pleasure of being introduced."

I chuckled and stared at Bob with eyes like lasers that could have bored a hole into him if I stared long enough. I said, "We met once before, Bob. I came to you for funding when I first had the idea to start Kelco. If I remember correctly, you sat right there where you are now, and you said, 'Son, that is the craziest and stupidest idea I've ever heard.'"

My words sliced through him to his core. The color drained from his face. He responded, bumbling his words, and said, "Well, I don't think…I mean…I wouldn't have…"

I reassured him. "It's okay, Bob. You don't need to apologize. You didn't believe in me, but I did. I swore I would prove you wrong. And here we are." I smiled broadly at him across his desk. I continued by saying, "We just closed more than three billion dollars in financing from a total of eighty-three investment banks on Wall Street."

"That's great, Mr. Keller. I'm really happy for you," he said, clearing his throat.

"But here's the best part, Bob: Kelco purchased your building."

We stared at each other across his desk. I let him squirm, remembering how my stomach clenched into knots at the feeling of rejection as I wondered how he could be so cruel. I watched as his Adam's apple jumped in his throat as he swallowed hard.

"Bob, I bought your building. Fifth Third Bank is no longer welcome here. Everyone in the building has until the end of the month to clear out. Starting June 1st, this building will be Kelco's headquarters."

He stared incredulously at me, and I could only assume he was wondering, as I once did, how anyone could be so callous.

I looked at him, growing impatient. I stood from the chair and buttoned my suit jacket and said, "As you once said to me years ago, 'Thank you for your time, Mr. Finley, and thank you for wasting ours."

LOOKING OVER THE HORIZON

I rode the Harley Fat Boy motorcycle, the free gift from United Benefits years ago, to our new office building. The nine-story structure loomed high overhead. Lettering, forty feet wide, at the top of the building read, KELCO. I made sure the lettering would dominate the outside of the building for all in Lexington to see. The brand towered among the small city skyline, and I couldn't help but feel a sense of pride swell within me. I rode my bike right into the lobby of the nine-story building and parked near the elevator. I loved the feeling of freedom the bike gave me every time I rode it. However, every time I rode the bike, it also reminded me of United Benefits, who happened to be under investigation for fraud in the state of Florida.

I sat at my office desk, looking over the rooftops of various buildings and then down to old slave-auction square, today known as Cheapside Bar. I thought of the corruption that was allowed by those in power during those days. It saddened me that such a terrible practice was corroborated by the mainstream public. It made me wonder what terrible practices still exist today, unvoiced by those most affected and unchecked by society for fear of retaliation from those in power.

United Benefits then came to mind again, along with some of the other scummy Ponzi schemes that were weaseling their way into our industry. Even though we refused to deal with the borderline fraudulent companies that were snapping at our heels, they still claimed to be a part of the industry, and any association with such a company could taint Kelco's fragile reputation in the marketplace. Another company, Personal Choice Opportunities, located in Las Vegas, played a shell game, moving money from one investor to another, showing forged and manufactured numbers as profits to encourage and manipulate investors. As a result of these fraudulent maneuvers, they were guaranteeing investors outrageous profit margins and making it difficult for legitimate outfits like Kelco to compete. Even worse, they paid doctors and created fictitious "patients," who claimed to have sold policies to cover up their fraud. From the outside looking in, PCO seemed to be a legitimate company, telling investors that their money was safe in a bonafide escrow account in a bank called Escrow Plus of Burbank, California.

I was beginning to feel a sense of power and control over our growing industry, and I was starting to feel the positive impact our small company was having on tens of thousands of lives. With that, I felt a sense of responsibility. I tapped my fingers against the glass window as I looked out over the landscape.

"I really need to get more solid laws in place," I said aloud to myself.

I pressed the intercom button on my desk to page our new secretary and said, "Hi, Heather, can you please ask Keith to come in for a talk?"

Moments later, Keith entered my office.

"So, how are we doing on finances?" I asked.

He nodded his head up and down with a big smile, "We're rolling. Why do you ask?"

"We need a new department," I said as I sat and offered Keith a seat.

This seemed to make Keith uncomfortable. He adjusted his tie as he shifted in his seat. He never liked conversations that involved spending large amounts of money.

"And what would that be?" he asked.

"We need an anti-fraud department, something that makes sure we keep all of our policies clean."

"That's not our responsibility. It's the insurance companies."

"Legally, yeah, but, part of me just feels like we should cover our asses. Now that we're claiming a bigger stake in the industry, we need to make a stand for what is morally right too."

Keith sat back in his chair. He removed his glasses and pressed the bridge of his nose while inhaling slowly. Finally, he stated, "You're worried about this whole Personal Choice thing."

"They're giving us all a bad name. We have to get out in front of this thing."

"I agree. We need to do something. So, what do we do? Who do we hire?"

"I've got no idea, but I know you'll find a way to make it work."

Keith inhaled sharply and breathed a heavy sigh before asking, "Anything else we need?"

I stood from my desk and looked out across the horizon, saying, "I got a call from an insurance company this morning: ATLAS GLOBAL. They want to meet with us early next week."

Keith raised his eyebrows so quickly that he had to correct his glasses' level as he responded, "Did they say what it's about?"

"No, but I've got my suspicions," I said with an excited grin

MEETING WITH ATLAS GLOBAL

Stainless steel elevator doors opened within the World Trade Center high-rise office building in Manhattan, New York. Keith and I stepped into the elevator, thankful that no one else joined us. I pressed the button for the 100th floor. The doors glided closed, and the elevator box lifted Keith and me high into the sky.

Keith noticed the button I pressed and squinted in my direction. He said, "I thought Wendy White asked us to meet on the 99th floor."

I nodded thoughtfully. "She did," I said. "She wants us to meet with Jerry Wendorf, the president of ATLAS GLOBAL."

Keith's mouth dropped open in surprise.

"You didn't tell me that!" he exclaimed.

I smiled at Keith, gauging his reaction as I continued to lay it on thick, hoping to impress my older, more seasoned CFO. I added, "We've had over two hundred meetings here in New York now, signed non-competes with each and every one of them. Something doesn't feel right about this one, and I think it might be good news. They refused to sign anything in advance this time. I want to show up on our usual floor, get the lay of the land, and see if we can get any info on what this meeting is about before we head in there."

Keith rolled his shoulders back in acceptance of the new information. He stood content, stoic, and patient while we watched the elevator floors climb higher.

50...60...70...80...90...100.

Keith and I exited and approached the floor-to-ceiling glass entryway to the reception area. A young dark-haired woman sat behind a long gray counter wearing a thin microphone headset. She greeted us with an impatient smile as we approached. I opened my mouth to speak but stopped short as she lifted a finger in the air, signaling for me to give her a moment. I spun my back to the receptionist while we waited and leaned against the countertop.

A bubbly woman with strawberry blond hair bounded around the corner and entered the reception area. She immediately noticed Keith and I standing at the reception desk. She called out to me across the lobby, "Steve! So good to see you!"

I greeted Wendy with a friendly handshake as Wendy charged forward with the conversation. She coyly remarked, "What a surprise. You know they're expecting you downstairs."

"Oh, that's right. We must have hit the wrong floor out of habit, or maybe it was just an excuse to come see you." I flirted, heavy with insinuation.

Wendy's pale complexion brightened to a rosy shade of red. She sauntered toward the elevators and said, "As flattering as that is, I'm going to have to guide you gentleman to where you need to be."

I laughed, acting like a scolded child being led to the principal's office.

"So, what gives, Wendy? Why the meeting with the top brass today?" I asked, watching her intently to see if I could glean any information from her response.

Wendy shook her head and looked at me with a hint of playfulness in her eyes. She stated flatly, "You'll just have to find out for yourself."

Wendy pressed the elevator call button, and the doors opened.

"Oh, come on, Wendy. Give me something," I cajoled as Keith and I stepped into the elevator.

The doors began to close, and Wendy said, "Must be something good..."

The doors closed, and the elevator lowered one floor to reveal another reception desk. A young man with short, dark hair sat behind the reception desk. He greeted us with a bright smile, addressing us, "How can I help you, Gentlemen?"

"Steve Keller with Kelco, here to see Jerry Wendorf," I announced.

The young man stood from his seat and guided us to a conference room. He said, "Right this way. Mr. Wendorf is expecting you." He then swung open a massive wooden door.

Three men who sat behind a sprawling mahogany and glass conference desk stood from their chairs to welcome us. Jerry Wendorf was the first to jump from his seat. His salt and pepper hair sat atop his head like a mop that had lost its purpose. I shook each of their hands firmly, and we all introduced ourselves. Keith and I chose seats across the table from where Jerry sat between his two colleagues.

My attention lingered out the window behind where the men sat. A jumbo jet descended below us down toward LaGuardia airport, passing the Statue of Liberty. The view nearly took my breath away and completely hijacked my attention. Jerry noticed where my eyes lingered and turned his seat sideways to observe my eye line. He asked, "Not bad, huh?"

"Not at all. I try to enjoy the view whenever I can." I smiled.

Jerry drummed his fingers against the desk. He thoughtfully watched his fingers' movement like a kid unsure of how to admit a guilty conscience. He lifted his gaze and said, "So, Steve, is my team doing a good job financing the pool of policies for you?"

"Frankly, Jerry, your team is one of the most cantankerous groups we have," I replied with a friendly grin to soften the blow. "To be honest, I don't feel like we have made any progress with your group. In fact, I don't even take them seriously at this point. I have too many other companies moving forward at rapid speed, and I can't babysit your group any longer."

"I see," Jerry responded, offering a glance up at me out of the corner of his eye as he continued looking down at his hand on the table. The corner of his mouth froze in a smug smirk that reminded me of a man holding a royal flush at a poker table. Something seemed to be weighing heavy on his mind, but I sat patiently as we studied each other's movements. After another few pecks of his fingers on the glass tabletop, he turned to me and addressed me head-on. He said, "Steve, look, here's the deal. ATLAS GLOBAL is not interested in financing your pool of policies. We are interested in buying Kelco. So, what do you say? Let me make you an offer."

I didn't hesitate before responding, "Look, Jerry, the bottom line is you can't afford Kelco."

Sitting by my side, Keith leaned forward in his seat. I could feel him staring at me out of the corner of my eye. With effort, I ignored him and focused on Jerry's response.

Jerry, tongue in cheek, considered what to say next. He resumed the drumming of his fingers against the tabletop. He then swiveled his chair toward the sky view from the window. He smugly replied, "That's a bold position, young man. You haven't even heard my offer yet."

I said, "Listen, Jerry. Kelco is a small company today, but I have raised three billion dollars in commitments to fund policies for next year. That means we are going to buy fifteen billion dollars' worth of policies and still have a reserve to pay premiums. So how do I even price Kelco? What will it be worth next year or ten years from now? You're not going to want to pay either one of those scenarios. Besides, I promised the employees that if they helped me build Kelco that they would all share in the stock down the road. I just simply can't consider a sell. I'm sorry, Jerry."

Jerry looked to his colleagues and shared knowing glances that didn't sit well in the pit of my stomach. Jerry nodded with a sigh, saying, "I don't recommend it, but I admire your fire, young man. I must say though, when you're up this high and get too close to the edge, well, that's how people catch a stiff breeze – or a stiff *push* – and tumble off. You were admiring my view here, watching a plane come in for landing, if I'm not mistaken. I don't know much about you, Keller, but I'd guess you're not up this high that often."

Jerry stood from his chair and shoved an arm across the table to shake my hand. While my hand was within his grip, he coldly remarked, "Like you said, enjoy the view while you still can."

NEW ARRIVAL

From the cold, sterile hospital waiting area, I looked out over the parking lot below. A thin January frost coated the Lexington landscape outside the window. I took a few deep breaths and continued pacing, reflecting on the past year. I was excited about the promise and hope the new year represented, pushing through any nervousness or fears that rose to the surface. My parents and brother and sister sat idly in hospital chairs near me in the waiting room. They mostly watched me pace back and forth.

My dad observed me with a gentle smile. He said, "It's going to be okay, son."

"Well, how long is this going to take? Shouldn't I be back there?" I asked him sharply.

With her reassuring presence, my mom said, "Your time will come soon enough. Just be patient."

My dad noticed me checking my watch every few seconds. He stood from his chair and put an arm around my shoulder. He walked with me a few steps and guided me away from the waiting area to a hallway where we could speak more privately. He said, "Son, just slow down. I can see your mind racing a mile a minute."

"Dad, we've been here all day. I'm worried about her."

He smiled softly. "Is that really all you're worried about? I know you better than that."

"I've got a lot going on at the office too," I admitted.

"Can I give you a bit of advice?" he said, his hand still on my shoulder. "You can only be one place at a time, son, so just be here – for now."

I nodded my head, acknowledging his words. "You're right, Dad, but we're opening an office in France. We're going global. You don't under-stand. I have to be on top of things around the clock."

My dad opened his eyes wide with amusement, saying, "This might be true, but how many times do you think you'll experience the birth of your first child?"

He let his words sink in before saying, "I've done a lot in my lifetime, and what I'm most thankful for is you and your siblings. It's family, son; that's what's most important in this world. Everything else comes second. The moment you forget that – you're in trouble."

My dad and I rejoined the group in the waiting room. I resumed my vigil, pacing the floor for what felt like an eternity. Finally, a door swung open, and a petite nurse wearing scrubs entered the waiting room. She announced, "Mr. Keller, you can come back now. She's asking for you."

I looked to my parents with elated surprise. The nurse led me into a delivery room, and I found my wife, Tammy, on a hospital bed with her feet elevated in stirrups. She noticed me, and a wave of relief seemed to wash over her. Perspiration matted her brown hair into thin strands across her flushed face. I approached her and put a hand on her arm. She smiled at me, only for a moment, and then labor pains contorted her face. She unleashed a primal scream.

The doctor, dressed head to toe in scrubs, addressed me with a slight nod. He said, "Now's your time to be the husband of the year. Your job is to be the pushing coach." He then spoke to Tammy, saying with finality, "When I count to three, you push. Bear down with everything you've got, and don't forget to breathe."

I vigorously nodded in agreement to let the doctor know that I was there to help and support Tammy as she looked to the doctor and pleaded, "I can't do it anymore! I just can't!"

The doctor turned to his nurses. "Administer the epidural." The doctor then turned back to Tammy. "Okay, we're going to give you what I like to call the Cadillac of feel-good medicine, so don't you worry. You're in good hands. Especially now that you have your breathing coach here."

After a nurse administered the epidural, the doctor resumed his position between the stirrups at Tammy's feet. "Okay!" he called out to us, "the baby is crowning. Here we go! One. Two. Three!"

Tammy tensed her entire body. She gripped my hand like an iron vice while she belted out a pained yell through hoarse lungs. I modeled the breathing exercises that we learned in Lamaze class and from studying baby books. I coached her through pushing the breath out slowly and forcefully, then drawing sharp inhales to recover.

"You can do it, Tammy," I reassured her. "I'm right here with you. Just push and breathe. We're almost there."

I could see the baby's head pushing its way into existence. Over and over, we repeated the drill. We pushed, and we breathed. We pushed, and we breathed. I reassured her, and she bore down with every muscle in her entire body. I felt exhausted, and I was only helping her breathe. I could only imagine what she must have been feeling.

Tammy pushed again, and the next thing I knew, the doctor cradled the baby in his hands. The nurses clipped the umbilical cord, and the doctor placed the baby, my baby, our baby, into Tammy's arms – *what a way to start out the New Year*. No coaching could ever have prepared me for the overwhelming feeling of knowing that I was now a father. Looking into my newborn son's eyes, my first child, almost changed how my eyes see. As I looked at this tiny, precious, life that came from the love Tammy and I shared, my perspective on the world reincarnated completely. Tammy handed our son, Cole Keller, to me. Holding Cole in my arms was the most incredible experience of my life. I watched him taking his own breaths and his little heartbeat pulsing life throughout his tiny body – what a miracle. I felt the truth of my dad's words echo within me, *"Family is what is most important in this world."*

As I looked into my son's eyes, a mighty flood of emotions engulfed me, swelled within me, and expanded my understanding of what I was capable of feeling. I realized that I was now a father, and this baby boy was my son. I felt the alignment of my life shift. As I held this little life in my hands, I understood that if it came down to it, I would gladly give my life for his. I couldn't understand why I felt that way, but I knew it to be true all the way down to the core of who I was.

Though at the time I had eyes for no one but my son and Tammy, other people had eyes on me. For a time, I thought I wanted to quit the whole world and just be with them every minute. However, I had started something too big to leave unattended, most importantly because I knew how many other people's lives depended on my attention and care. Home felt like heaven, but that fucking phone wouldn't quit ringing.

Damn their eyes.

A STORM BREWING

A no-nonsense attorney, Jolene Fullerton-Sharp, briefed Keith, Grant, and me in the conference room at the home office in downtown Lexington. Getting right to it, she said, "Okay, guys, I've compiled a report, and here's the skinny. You're being audited. The state of Florida is looking into Kelco's practices."

"We have nothing to hide," I said earnestly. Keith and Grant both nodded in agreement by my side.

She frowned, saying, "I'm afraid it gets worse. I spoke with Kevin McCarty of the Florida Department of Insurance. They found six clean-sheeted policies."

"What the hell is a clean sheet policy?" Grant asked, scrunching his face in annoyance.

"Yeah, I gotta say, that's a new one on me," I agreed.

Jolene continued at a measured pace. She informed us that, "It's because it's not in any state or federal laws. Some insurance companies came up with it. Now they are all doing it because there's no regulation against it."

Keith interjected, "I'm still not getting it; what exactly does it mean?"

"It's simply a term used to define a life insurance application filled out incorrectly by an applicant."

"Yeah, because no one ever does that on an insurance application," Grant said, rolling his eyes.

Jolene allowed herself a smile. "True. Oddly, most insurance companies didn't even bother investigating these answers until the viatical industry came along to put a dent in their profits."

"Imagine that," I snorted, feeling a twinge of pride that we kept those dirty insurance companies' noses bleeding.

Jolene continued, "The way the system operated previously is if a person who smoked answered the question on the insurance application stating that he doesn't smoke, the insurance companies have two years to identify and correct the falsified application. Now, however, companies are extending that two-year term, indefinitely. They are retaining the right to cancel any policy at any time, thus, the term, clean sheet."

I couldn't help but feel angry. My voice raised as I responded, "That's not right! Insurance companies bend or even break the rules whenever it serves their purpose, but when someone threatens their profits, they all of the sudden become Moses coming down from Mount Sinai with a new declaration."

Jolene raised her eyebrows and observed the report in her hands. Inquisitively, she asked, "What's this about a Harley Davidson motorcycle being gifted to Kelco from a United Benefits?"

The color drained from my face. I could feel Keith and Grant staring at me.

"United Benefits is bad business, guys. The state of Florida is building a fraud case against them. You need to stay clear."

"We did, and we have!" I protested.

Keith agreed, saying, "We refused to do business with them multiple times. We recently became aware that they had been using the Kelco name to illegally purchase policies in Florida. We never authorized that."

"We immediately issued a cease and desist," I added.

"Then how do you explain the motorcycle?" Jolene probed.

Keith exhaled sharply and glared in my direction, saying, "We shouldn't have accepted the gift, but legally, Jolene, this doesn't put us in jeopardy, does it?"

Jolene placed her report down on the table. She stated sternly, "Gist of it is Florida has no grounds to find fault with Kelco's practices, the motorcycle included. It gave the auditors pause, but there is nothing illegal about receiving a gift as long as no favors were given from Kelco in exchange. In talking with Kevin McCarty, he said that Kelco needs to have more precautionary measures in place and that you need to steer clear of clean sheet policies."

"Yes! Exactly – Keith and I were just talking about this," I stated.

Keith continued, saying, "I couldn't agree more. Like I always say, the Devil is in the details. We've steered clear; trust me. The problem is, how do we know if we're at risk under the new clean sheet practice? We couldn't investigate every policy we ever bought. That would be impossible, completely impractical. We aren't obligated to do that, are we?"

I answered before Jolene could respond, saying, "No, that's the insurance company's job. Still, I think Jolene is right; there's too much gray area in this industry. Big Insurance is trying to claim that uncharted territory. Keith, I say we keep moving forward with an anti-fraud department, as we discussed a few months back, and, Jolene, I want to get proactive. Kelco and the viatical industry as a whole needs representation on these issues. I want to initiate our own legislation. Can you help us with that?"

Jolene nodded thoughtfully and allowed herself a small smile. "I think that is a prudent move. I'd like to work with Ron Kreiter on this if he is available."

"The Deputy Insurance department guy?" Grant asked.

I answered, "Yeah, he works for George Nichols's department. Remember, we met him down at the conference in Florida? I'll see if we can set up a meeting for early next week."

FRANKFORT, KENTUCKY

The grass grew thick and dark green, almost blue, on the lawn of the Kentucky State Capitol building. The smooth gray stone of the Capitol building dome reached high before us and into the bright blue spring sky.

Jolene led me through the front entrance of the building, where we met George Nichols in a conference room. I extended a hand in greeting, and George gripped my hand with a firm shake. With a warm smile, I said, "Great to see you again, George."

"The feeling is mutual, Mr. Kelco," George said with a deep-voiced chuckle. "I take it you're still running full tilt. Kelco has made quite a name for itself in the industry. You've come a long way since we ran into each other at the National Association of Insurance Commissioners in Florida."

I laughed and quickly felt a camaraderie with George that took me back to my college football days. His athletic build and clean-shaven look reminded me of some of the guys I knew while playing college football. I felt a camaraderie with him and his competitive spirit. "I could say the same about you," I quipped back. "Your stock seems to be rising higher every time we meet." I replied, buttering him up.

"Well, then maybe we should meet more often," George jested, jabbing me in the ribs to goad me. He offered me a chair at the conference table and took a seat of his own. His jovial demeanor shifted suddenly to business formal. He cleared his throat and adjusted his tie and said, "Steve, I understand you want to introduce legislation for your industry?"

"Yes, sir, I very much do," I firmly reiterated.

"Well, since being elected as the president of the National Association of Insurance Commissioners for the country last quarter, I know that a lot of states have already passed legislation in that space. You're already regulated, are you not?"

"George, Kelco is the most licensed company in the viatical and Life Settlement industry in the country. I know all too well what you are talking about, but the fact is all the states got it wrong."

"What do you mean?" he asked, as if personally offended.

"You see," I responded quickly, hoping to ease the tension, "all the states have regulated the policy-sellers' side of the business. This seemed to be the politically correct thing to do since it involved AIDs patients and the elderly, but, frankly, this is useless because it comes down to supply and demand on that side of the business. To clarify, if I am selling a policy, either someone offers me the money that I want and I accept it, or I don't have to sell my policy. It's that simple. I walk away and wait until a later date to try again. There is not really a concern for fraud on that end."

"This makes sense when you break it down like that. Where is the need for the regulation then?"

"It's on the end where there is real fraud taking place. The end that is not even being talked about. You see, the money to buy the policies comes from investors, and I use that money to pay more money for a shorter-term policy or a lower rate for longer terms. If I only have to wait one year for a return, then I would pay upwards of eighty-five percent. If I have to wait, say, five years, I may only pay twenty-five percent of the face amount. Now, here's where things go wrong. Companies are hiring in-house doctors that do nothing but place a life expectancy on a policy. Usually, there wouldn't be anything wrong with this, but when those same companies tell that doctor to put a three-year life expectancy on a policy when the policyholder may have ten years left to live...they can get more money from the investor, and the company keeps the difference between the ten-year price and the three-year. "

George leaned his sturdy frame over the table, listening intently. He replied, "That is disturbing. And how do you know this if you don't mind me asking?"

"Good question. You see, I am bidding against these companies every day. Sure, I am going to lose a case here and there for three to five percent. You can't win them all, but when I go against one of the fraudulent companies and lose a bid by twenty-five percent, something is very wrong. It hurts our company, and it hurts the investor and, ultimately, the industry. Now listen, George; I don't want the credit for this. You take the glory, and let's pass a bill that other states and other insurance commissioners can adopt for their states. You will look like a hero and a genius. It will be good for all of us."

George rocked back in his seat and said, "That's heavy. Steve, I have to say, that's the most understandable explanation of the viatical industry I've ever heard. I see why you want more regulation. Ron, my deputy, couldn't be here today, but I'm going to put him on this project. He's an attorney as well, Jolene, so you two should get along."

Jolene brightened at the idea of working with Ron Kreiter, the exact partnership that she was hoping for to help complete the legislation. "Thank you, George. Ron will be a perfect addition to the team. I couldn't have picked a better man for the job myself," she said with a smile in my direction.

"Thanks, George," I said, standing to leave.

George looked at me sternly before adding, "Don't thank me yet, Steve. You know you're going to make a lot of companies unhappy, right? I'm telling you, be careful. These guys are cutthroat."

I ignored his warning with a playful grin and responded, "Well, the worst they can do is run me out of business. I've been broke before."

George frowned. "No, it could be much worse, buddy, so watch yourself, okay?"

I nodded as I shook his hand and said, "Sure, no problem, I'll be careful."

As Jolene and I left the room, I walked out wondering what George was trying to tell me.

POLITICS AND PAPPY

Months later, an old man named Pappy stood shivering in the cold wind by the front entrance of the Capitol building. Huddled beneath a heavy winter overcoat, he looked like a cross between Rooster Cogburn and Mr. McGoo. Long before meeting Pappy, I was warned not to be fooled by his withered appearance. Underneath his aged frame stood the most grizzled political fighter in Frankfort politics. As I approached him, I braced myself for the abuse of his sharp tongue as if shielding myself against the cold wind.

His eyes lit with recognition under his thick-rimmed glasses, and he barked in my direction, "Keller, where the hell you been, boy? It's as cold as a witch's titty out here."

"Well, it seems as if all the important people took the parking spots," I said, smiling as I stuck out a hand.

He grunted and relented to shake my hand. "Ain't that the damn truth. All right, let's go, boy; Representative Gooch's office is on the second floor."

We entered the Capitol building, and I felt like I was walking with a celebrity. Everyone we passed in the hallways seemed to know Pappy, and he made a point to stop for a moment to talk with each person we encountered.

Pappy approached a man and quickly shook his hand with a playful smirk. He said, "Orin, I thought I told you never to show your face around here."

The man laughed and brushed Pappy's comment aside with a smile. Wide-eyed, I stared at Pappy, trying to refrain from laughing. We moved along from the brief encounter, continuing down the hallway as Pappy barked in my direction, "The man's a son of a bitch, but his wife makes a hell of a casserole."

A rotund man wearing a suit waddled in our direction. Pappy shouted, "Mark, my brother from another mother! Get over here."

Pappy shook the man's hand as we continued on, and Pappy growled a running commentary in my ear as we worked our way down the hall. "He's got the eye, that Mark does. Mark my words; he's gonna do well in this shit town. Mark my words – hear that? Get it, boy? *Mark my words. Ha!* There's a reason I've been surviving in this hell hole for this long. Stick with me around here, and you'll go far."

"You got it, Pappy. You're the boss," I replied, biting my cheek to keep from bursting out laughing.

"Smart boy," he grunted.

Representative Gooch greeted us in front of a glass doorway. He ushered us into his office, saying, "Gentleman, it's a pleasure. Let's go back to my office." We each lounged in seats in Representative Gooch's office, and he said, "So what can I do for you all today?"

Pappy sat forward in his chair with effort and spoke with force. He bellowed, "Representative, this is Mr. Keller, the president of Kelco. Now let me explain to you, Kelco is a company that purchases life insurance policies from people who no longer want them. We feel that Kentucky needs legislation for this industry, just like the other thirty states that have enacted similar regulations. Mr. Keller's firm is presently working with George Nichols of the Department of Insurance and the deputy commissioner, Ron Kreiter, to draft a bill for you to see. We also have the support of Senator Tom Buford, the Chairman of the Insurance and Banking Committee and the House Chairman of the Insurance Committee."

"When do you project to complete the bill?" the Representative asked.

I replied eagerly, "I have a full-time, in-house attorney involved on this bill. We have met with the Insurance Department several times and are working hand-in-hand with them on this. I think it will be finalized over the course of three months."

He nodded without emotion and jotted down a note in a small leather book on his desk. "Mr. Keller, why do you think this bill is needed?"

I swallowed hard. Then I projected my voice, as I had observed Pappy do. I said, "Sir, the viatical industry is pretty new, and there is a lot of room for fraud. Sadly, there are a lot of people wanting to make a quick buck."

"Why do you want to stop them? Aren't you in it for the money too?"

I smiled and implored him to see my good-natured humor in the matter, saying, "Of course, but fraud, lies, and cheaters are bad for business."

He chuckled. "Good answer, Mr. Keller."

I pounced on the opportunity to build on his positive reaction. "On a personal level, my dad taught me to be fair. I still believe in that, despite everything, and it's important to me that our growing industry is built on a fair playing field."

The Representative nodded slightly and said, "So what is it that you are proposing in this legislation, and why is Kelco the one to draft it?"

"Well, the greatest chance for fraud in this industry is through the medical underwriting process, and we know, better than anyone, the adverse effects of this corrupt practice because, as the largest brokerage in the country, we are constantly combating the unscrupulous, wild west types that delegitimize our market. We know this industry inside and out, and we know how to keep it clean, profitable, and, most importantly, fair to those people who need the relief we provide."

This piqued the Representative's attention. "Go on," he insisted.

"Well, you see, Representative Gooch, no offense, but industry leaders who understand the industry need to draft the legislation, not political folks who don't have a clue about how all of this works. Up to this point, one state passes regulation, and the rest follow suit, thinking the first state got it right when they didn't. It's literally the blind leading the blind out here. Almost constantly, I am running into fraudulent firms who get a bogus life expectancy report from a doctor willing to take a bribe. They then sell the inaccurate policy to an unsuspecting buyer, or investor, for way more than it's worth. You see, the shorter the life expectancy, the more money it's worth, and people are stealing millions every day in fraudulent transactions, right under the regulators' noses. I want to get the broken regulation back on track. And you, Representative, and the state of Kentucky have an opportunity to set the benchmark for the country."

Representative Gooch sniffed the air as if he caught a whiff of something he liked. "I understand that is wrong, but how does that affect you? And why do you want legislation to stop it?"

"We can't compete with these firms. I have to bid on these policies, and if a guy has a ten-year projected life expectancy, I may offer forty percent of the face amount, for example..."

He interjected, "That seems awfully low."

I gestured with my hands for him to slow down and allow me to finish. "You forget that we have to pay the premiums all of these years. There's a lot that goes into this equation, but bear with me for simplicity's sake."

"Okay, get to the point. I'm just trying to understand," he said, easing the abruptness of his tone with a smile.

"You got it. Here is the bottom line. If I am offering ten cents on the dollar for a long-term policy and my competitor is offering twenty-five or higher, there is no way I can compete with that. That other firm may have a doctor that they are paying off to fudge the medical records to make the person look sicker on paper than they really are. It knocks me out of the saddle, and the investor expects a three-year payoff, for example, while the guy may live ten years. Do you think the investor is going to be happy with that company and this industry? With companies participating in practices like that, this industry is going to make national news soon! And then everybody is going to wonder why the regulators failed to address regulations to stop this fraud in its tracks. You, sir, can be that champion. It's the right thing to do on all levels," I said, satisfied with the argument.

He clasped his fingers atop the table in front of him, saying, "I like the sound of this, gentlemen. I'm not a huge fan of the insurance business – too many people trying to keep the letter of the law while shitting on the spirit," he jested.

Pappy chuckled. "So, when we're ready, we can count on you to introduce it to the House?"

The Representative abruptly stood. He tucked his white shirt into his beltline that hid beneath an overhanging belly that seemed to reach out hungrily in front of him. "Let's see what we can do," he said with a wink. "I only work with winners."

I stood, not fully understanding the implications of his words, and said, "Thank you for your time, sir."

We shook hands firmly across the desk, and I felt accomplished in our exchange. I also noticed a novel feeling for me, one that, strangely, involved Cole and Tammy. This lobbying to protect our industry was a logical step in protecting Kelco and our partners' interests, but it also felt like we were protecting people who depended on us. These attempts at pre-empting disaster made me feel good for my boy and my love, and when one is consumed as much as I was by work, a moment to feel like a father, for me, was like taking a deep breath up in the Cumberland Mountains.

Pappy extended his hand across the desk as well and croaked, "Great, we'll be in touch as things move along. Here's my card. If you need anything, let me know."

As we turned to leave the room, the Representative looked intently at Pappy's card. He called after us, "Well, now that you mention it, Pappy, Bruce from the Insurance Committee said you might be able to hook someone up with Derby tickets," he stated, though in the form of a question.

"I might have a source to refer you to. How many are you looking for?" Pappy asked.

"Oh, just a couple."

"You got it, Chief. I'll work on that and be in touch."

Pappy and I passed through the glass doors and returned to the grand hallway. Pappy quietly leaned toward my ear and whispered, "Well, we've got a sponsor!"

"Great job, Pappy. Thank you!" I responded with a big smile as I vehemently shook his hand and clapped him on the back.

Pappy grunted, "Don't thank me yet, boy. Politics is a strange game."

THE OFFICE MADE OF GLASS

The ninth floor of Kelco's new offices were entirely wall-to-wall glass. Sitting behind my desk felt like being perched on top of a mountain. The sensation reminded me vaguely of summers and family camping trips in the Appalachian Mountains. Grant and I both had corner offices on the top floor, separated only by the glass walls of Karen Lockridge's office. I glanced over at Grant periodically throughout the day, checking on him. We both kept our doors open to stay connected to the ebb and flow of the organization. I looked in on him and noticed him talking animatedly into the phone. A look of shock crossed his face. He placed the phone down on his desk and yelled from his office, "Steve, can you come here for a minute?"

He was capable of handling nearly any situation that came his way during business operations. I trusted him completely. Sometimes, though, he needed help negotiating a new broker's contract while enticing them to come on board with Kelco. This seemed different. I stood from my desk chair, and from the look of panic on his face, I knew he had a situation on his hands. Always caring about my man, my lost loyal partner, always at his back, I hurried to Grant's office.

Grant met me in the doorway, closing the glass door behind me. He pointed to the phone on his desk, insinuating I pick it up. He said, "Wayne Holcombe is on line one. He is very upset about a conversation with Chuck Cole. It sounds like he's got much bigger problems than just drinking too many 7-Ups." Grant rolled his eyes.

"Put him through," I responded.

All policies that passed through Kelco first passed through Wayne Holcombe and his attorney firm, one of the largest in Pittsburgh, called Klint, Lieberman, and Rooney Attorneys at Law. Wayne handled so much of Kelco's backend operations that I believed Kelco was his primary source of income. Wayne not only advised us on what policies to purchase and what insurance companies to stay away from but also handled all the paperwork from each transaction. Wayne was the epitome of a hands-on attorney, and he didn't mind rolling up his sleeves when the workload piled high. Wayne was a cornerstone in Kelco's operations, and over the years, he had become like family. He was so involved with each policy we bought or sold that Keith would sometimes worry about what would happen to Kelco if, God forbid, something ever happened to Wayne.

Grant hit the connect button and spoke into the phone, "Wayne?"

"Yes, I'm here," Wayne stated.

"I've got Steve with me."

"How you doing, Wayne?" I said cordially.

Wayne spoke slowly, grasping for the right words, "I'm...I'm doing okay here, but I just had a bizarre conversation with Chuck Cole. No, that's not right; bizarre is the wrong word...Disturbing – disturbing is a more fitting word."

"What do you mean, Wayne?" I asked.

"Well, Chuck called me this morning inquiring about certain insurance companies. He asked what my experience has been with these companies and how they contested policies within the new two-year clean sheet regulations. It was like he was fishing for a loophole or for something he could use. Since I've been overseeing the trusts, I've noticed the patterns of what types of policies certain insurance companies are going after as contestable policies. Well, after my discussion about the contestables, Chuck started talking to me about his enlightenment."

"His what?" I asked.

Dead air as Wayne searched for the words. He finally said, "His... His spiritual awakening, I guess you can call it. He told me that God has given him the task of helping all his gay brothers who attend his church. He stated that some of the things he was doing went against man's laws, but God insists that he continue on His mission."

"I'm confused here, Wayne. What exactly was he talking about?" I asked.

"Well, I share the same sentiment with you there, Steve. I pushed Chuck for more information, and he stated that he is doing whatever he has to do to sign up the members of his church for policies. I told him that I was deeply troubled by this conversation and that I wanted to talk to you before getting back to him. My recommendation is that we distance ourselves from this guy." Wayne urged.

"Wayne, that's an understatement. We need to cut all ties with this guy immediately," I insisted.

"This guy has lost it," Grant commented. "The warning signs were all there!"

Wayne said, "I knew you guys would say that. I've already drafted a cease-and-desist letter, terminating our brokerage agreement with him. It currently states that we are not going to deal with him again due to actions that we find inappropriate. I can simply leave it at that...and off the record, the man is a wacko."

I nodded fervently in agreement. "We have had our share of characters, but The Whale takes the prize. I should have severed the brokerage agreement with that nut job a long time ago. When he first started, he created an unauthorized web page, purporting to be the Manager of the Genesis Company, Trish Sill's company, solely operating their California Branch. Talk about a red flag...this is bad timing, Wayne. You're aware of the audit?"

"Of course. I thought that was cleared up months ago."

"It was, but we received notice this week that we are now being audited by the state of California..." As the words rolled from my mouth, a realization hit me. "Shit! Wayne, I'm going to have to call you back. Cease and desist! whatever you have to do – completely separate us from Chuck Cole. Sue him if we have to!"

"Don't worry; I'm all over this," Wayne stated emphatically as I hung up the phone.

That's what we pay you for, Wayne, I thought. Fix this.

To Grant, I said, "Call a meeting – everyone you can get on short notice."

FIRES ON THE MOUNTAIN

The Deputy Insurance Commissioner, Ron Kreiter, was now a full-time member of our team thanks to our friend, George Nichols, at the Kentucky Insurance Commission. Next to Ron sat Jolene Fullerton, Scott Brown, Michelle Kuykendall, Grant, Keith, and I, all huddled around the table.

"The Devil is in the details," Keith confirmed as he scanned the faces seated around the third-floor legal team's conference table.

Michelle was the only non-attorney who regularly worked on the third floor. She was responsible for acquiring all state operations licenses for Kelco and maintaining our good standing with each state regulator. She was as good as any of our attorneys on staff at obtaining research within our database.

I responded to Keith's "Devil is in the details," remark, saying, "You've said it a thousand times before, Keith, and you couldn't be more right. We need to be more proactive in that way. I thought that's what we were doing when we created the anti-fraud department." I looked to Ron Kreiter across the table for answers.

Ron opened his palms atop the table, empty-handed. He answered with a sigh, "Working with the state regulators hasn't been as black and white as we hoped."

Grant responded, "Don't sell yourself short here, guys. Remember, we just got a bill passed that other states are adopting like dominos. That's no small feat. You're right, Steve; we just need to stay proactive."

"Proactive, yes, but with caution," Keith implored, shaking his head, "details, details, details."

Ron added, "The bill was a good measure for us to take, yes, but in addition to our California troubles, my office just received notice that we are now being audited by Kentucky and Iowa too."

Jolene responded firmly, saying, "That's the nature of this business, gentlemen. When we push, they are bound to push back. I've seen it before, time and time again."

Michelle, our state licensing specialist, jotted notes on a pad as she said, "The Florida audit was a breeze. With proper due diligence on our end, we will handle this multi-state audit in the same way. We're going to open our books and expedite the process to get them out of our hair as fast as possible."

Everyone seated around the table looked to me. I rub an open palm atop my fist, searching for answers. "Four state audits in only a matter of months," I said grimly, "Keith, you were right; we poked the bear. I feel like we're being targeted."

Keith looked down the bridge of his nose at me through his glasses as he said, "I can't say that I'm happy to take credit for the prediction."

Grant leaned toward me in his chair. "Let's not jump to conclusions here. We've handled audits like this before, and we'll handle it again."

I lifted my eyebrows with a tight-lipped nod, responding, "Right, well, on top of all this, we've got another, even bigger concern. It's big."

Grant sensed a hint of sarcasm in my voice and asked, "The Soda Whale?"

"Chuck Cole," I affirmed, "the good reverend as he calls himself. Michelle, what were you able to dig up, and what are your concerns?" I asked, holding my breath as I prepared for the adverse news.

"I ran a search of agent activity versus policies brought in or tendered for sale. Chuck Cole sold one hundred and thirty-four contestable policies to us, all of which were policies that he acquired and oversaw the filing procedures himself. None of the other brokers were anywhere near this amount."

Keith looked at the attorneys, reading their reactions. He then said, "Well, guys, Florida took exception to six contestables, leading to their audits. What do you think California will say about one hundred and thirty-four?"

Ron Kreiter, our on-staff Deputy Insurance Commissioner, weighed in on Keith's question responding, "Keith, Florida is the only state that has passed any state-level laws limiting one's ability to purchase contestable files. California laws are much more open."

Keith quickly replied, "I'm aware of that, but I do not trust Chuck Cole. I'm afraid of what he might have done in the course of attracting business. We need to bring in another attorney firm to help with the audits."

"I agree," Michelle stated. "I'm sorry to be the bearer of more bad news, but we do need to also address the Ann Dileo situation in California. She was also red flagged for contestables."

I stood from my chair in frustration. "Why am I just now hearing about this?" I shouted. I scanned the faces around the conference room, demanding answers.

Grant interceded, "We didn't think it would be an issue. Wayne Holcombe drafted a cease-and-desist, first quarter. She's been compliant as far as we can tell. The auditors can't fault us for something we've already remedied."

The phone rang on the conference room table.

I ignored the noise and continued addressing the team, "We need perfection right now. We don't have any room for a fly in the ointment."

The phone continued ringing. Jolene lifted the phone receiver and answered the call.

I pressed forward, saying, "These deals with Wall Street require us to be better. We can either rise to the expectations, or they'll bury us in paperwork."

Jolene interrupted, covering the phone with her hand. "Steve, it's your wife. She says she needs you at home."

The color drained from my face as worries about our one-year-old son, Cole, ran through my mind. Everyone fell silent, waiting for me to respond. I shook the thoughts with a determined nod.

"Tell her I'm busy right now, Jolene. We're right in the middle of something here," I insisted. Jolene relayed the message quietly as I said, "We have over four thousand senior policies in our portfolio with a total insurance value of six billion dollars. We have raised over two billion dollars in investment bank financing, and we're on track to open a pipeline for thirteen billion in funding by quarter four. I don't care what it costs or who we have to hire. We have to be proactive!

We have to outgrow these issues! We have to go bigger!"

Jolene interrupted, "Steve, I'm really sorry. She wants me to tell you she needs you to come home."

An exasperated sigh escaped my lungs. "Fine…Jolene, tell her I'm on my way." I packed my briefcase as I continued addressing our team, "You've heard me say this before, but I'll say it again. There are two great fears in business: failure and success. We've grown exponentially. We're growing in stride with the dot com companies going public and making millionaires and, hell, billionaires overnight. I want that for everyone in this room, and unlike most of them, I'm proud that we can go forward with the satisfaction and levity of conscience that we're making our fortunes by helping vulnerable people. I'm willing to do whatever it takes to get us there. I'm proud of you all for getting us to where we are, but we need more. We can't let our success outpace our capabilities. We have to do better."

I closed my briefcase and exited the conference room without another word.

TROUBLE AT HOME

The gate to my property opened. The dark of night enveloped our property, but warm lights glowed from our windows, welcoming me home. I drove into our garage, and our dog, a brown labrador retriever named Buster, greeted me with a friendly wag of his tail. Tammy stood at the island in the kitchen. She refused to make eye contact with me as I entered the room. Suddenly, she began sobbing into her hands. I dropped my briefcase by the door and hurried toward her, fearing my worries about Cole were true. Tammy's shoulders shuddered as I approached her. I instinctively draped my arm over her to comfort her. "Hey, I'm here. What's going on?"

She recoiled at my touch and lunged away from me. *"Don't* touch me!"

I stepped back, shocked. "What's wrong? Is Cole okay? Are you hurt?"

Tammy stepped toward me, furious. *"Am I hurt?* Of course, I'm hurt, Steve!"

I opened my arms to embrace her, and she pushed me, shouting, "I said, don't touch me!"

Confused, I scanned the room for clues. "Where's Cole?" I asked.

"Oh! Where's Cole? You're his *father*, Steve! and you don't know where your son is? If you were ever here and actually gave a shit about me or your son, maybe you'd know!"

"Tammy, what are you talking about? I love you! I'm here now!"

"You're never here! You leave me here all alone, and you just expect me to raise your child all by myself! What kind of man are you?" she screamed, stepping forward with rage in her eyes.

"Damnit, Tammy! I work for a living! Look around you! You're living in a twelve –thousand-square-foot home! You have everything you could ever want and then some, so I don't want to hear it!" I shouted.

"I want a husband! Is that too much to ask?" Tammy shrieked.

The reality of the request she was making, I could not fulfill. I was married to Kelco, and it consumed me. I felt I had no room in my life for anything or anyone else. I so wanted balance in my life, but it was beyond my grasp. I felt frustrated, confined by my own dream, in some ways, trapped in the sad reality of what I had become and where I was in life. I felt hopeless as I looked back at her as she pleaded. The only way I could reconcile the demands and pressures of running Kelco was to, in the short term, set my family aside to take care of what needed to be done now and then, one day, come back to them in full force, hoping desperately Tammy would understand.

Instead of expressing that, instead of responding with empathy for Tammy, understanding her request for my love and attention, I responded defensively, barking back, "I'm running one of the fastest-growing companies in the country, and I just can't do it all! I can't give you anything more right now. You can't have it all, Tammy. I buy you cars and jewelry and clothes, and you can't tell me you don't love it! You might even love all this shit I buy you more than you love me!"

Quick as a coiled cottonmouth, Tammy smacked me across the face. She insisted, "Don't you dare turn this around on me!"

My pride hurt more than the sting rising on my cheek. She covered her mouth and turned away from me. A fresh wave of tears fell from her eyes. I immediately felt terrible and regretted what I had said and how I had behaved. I breathed heavily, wanting Tammy to look me in the eyes, but she refused. Then another scream came shrieking from another wing of the house.

Tammy sniffled and wiped her nose with the back of her hand. "Great," she said, "now you've woken up the baby. Why don't you be a father for once and go check on your son?"

Just do it, I thought. Go be with your son, and all of this will blow over. But I'm not in the wrong here; she is. She's acting out of line. As much as I wanted to, my pride wouldn't let me do what I knew was right. I couldn't admit my part in Tammy's anger. Instead, I responded again with anger, doubling down on my position while Cole's cries beckoned us.

"I can't. I'm sorry, Tammy. I have to go," I said, bluntly.

I turned my back, picked up my briefcase, and opened the door.

"Steve! where are you going? Damn it, Steve! answer me! I said..."

I shut the door behind me, and shut out the compassion I should have had for my love.

THE HIGH LIFE

A 747 commercial airplane sped along the runway as I watched from the driver's seat of my Porsche. The nose lifted into the air; then the front wheels rose from the pavement. I turned the steering wheel hard left, following the orange cones on the Bluegrass Airport tarmac. The twin turbine engines of the plane roared as I watched the plane first leave the ground in my rearview mirror. Airplanes and the idea of flight had always fascinated me. I relished the moments looking down from the vantage point of the clouds while flying – those moments when the world below became quiet and calm.

I drove through an immense entryway to the hangar designated for private jets. Flight crew met me at my car and began unloading my luggage. I hurried up the drop stairs of the Cessna Citation 1 jet and entered the main cabin where Keith and Grant greeted me with friendly smiles. I chose an open seat and strapped in for take-off. As the jet lifted into flight and then rose above the clouds, relief washed over me. I felt I could finally leave my personal problems on the ground below, if only for the flight's duration.

I poured a stiff drink and knocked back the first bourbon in one gulp, perhaps hoping the alcohol would help me forget temporarily about my wife and my callousness.

"This bottle isn't going to drink itself. Want a drink?" I asked, gesturing with the bottle.

"Sure, I'll drink with you," Grant volunteered.

I poured Grant a double and passed him the glass as Keith watched me with a nonjudgmental warmth.

"Keith?" I said, offering him the bottle.

"No, thanks, I better not." Keith said.

"Keith, really? You okay, buddy?" I joked.

"Yeah, I'm fine – just want to stay focused," he assured me, leaning back in his chair to find a more comfortable position.

"Come on, Keith. Live a little. Let's celebrate," Grant insisted, prodding him.

"Thank you, guys. I'm fine. Really, thank you though."

Keith responded, remaining tight-lipped and firm.

I raised my glass in toast with a nod, saying, "Well, anyway, here's to you both. Congratulations on sealing the Arizona deal this week!"

Grant lifted his glass to tap mine. "Cheers to that. Twenty-five million reasons to celebrate!" he added with a wink.

Grant and I shared a laugh as we gulped down the drink with gusto.

"Wooo!" I yelled as the whiskey burned down my throat. I slammed the glass down on the armrest to then pour another.

"New York better get ready because here we come!" Grant cheered.

Keith smiled in our direction, and then the smile slowly faded as he turned toward the window to watch the clouds pass by.

THE GLASS HALF FULL

Floor-to-ceiling glass windows opened to a breathtaking view of the Manhattan skyline from a World Trade Center conference room. Keith sat at the conference table waiting for our meeting to begin as Grant and I stood near the window. Heights always scared me, but I loved being in the air or being high above it all in a towering building, looking down on the world laid before me. In the World Trade Center Tower, even the distant horizon seemed both impossibly far away and beneath me. A sense of pride and power swelled within me as I stared into the sun.

I leaned closer to the glass, imagining the free fall down one hundred and ten stories to the ground below. The thought dizzied me, and I felt my chest constrict. The more I feared the fall, the more I tried to mentally fight my body's reaction to it. I refused to be afraid. Gridlocked in concentration, something suddenly touched my back. It pushed me forward. For a split second, I felt the sensation of plunging headfirst toward the earth.

I snapped back to reality and noticed Grant standing beside me with a big goofy grin of amusement. "Don't tell me you're still afraid of heights, Steve, especially not after we survived that McMinnville flight together!"

"After that experience, I think I'm more afraid of heights than ever, or maybe just of flying with you!" I said with a laugh, shaking my head in disbelief.

Flustered, I stepped away from the window to return to the conference table.

A door opened, and a procession of businesspeople filed into the room. I recognized Dick Longear of AON Insurance, accompanied by a woman, presumably his colleague, and Ian Mimms from Lloyd's of London, flanked by two attorneys. Ian and I shared a cordial smile in remembrance from a previous meeting at the Kelco offices in Lexington, nearly a year prior. Knowing Ian as one of the top representatives of Lloyd's of London, I understood how rare it was to meet in-person with one of the men behind the curtain of such a prestigious firm, especially outside of their ivory towers and so far from home in our own Bluegrass state. I imagined Lloyd's of London playing a grand game of chess, typically choosing to send their pawns, the syndicates that comprised the majority of Lloyd's labor force, to negotiate the deals. That way, if anything went wrong on a deal, the pawns took the fall, not the bishops. I felt a sense of pride and accomplishment in no longer dealing with the pawns, instead, mixing it up with the bishops in the global game of finances.

Dick Longear entered the room and threw open his arms as he barked a greeting across the room. "There he is! Steve Keller. I swore I'd never meet with you again and look at us all! Here we are."

Grant, Keith, and I shared a nervous laugh as everyone seated themselves around the table.

"Good to see you again, Dick," I said warmly.

"Keller, we lost a hundred and twenty-five thousand on our last deal with you." Dick ranted. "We didn't see a dime back! Why in the world would we do business with you again?"

I glanced to Keith for answers, who only shifted his eyebrows in response. Grant turned to face the windows, pretending to take in the view.

"Well, Dick," I started slowly, searching for a response, "I didn't want to start my Wall Street debut with a dead loser. We would have lost a hell of a lot more than one hundred and twenty-five thousand. The viatical industry is roughly two billion dollars in market share. That sounds like a lot, but it wouldn't be enough to support the deal you and I discussed and make it profitable. However, I'm going to tell you what does. We have created the Life Settlement industry, which is the practice of buying policies from seniors who are sixty-five years or older, a market estimated to be four hundred and ninety-eight billion dollars. Do you want to get pissy about a hundred and twenty-five thousand dollars, or do you want to make some serious money? Your call."

Dick leaned forward in his chair with a chagrined smile.

Ian dropped his elbows on the table. "To weigh in here, if I may, Mr. Keller, we acknowledge your track record as a disruptor in this market segment. We are quite keen to take part in any new opportunities that may hedge our exposure to payouts. However, Mr. Keller, in Kentucky, we offer reinsurance on your racehorses. Your product, in comparison to the racehorses, is a no-brainer for us. We love your product, and here's why. When we have to pay out on a racehorse from an injury, guess what happens to our asset?"

"I'm not sure," I responded.

He leaned over the table with a grim expression, captivating my attention, and said, "We shoot it. If we have to pay out reinsurance on your policies where somebody has lived beyond the actuary tables, we then take control of the policy and then collect it when it comes due. It's a win-win. We emphatically love your asset."

"With that said, Ian, how much can Kelco count on Lloyd's to back us?" I scooted my chair closer to the table. "Listen, fellas, the market is changing. Beyond that, people deserve payouts. They pay into the policies for a lifetime, and then when they need it most, that's where we come in. Now I'm offering you both an opportunity to get in on this side of the business before your competitors have a crack at it."

Dick and Ian both shared a glance. I knew then that I had them both on the hook. I then continued to reel them in by saying, "Stocks are packaged, securitized, and then sold on the open market. Bonds, real estate are the same. Gentlemen, my question to you is this: why not life insurance policies?"

We shared a moment of silence. I could see the wheels spinning in their heads, calculating the colossal possibilities of such a shift in the market. I pounced on the moment with increased excitement in my voice. "Package the policies. Securitize them. Bring new investment dollars into the market. Exponentially grow this market by the billions. That's not even the best part yet..."

I let the silence linger. *Okay, here we go. Set the hook, Steve,* I thought to myself, hearing the words not in my own voice, but in the voice of my father when I was a child, fishing the Licking River in rural Appalachia. The thought brought a humble smile to my face as I scanned the wide-eyed, anticipatory expressions on the faces seated around the table. At the height of expectation, I finally announced, "The best part of this deal for you is that AON and Lloyd's benefit from the upfront financing on every deal you take part in, and you also profit on the other side of the deals by offering *reinsurance* on the newly packaged policies."

My dad always taught me that once you feel the hook set, always keep tension on the line and reel it in with everything you've got...so I kept my line tight. "Dick, you can either be hung up on the fact that you lost a hundred and twenty-five thousand, or you and Ian can both get involved in this deal where we're all going to make millions. What are you going to do?" I said bluntly, followed by a capturing silence. They looked like fish on a hook.

Dick looked to his colleague, a woman in her mid-thirties, and then he and Ian shared a quiet look of surprise. After several tense moments, Dick broke the silence by slapping a meaty palm down against the table, bursting into laughter. "I knew you'd pull through, Keller! I had my doubts, but you've always been my dark horse in the race!"

I shared a laugh of relief with Dick.

Ian then addressed me with a concerned expression that bordered on a smile. He said, "This is more than a hedge play. This changes everything. How much initial capital do you require?"

"We're revolutionizing the whole industry here. The sky's the limit!" I said bursting with excitement, then quickly realizing that I needed to reel myself in and maintain a calm demeanor. *I'm the fisherman here, I thought. Let's take these catfish to the filet table.*

They let me hang in the silence for what felt like an eternity.

Dick looked to Ian and said, "The deal hinges on you. How much reinsurance are you willing to give these boys?"

"We feel quite comfortable with five billion."

Dick said, "Well, shit, that's bigger than we can do on our own, but we can source other funders on Wall Street to raise the cash."

I tried to keep my resolve after feeling like I had won the lottery. Never in a million years did I anticipate these numbers being thrown at us. The reality had become more sizable than even my dream. I reached across the table, and we shook hands, sealing the deal. I just hoped my chin wasn't on the floor.

LONELY AT THE TOP

The gate opened to my property, and I pulled into the garage. My thoughts reeled with visions of New York dancing in my mind – the flash, the glitz, the speed. I enjoyed the pace of the big city lifestyle – fast money and the adrenaline rush of making deals. With the ink barely dry on the Lloyd's of London and AON deals, I set my sights on becoming the next business behemoth of our time. I imagined my face on the cover of *Forbes*, I, and *The New York Times* – maybe even towering in lights above Times Square, paired with bold lettering, *KELCO.*

Being in Lexington felt slow but comforting. In truth, I was happy to be home. I withdrew a small, delicate box from the glove box of the Porsche. Inside rested a diamond tennis bracelet, dazzling in the low light of the car.

Buster greeted me happily as I entered the house. I flipped on a light and yelled through the house, "Tammy! I'm home!"

I walked through the dark house, turning on lights in each room. Buster followed me, wagging his tail by my side. "Tammy! Are you home?" I dropped my luggage by the bedroom closet, eager to get out of my business clothes and take a hot shower to wash off the travel. "Tammy? Where are you?" I shouted, growing concerned.

I opened the door to the dressing room. Tammy's closets were empty.

"Shit," I muttered.

I rushed to the next bedroom. My heart sank into the pit of my stomach as I turned on the overhead light. Cole's room was empty, completely barren without furniture and without my child. I slowly stepped into the hollow space. Emptiness crawled into my chest and expanded, breaking down my pride and ego with each step I took into my son's empty room. A lone piece of paper rested on the floor where his crib once stood, the indentions from the crib still fresh in the plush white carpet.

Steve,

Cole and I moved out while you were gone. I love you, but I'm sor-

ry. I can't live like this anymore. If you think all I want is your stuff, then you can have it all to yourself. We're living in an apartment on our own. I'm sorry. I'll always love you – Tammy

I folded the note gently in my hands as a burning sensation welled behind my eyes and an emptiness spread inside my chest. Loneliness, a feeling of abandonment, pulled at my heart. I began to doubt myself. *Why would she do this to me? Can't she understand what I'm trying to do and how hard it is? Why won't she support me? I don't get it. I'm trying my best. Is there something wrong with me?* Guilt flared inside me as images of all of the New York nights danced seductively, vying for attention in my thoughts. *Maybe she's right; maybe I don't deserve her.*

"I love you too, Tammy," I spoke aloud to the folded note in my hand.

A light suddenly dimmed within me. I sank into sorrow and self-pity. My eyes explored the empty space around me, and as I did, I swore to myself that my words were true. I spoke the words aloud again, "I love you, Tammy." I shook my head, disappointed at myself because I couldn't feel the truth in my own words. A lump grew in my throat as I spoke the words louder. "I love you, Tammy." The lump in my throat expanded into a burning sensation behind my eyes. I began to glimpse the truth that I didn't want to face. I shut it out. I turned my thoughts of disappointment inward. I began to taste the salt from my tears that ran down my cheeks as I hung my head in despair. I tucked the note away in my pocket, dragging my feet heavily away from where my child should be but wasn't.

With a look over my shoulder, I flipped off the light to the room. Darkness.

I went from room to room throughout the twelve thousand square foot home; it felt empty and cavernous everywhere I went. I turned off the lights – darkness. Every room felt lonelier than the last. The darkness outdoors called to me.

I sat for a long time on the veranda overlooking the expansive property, silently observing the well-manicured, moonlit field. The noise from the nocturnal creatures surrounded me. The cicadas were buzzing. The lightning bugs glowed bright, flickering yellowish green in the darkness, showing off their bioluminescence, hoping to attract a mate. The crickets chirped, calling out for companionship. It seemed like all life that

surrounded me was seeking and finding something that I didn't have –
something that I had...but squandered.

I had never felt so alone. I reflected on how evitable it truly was,
thinking back, *I had unintentionally distanced myself by allowing Kelco to consume my whole life, allowing distractions to fill the void, even
though my life with Tammy and Cole should have felt full.* I suddenly felt
like my whole life was an empty cavern, and I wondered, *Had I always
been this alone?*

CLOUDS ON THE HORIZON

I had everything to think about at home – every gesture, every rededication I would make to get Tammy and Cole back into my life – but once again I stood in front of an elevator door, waiting for it to open to the third floor of Kelco's office in Lexington. *I love what I do, but is this all worth it if it alienates me from the people I love most?*

Ding. The elevator doors sweep open.

Wall Street auditors from both Moody's and Standard and Poor's had nearly established permanent residence among the third-floor offices to conduct their weekly audits. Arthur Andersen, one of the big five accounting firms, had a full-time office set up on the ninth floor designated entirely to the purpose of developing a financial model for their clients by analyzing Kelco's buying history. I made a point to walk a lap through the third floor of the building at least once per day while in the office, making sure they put a face, my face, alongside the numbers they crunched when reviewing our books. Sipping my morning coffee, I strolled through the cubicles and peeked inside the open office doors. I raised my cup to familiar faces who lifted their heads from their paperwork and greeted me with lukewarm smiles.

Putting on the front at least allowed me to concentrate on something exterior from the vacuum pressure I felt in my chest, but I imagine my rounds looked lukewarm as well.

The elevator carried me to the ninth floor. I strolled past the Arthur Anderson team behind their office's glass walls with a friendly raise of my coffee mug. After my morning stroll through the building, I stepped into my office and sat behind my desk, where I felt most at home. Within minutes, Keith entered the doorway. His tall, statuesque, and proud figure waited patiently until I acknowledged his presence.

"Hey, buddy, what's up?" I said, observing him above a stack of documents.

"Hi, Steve, do you mind if I come in?"

"Of course not, come on in."

Keith closed the door behind him. He never closed my door, not by choice. My brow furrowed with concern as I offered him a seat across from my desk. "Are you all set for the meeting coming up with the Insurance Commission?"

Keith swallowed hard. A pained expression clouded his face as he stared at the floor for a few moments, hesitant to meet my worried gaze. He removed his glasses and rubbed his eyes. For a moment, it seemed like he may have wiped away a tear. Finally, he said, "I'm sick, Keller. Something is wrong with me."

His words pierced me. I looked to him for clarification. "What is it? Do you know?"

"You might have noticed...I haven't exactly been myself lately. I've wanted to tell you, but I didn't want my stuff to get in the way...with all of our meetings in the past few weeks..."

"Buddy, you can always talk to me," I insisted.

"I haven't been feeling well — just feeling weak, kind of off — so I went in for tests last week." Keith's voice began to strain. He released a slow sigh and continued softly, "The doctors confirmed it, Keller; I have cancer."

I closed my eyes, absorbing the pain in his voice. My gut clenched, and I realized I was afraid for him. I had never seen him be vulnerable or show any signs of fear. I looked to my friend as he sat with shoulders more rounded than usual. His proud, lean face appeared less full. Sadness tumbled through me as I pushed against the mountain of pain I was feeling for Keith. I felt buried after not seeing Tammy and Cole for several weeks, but the idea of Keith's family losing him, this wonderful, pillar of a man, made my personal pain feel self-inflicted and childish. From the inception of Kelco, Keith had been a guiding light to me. He stood beside me through good times and bad, always standing tall. He carried himself with such confidence, such class, and a subtle but powerful presence. In my mind, he was still invincible. He was one of my life's most treasured friends. I walked around the desk to meet him with as earnest a hug as I had ever given. We squeezed each other tight in a brotherly, fortifying embrace.

I clapped him on the back. "Listen, buddy, we will get through this; I promise. Whatever you need, I'm here. We will find a way to fight this battle together."

He clapped me on the back in acknowledgment, and we both pulled away. He returned his glasses to the bridge of his nose and pressed them into position with a forefinger. He inhaled sharply, rolled his shoulders back to once again lengthen his posture. He lifted his chin, stoic and strong. In my mind, cancer or no cancer, he was still invincible. He was still one of the toughest men I knew.

He nodded. "I appreciate you, Steve, but the fact of the matter is that you are not in these shoes. I have to walk this alone – nobody else, just me," Keith stated with the determination of a man staring death in the face. He was choosing not to look away.

"What do you mean? You've got us, you've got Susan, your kids, your church. We'll all rally around you."

"Yeah, but I'm the one who has to do the chemo, go through the puking and feeling helpless and weak."

"You're right, but with us around you, you can lean on us. It's your fight, but you don't have to fight alone."

Tears formed in his eyes as he swallowed and shook his head in an affirming manner.

I smiled with admiration at his inner strength.

He sighed and looked out of the office toward Grant.

"Guess I should go tell him, huh?"

I nodded.

"He's just a kid – thinks the world will never end and he's immortal. Twenty-four years old...do you remember feeling that way?"

"Yeah, and before you walked into this office, I felt that way. Guess we're not invincible," I confirmed.

He nodded solemnly in agreement. "Keller, you've got to get a hold of your life, you know? This pace is going to kill you, and it's not fair to your family. You're like a runaway freight train."

I hated to admit it, but I knew he was right. "Yeah, I will try and get a handle on it." "Don't try. You don't know how much time you have left – none of us do."

Keith walked out of my office without another word. He entered Grant's glass office, and I watched as the kid's face crumpled, and they hugged. Tears formed in my eyes, but I fought the impulse to lose control. Not here, I reminded myself, not in my office.

KELLER:

No matter how chaotic things grew around me in the office, I felt I had to always maintain the outward appearance of composure. As CEO, as our leader, I had different, unspoken rules. I had to be perceived strong on the outside, even if on the inside I was being ripped apart. I knew that I set the tone for the office, and my employees looked to me when times were uncertain. It was during those times of uncertainty that I could have won an Oscar for best actor. I had to learn to compartmentalize all emotions and stay focused. This is not something I learned in college. This is a lesson learned on the fly, a hazard of the job. Maybe it was the constant spotlight of everyone viewing my every move, constantly gauging the validity of their own concerns by taking my pulse. I am not sure, but I was very conscious of how I had to be perceived. A CEO is the ship captain, and if the ship sank, I would surely go down with it. The last thing anyone needed was a catastrophizing captain. I had to be perceived as in control – at all costs – one of the hardest parts of the job.

SHIFTING WINDS

A gust of crisp autumn air blew through a row of ash trees on the lawn of the Kentucky Capitol building in Frankfort. A torrent of dying leaves dropped from a cluster of trees and swirled in the wind. A cascade of yellow, orange, brown, and a bloody shade of red tumbled down to the barren lawn.

Jolene, Kelco's in-house counsel, walked with me along the sidewalk toward the state Capitol building. As an attorney, Jolene had a long history of working hand-in-hand with the state Insurance Commissioner's office. I felt grateful to have her with me as we approached a meeting with George, the acting Insurance Commissioner. I usually enjoyed the chance to chat with George about the industry. It always felt like catching up with one of the guys. In recent correspondence from his office, though, something seemed different.

"Don't you just love this weather?" Jolene commented, admiring the colors that swayed and dropped from the trees in the brisk autumn air.

I pulled my jacket tighter around my chest as a cold wind cut through to my skin. "Not me – give me sunshine and eighty degrees every day," I countered.

We passed through the security checks in the entrance lobby to arrive at the Insurance Department a few minutes early for our 9:00 AM meeting. We announced ourselves at the desk and were ushered back to our usual setting, a rectangular conference table surrounded with spring-enforced chairs that tilted backward to recline like the driver's seat in a low-rider convertible. I chose a place at the corner nearest the head of the table with Jolene to my right. Department staff members soon filled the remaining four seats on the other side of the table. Sharon Miller sat across from me, and I didn't recognize any of the other faces seated around the table. Perhaps they're legal staff, I pondered, smiling at Sharon. She nodded in my direction, tight-lipped and unlike here usual jovial self. I'm glad *I'm not a comedian; otherwise, this would be a really tough crowd.*

George entered the room with his usual larger-than-life presence. He instantly commanded all the attention in the room. He stood over six feet tall, and his body was built rock solid. As far as I knew, he was the first black Insurance Commissioner for the state of Kentucky. As a former collegiate football player myself, I imagined George had his fair share of days on the field. As a businessman, I admired his ability to position himself masterfully into angles of advantage in the political arena. As a Republican, he managed to stay on as Insurance Commissioner after the Republican administration shifted to a Democratic-run office. George seemed to tread well in any water. *He would be a terror to confront in shoulder pads on the open field.*

"Sorry I am running late," George stated in a booming voice.

"No problem at all, George. Good to see you." I said with a grin, standing to shake his hand.

George shook our hands with forced formality and quickly sat at the head of the table. He placed his hands atop the table, fidgeting with his fingers, appearing uneasy and irritable.

Sharon Miller broke the ice. "So, you two are here to discuss the proposed amendment of H.B. 434, the Viatical and Life Settlement Bill."

Jolene opened her folder and readied herself to take notes as she replied, "Yes, we're very appreciative of your time this morning. I conducted a conference call with leaders in the viatical and Life Settlement industry yesterday. I am here representing not only Kelco but also innumerable colleagues in our industry who share our concerns for the proposed bill."

"And what are your concerns?" Sharon asked.

"Well, Sharon, to be frank, this clean-sheeting bill threatens to shift the entire landscape of the industry, and to put it simply, it's unreasonable. The language in this proposed bill asserts that any policy purchased by a viatical company would be deemed 'contestable' — forever."

I interjected, saying, "George, who would want to buy a policy that could be voided at any given time, for any reason?"

Jolene continued, "The two-year contestable period afforded to the insurance underwriters has been a longstanding law and for a good reason. This bill threatens to change the status quo of this industry simply to deepen the pockets of big insurance and allow them to get away with not paying policy benefits."

George tilted his head away from us, looking down at his clasped hands on the table. He began speaking slowly as if he struggled to recite a memorized passage or read a script from a teleprompter. He said, "Let me be clear, Jolene; we feel that the language affords the underwriters time to review the policies and determine if there was any influence or wrongful intention in acquiring the policies. If there are no wrongful intentions, then there should be absolutely nothing to be concerned about."

Jolene cleared her throat, retorting back, "George, these contestable laws have been on the books for two hundred years. They were created to prevent the insurance companies from getting out of paying widows after their husbands pass. The insurance industry is the only industry I can think of who has two years to determine if they want to accept a contract or not. Two years is a long time. Making indefinite that time-window to void someone's policy is not in line with what they are calling contestability. It is just plain wrong."

"I'm fully aware of the contestability clause," George shot back.

Jolene quickly countered, "Then why should Kelco be responsible for the costs of reviewing the underwriting? That is, by definition, their business and, therefore, the responsibility of the insurance providers. They choose whether or not to issue a policy. We have no control over this. To make us, and companies like us, responsible for conducting reviews of their policy underwriting for us to act as a third-party purchaser or re-seller is completely out of line, especially when the industry market cap of the insurance providers is in the hundreds of billions. With a fraction of their market cap, our viatical and Life Settlement industries do not have the infrastructure in place for this. We cannot afford to do their jobs for them. This bill is effectively a death sentence to the viability of our industry."

George squeezed his clasped hands tighter atop the table, clearly attempting to restrain himself as he responded through gritted teeth,

"Jolene, I hear what you're saying, but it's not really your call."

Jolene's eyes widened at his remark. "You are right. It's yours, George. Now you know that the two-year contestability clause is more than enough to allow big insurance due diligence. If this new bill passes, you are effectively declaring that any policy ever issued to a consumer could be contested and made void, not only within two years after issue but indefinitely! Sounds to me like the big insurance companies are looking for a way to get out of covering their death benefit payout!" Jolene pressed the issue, suddenly personally offended. She dropped her pen and wagged her finger at George. "George, I don't know what's gotten into you, but I'm here to speak on behalf of all the people this will affect. And you have a responsibility, a moral obligation to listen."

George unclasped his hands, a fury building and tensing within his body. His eyes flared wide, staring hard at Jolene.

Jolene didn't budge. She didn't back down for an instant. Before George could respond, she trudged forward, rechallenging George. She continued with a finger pointed at George, "Sounds to me like big insurance already got to you and got you to switch sides."

Quicker than a cornered hyena, George lunged across the table.

I careened back in my chair, barely dodging his arms as he reached to grab Jolene. Jolene recoiled back in her seat, nearly toppling the reclining chair onto the floor. He pointed a long, tense finger in her face as rage burned in his eyes. "Don't go there! Don't you go there, girl! You hear me? Don't you go there!" he shouted at her with spit flying from his lips.

Silence...

The wall clock *ticked, ticked, ticked.* Everyone seated around the table stared at George as his body was stretched atop the conference table. George quickly came to his senses. He seemed instantly embarrassed by his actions. I felt shocked...and embarrassed for him. I felt angry and outraged at his outright disrespect toward my staff member, but I sat in silence, knowing that George was in a position of power in our industry and we needed him as an ally. George slowly slid his body down from the table and back into his seat. He placed a hand over his mouth, unwilling to make eye contact with anyone seated around him.

I broke the long silence and said, "George, I don't know what happened there, but I think we can all move past it and return to the issue here. You got to admit; Jolene has a point. Why should Kelco be responsible for the insurance underwriting? I'm not obligated in any form to the insurance companies, and they have a responsibility to the consumer. We all do."

George didn't respond. He stared blankly across the conference table.

Seated at George's left hand, Sharon responded for him, "Why don't we table this discussion for a later date? Submit your changes to me for consideration. Once I compile all the arguments, we'll have another open forum meeting."

I nodded to Sharon in agreement. We all stood from the table, and I reasoned, "Listen, George, I'm trying to work with you."

George avoided my eyes with a look of shame. "I know, Steve. Thank you for coming up. I'll talk to you later," he stated flatly.

I shook George's hand. His grip no longer felt like the embrace of a friend.

LIGHTNING IN A BOTTLE

Stainless steel elevator doors opened within the World Trade Center Tower. Keith and I stepped into the elevator together as we had hundreds of times during the previous several years. I pressed the button for the 99th floor. The doors glided closed, and the elevator box lifted Keith and me high into the sky.

Keith stood in silence, presumably lost in thought. I gently clapped him on the back. "Hey, buddy, I really appreciate you making the trip," I said sincerely.

Keith nodded. Pain and warmth lived behind his eyes. "You and I both know how important it is to have a gray hair with you in these meetings. To be honest, Keller, I'm just glad I've still got hair!" Keith jested playfully.

"Are you kidding me? Cancer has never come up against someone like you. In my eyes, you're invincible, Keith."

"We'd like to think so, wouldn't we?" Keith smiled.

Silence

Floor 60...70...80...90...99 I stepped out of the elevator, leading the way. I strode forward with my shoulders thrown back and my head held high, bracing against what felt like the weight of the world on my back. I walked with the momentum of nearly one hundred full-time employees on staff at Kelco, who depended on me for their livelihood; the sales network we had assembled of thirty thousand affiliated sales agents worldwide; the industry at large, and the thousands of consumers globally; their friends and family, ensuring financial peace of mind when they needed it most. *I have to stay strong – if not for me, for them and for Keith. If he can fight this battle, then so can I.*

We approached the floor-to-ceiling glass doors of ATLAS GLOBAL. I pushed open the door and smiled fondly at Keith as he stepped into the reception area with me.

A bubbly woman with strawberry blond hair, Wendy, awaited us as we approached the reception desk. "Steve! We've missed you!" she chirped.

I greeted Wendy with a friendly handshake and my most charming smile. "You know us, Wendy; we wouldn't miss an opportunity to come to see you."

Wendy's face warmed to a rosy shade of red. "And Keith, so good to see you. I hope you're doing well."

"As well as can be expected," Keith replied with a curt nod.

Wendy's smile turned to the business at hand. "Now, if you both will follow me. We have the conference room ready."

Wendy led us through the office and into a nearby conference room. The doors opened to tall glass windows that overlooked the New York Bay and the Statue of Liberty. Jerry Wendorf, President of ATLAS GLOBAL, sat alone behind an enormous mahogany conference table. His salt and pepper hair sat lifeless atop his head. Large round glasses framed his stern face. He rose from his chair to greet Keith and me with firm handshakes.

"How are we, gentlemen?" Jerry asked.

"We've been putting out a few fires since we last saw you," I responded sharply, locking eyes with Jerry to gauge his reaction.

"Is that so?" Jerry responded, his face revealing no outward expression, like a poker player sitting behind a mountain of chips.

"Financially, though, we're healthier than ever," Keith stated firmly.

Jerry watched as he tapped his fingers against the mahogany table. He looked up from beneath his eyebrows at me. He said, "I can help you with your fires, Steve," then turned to Keith, "and breathe new life into your finances."

"And how do you propose to do that, Jerry?" I asked.

"Listen, boys, you've had a good run. It's impressive, really, but you're getting in over your head. The water only gets deeper from here on out," Jerry implored.

"Jerry, we have a portfolio with a face value of more than six billion dollars, and we recently raised our line of financing to ten billion for new acquisitions. We're swimming in the deep end with you now," I said boldly, pointing across the table in his direction.

Jerry threw his head back and laughed heartily. He adjusted his glasses and focused a laser glare in my direction. "That's where you're wrong, son. You don't even know how deep the water really goes."

Growing frustrated, Keith said, "If you're just here to give us swimming lessons and veiled threats, we'll be on our way, Jerry."

Jerry placed his palms down on the table. "Right. Okay, so I'm aware of your current situation: your growth opportunities, your current challenges with the audits – multi-state audits, I might add. That must really put a strain on operations," he said, pausing to read our reactions.

Keith and I remained steady, holding our stack of chips close to home.

Jerry continued, saying, "And a shifting landscape on the lawmaking front too. Kudos on getting your bill passed. I'm sure you're aware of the state-level changes being implemented by our lawmakers in response."

I resisted the temptation to glance in Keith's direction, affirming our suspicions.

Jerry sensed my urge. He said, "Here's the deal, and you're not going to find another offer like this anywhere else. I can make all your troubles go away. I want to buy you out. A straight equity deal to take over Kelco's stake in your asset portfolio – three hundred million dollars, on the table. What do you say?"

The number bounced through my thoughts. *Three hundred million dollars...I'm only thirty-three years old. What would I do? Retire? And what about all my employees? Would they lose their jobs? What about the dreams we built together of going public and all becoming millionaires? By selling out, would I be selling them out? With three hundred million dollars, I could buy an island and provide for my family with generational wealth to support my great, great-grandchildren; however, I worked so hard to create this vision and build this business from the ground up.*

Along with the thought of selling Kelco, the image of my face on the cover of Forbes faded; The Wall Street Journal faded; *The New York Times* faded. My vision of who I believed I was and whom I believed I could become faded.

I responded reflexively, pointing a rigid finger at Jerry. "The answer is no, Jerry, and here in a couple years, I'm going to be buying you out!"

Jerry clenched his jaw, revealing his hand for the first time. Keith watched me with a sideways glance, unflinching.

Jerry quickly released his tension as he responded with a heavy sigh. "Keller, you're making the biggest mistake of your life. Take the offer."

I didn't budge. "You heard me. The answer is no."

Jerry leaned back in his chair, "Do you have any idea how big we are, young man?"

I stared back at him, unwavering.

Jerry said, "You're about to find out."

PART THREE
WHEN A GIANT FALLS

THREE WEEKS LATER

NO REST FOR THE WEARY

My cell phone rang and buzzed. My eyes opened to a room of darkness. *Where am I? What time is it?* The clock on the hotel room nightstand read 7:00 AM. The phone insisted on being answered. I crawled out of bed, disoriented after only a few hours of sleep and a late New York night. I stumbled around the dark room in search of the ring, buzzing, and buzzing.

I tracked the sound to my suit, draped over an armchair. I fumbled through the jacket pocket and opened the phone. Nothing happened. I hit the call button. The phone connected me to whoever was on the other line while I searched for a light-switch to break the darkness.

I slurred my greeting, breathing heavily into the phone. "Uh, hello? Hello?"

I recognized the frantic voice of my assistant, Karen, as she shouted, "Keller!" She composed herself and said, "I've got some news for you, and it's not good."

"What is it?" I asked, plopping down on the bed in my boxer shorts with my hand on my forehead to shield myself from unwanted news. I braced myself for the death of a family member or an employee. *I hope Keith is okay, I thought.*

"The FBI has taken over Kelco!"

Her words didn't register as valid in my thoughts. The FBI? I sat on the edge of the bed, confused, staring at a blank TV screen. I scratched the scruff on my face trying to register the meaning of her words.

"Keller, are you there?"

I breathed a heavy sigh and stood from the bed. My confusion quickly turned to frustration. "Karen. What time is it anyway?" I said sternly.

"It's 7:00 in the morning."

"Karen, I was out with the insurance guys last night after closing a couple deals yesterday. I got in around three in the morning. This isn't funny. Do you understand? I don't need these shenanigans this early in the morning."

Karen raised her voice an octave, suddenly shrill with anxiety. "Keller! This is no joke! I'm in the parking garage across the street, looking at Kelco. There is yellow crime scene tape around the whole block! Loads of FBI agents are swarming the building."

I began to pace without even realizing it. My hand was still on my forehead as I stumbled over the clothes on the floor from last night. "Shit!" I said aloud to myself. Think, Keller. Think.

"Okay, Karen, talk to me. I'm here. How many do you see?" I asked.

"Keller, it's not good. It's hard to say – maybe a hundred. I don't know. You gotta get back here!"

"A hundred? What the hell? Where are Keith and Grant?"

"They took them."

"Where?"

"I don't know! Our people are hiding out at our attorney's office – the Frost, Brown, Todd building across the street."

"Karen, keep that phone with you. I'll be on the next flight back. I gotta go."

"Be careful, St...!" she shouted as I ended the call.

HURRY HOME

I stared blankly at the lifeless phone. My hands shook. My nerves pulsed with anxiety and fear as I sat paralyzed. I planted my feet firmly on the floor as the world around me began to spin, threatening to drop me down to my knees. I swallowed hard. A lump in my throat refused to pass. Nausea floated toward the surface as the hotel room walls felt like they were closing in around me. A cold sweat beaded on my skin. I rushed, stumbling, heavy-footed toward the toilet, where I vomited violently. My hands gripped the toilet for support. I refused to kneel.

I spat into the sink and wiped my mouth with the back of my hand, splashing water on my face as I stared at myself in the mirror. Shock and horror stared back at me. "Get a grip, Keller," I said aloud. "They can't do this. I won't let them." It reassured me to hear the confidence in my words. "That's right. They can't do this. I won't let them. Let them try. They don't know who they're messing with!" My muscles tensed, and my fear turned to an indignant fury, snapping me back to reality, clearing my thoughts of all the clutter.

I frantically searched for my cell phone. *Shit, my jet is in the shop.* I found it on the floor and quickly pounded the numbers for a private airport, called Teterboro in New Jersey, where my jet was in for maintenance.

Upon answering my call, I recognized the familiar voice of a woman named Norma, whom I had met several times before. She said, "Hello, Million Dollar Air, how can I help you?"

"Norma, it's Steve Keller. I have an emergency, and I need a ride back to Lexington, ASAP. Can you help me?"

"Steve, your jet isn't ready yet. They have it broken down in pieces. It won't be ready for another day or so."

"Norma, I don't care what you've got to do. I've got to get back to

Lexington. It's beyond an emergency there."

I heard the clacking of keys, and Norma responded, "Okay, we don't have anything available but tell you what...You just get down here, and I'll figure something out."

"I owe you, big time."

Norma laughed and said, "I have a long memory, Steve."

I rushed to throw my scattered clothes into my suitcase.

The hotel clerk greeted me with a warm welcome in the hotel lobby, and before I reached the counter, I shouted across the room, "I need a cab! To Teterboro!"

The clerk responded, waving his hand, "Sir, you've got to wait your turn. Our cabs are backed up. There's a wreck with an eighteen-wheeler on the parkway."

"Like hell, I do!" I shouted as I scurried into the revolving doors. I pushed against the automatic door, forcing it to rotate faster. Outside, in the valet area, I found a line of cabs that trailed back to the overflowing traffic in the street.

I rushed to the first cab in the line. A dark-haired man with a beer gut and thick forearms sauntered toward the taxi. I jumped in front of him and lunged for the rear door. The man shouted, "Hey! What are you doing, pal? That's my cab."

I dropped my luggage and blocked the man's path as he plowed toward me, reaching for the door handle. I shouted, "Listen, I've got an emergency! I need this cab!"

The man raised his voice as he reached for the handle, "I got places to be!"

I forcefully pushed the man's hand aside. At the slightest touch, he recoiled his arm, about to throw a punch. I held a hand in the air and reached into my back pocket to withdraw my wallet. "Listen! Listen to me. I just found out over a hundred FBI agents are raiding my business." Anger rose within me as I felt myself unraveling at the seams. My voice began losing control as I screamed. "Now you listen to me. I know you want this cab. You've got two options. I'm going to give you a hundred dollars right now to let me take this cab, or we can fight it out right here! And the only ride you'll be taking today is in a fucking ambulance!"

"I don't care how much money you got!" the man shouts, grabbing my shirt.

The clerk from inside the hotel appears at the man's side, trying to separate us. "Security!" the clerk yelled, struggling to push us apart.

At the first chance of separation, I dodged the man's grasp and jumped into the cab, slamming the door closed. "Go!" I shouted to the cabbie.

"Where do we go?" The cabbie says in a thick Indian accent.

"Teterboro airport!"

"Sir, I am very sorry. Traffic is terrible."

"Just drive!"

The cabbie slowly pulled into the traffic line in the street as the man tussled with the clerk. He broke free and approached the cab door as we stalled in traffic. I balled up a hundred-dollar bill in my fist and threw it out the window. The man smacked the cab window, shouting, "Fuck you! Asshole!" He then picked up the hundred-dollar bill from the street as the cab drove forward into traffic.

Cars quickly piled around our cab. I fidgeted in my seat, feeling trapped. I looked to my phone as an escape but felt fear as I realized I needed to make a call that I should have made weeks ago. I dialed the number.

"Hello," a familiar voice answered.

"Tammy, are you awake?" I asked.

"Sort of. What's going on?"

"I'm in New York. Karen just called. Something horrible is going on at Kelco. The FBI has taken over the company."

"What? Why?"

"I don't know, but Karen says there are a hundred FBI agents and cops down there. The news media is there too. If you can keep from it, don't go out. If you do, don't talk to any media. I'm trying to get back to Lexington as soon as I can," I said, breathless.

While I waited for her to respond, I suddenly felt uncertain about every aspect of my life, as if it had become like an Alice-in-Wonderland fantasy; my reality was tumbling down a strange and terrifying rabbit hole. Every thread that held my life together felt frayed and loose. *Tammy, how did I let you go? I felt an urge, wishing to rewind time and start over. I need to piece my life back together again. I will – stitch by stitch if I have to. I need something, anything that feels normal and stable right now.*

I swallowed my pride and spoke softly into the phone. "Tammy, this may not be the time, but I'm sorry that I let our relationship erode. I realize that my family is the most important thing in my life. Tammy, can I come home?" I pleaded, understanding that home was not the grand house we built together. Home was wherever she was, her and our baby boy, Cole. Home was with our family.

Silence hung on the line, only seconds long, but I felt the miles between us.

Finally, she replied, "Yes, Steve, come home."

I hung up and exhaled a deep sigh of relief. *Home...if there's even a home left when I get there.* I called a friend, the only criminal attorney I knew, Bob Webb, with Frost, Brown, Todd. Their Lexington office was located directly across the street from Kelco's office building in the Financial Center.

After a few rings, a receptionist answered, "Frost, Brown, Todd – can I help you?"

"Bob Webb's office, please," I said in a rush.

A lady answered the phone, "Kris speaking."

"I need to speak to Bob Webb. This is an emergency."

"Who's speaking?"

"Steve Keller."

"He's at a conference in Houston, Texas."

"Kris, my company, Kelco, has just been raided by the FBI. There are about a hundred agents in downtown Lexington. My employees are all seeking shelter in your Lexington office as we speak. I'm in New York, trying to get back to Lexington. I don't care if Bob is in Russia. I need him there now! What's his number?"

"His cell phone is 859-257-1333."

"Thank you, Kris."

I ended the call and dialed Bob's number. He answered in a whisper,

"Hello."

"Bob, this is Steve Keller. All hell is breaking loose in Lexington. I need you there ASAP."

"Hold on, Steve," he said, pausing, "Okay, I had to step into the hallway. I'm at a conference. What's going on?"

"Bob, I'm in New York. I got a call from Karen in Lexington telling me that the FBI has taken over Kelco. She said there are about a hundred FBI agents and cops swarming through the office. I don't know what's going on, but you need to get there now."

"I'm in Houston."

"Bob, rent a jet and fly back now. I've got to have you there now. These people are carting my company away in U-Haul trucks as we speak!"

"Okay, Steve, I'm on my way."

"Thank you, Bob. I'll meet you there as soon as I can."

"Don't worry. I've got this," he assured me.

"See you later, Bob," I said flatly and ended the call.

"If I can ever get there," I said to myself aloud. I soon turned my frustration toward the cabbie and shouted, "Get me to the airport, damn it!"

The cab driver lifted his eyebrows and glared at me in the rear-view mirror.

WHEELS UP

I ran to the jet with my carry-on rolling behind me. The door of the Lear popped open and thrust forward onto the tarmac as I approached, exposing the steps to the plane. A round man squeezed through the plane's open doorway to stand atop the steps. He waved proudly in my direction. His wave's vigor caused his shirttail to gape open, exposing the bottom of his overhanging belly. I hurried up the steps and examined this pilot. His wrinkled white shirt was splattered with grease stains, and his unkempt, jet-black hair seemed overgrown as if his barber stopped returning his phone calls. He looked like a New York cab driver, not an airplane pilot. I paused on the steps before entering the plane and asked this character, "Hey, can you fly this thing?"

"Yes, sir, I've been flying for years," he assured me and then coughed into his hand.

If I wasn't in an emergency circumstance, never in a million years would I step on this plane. *I don't have much of a choice,* I considered quickly.

"Look, I've got an emergency in Lexington, Kentucky. I've got to get back there in record time. I need you to redline this bird," I insisted.

"Then get in here and let's go!" he said, grinning through only one side of his mouth.

I stepped past the pilot and into the plane. When I saw the fuselage, I stopped in my tracks. The dirty walls and ceiling looked like they recently hauled used car parts. The seat was covered with worn-out gray leather but seemed relatively clean. I hesitantly sat down, and the fat man pulled the door closed. He hunched over painfully as he entered the fuselage and maneuvered toward the cockpit. He squeezed himself into his seat with a few grunts and deep breaths. The co-pilot seated next to him, who could have passed as the pilot's twin brother, turned to me and waved. I waved back, thinking, Oh brother, here we go.

The co-pilot shouted, "You might want to strap in!"

I never strap in on my plane, I thought and then realized his words were not a suggestion but a warning. "Okay!" I shouted back, strapping my filthy seat belt tight. Click!

The supersized jet-jockeys fired up the engines and headed out to the end of the runway. Once cleared for takeoff, they throttled down the levers and threw me back in my seat. We quickly rose into the air, and I understood the need for the seatbelt. The jet twisted and turned like a fighter plane and hooked a hard right toward Kentucky, pushing as much power through the jet engines as possible.

Once we reached thirty thousand feet, all my problems suddenly seemed so far away from me, yet I knew my hour was approaching. When I landed, I would be heading into a combat zone. I stared out into the clouds and reflected on my conversation with Karen. I hung up before she could tell me something. The curiosity spun quickly into paranoia. If the Feds know about my plane being in the shop, they'll expect me to be flying commercial. There may be agents waiting for me at the Lexington airport...maybe even the media.

"Change of plans, guys!" I shouted toward the cockpit. "Take me to the private airfield nearest Bluegrass Airport!"

The pilot leaned back in his seat and flashed a thumbs up and a smile. "You got it, Mr. Keller. We're almost there!" he yelled.

I took a deep breath and then another, trying to prevent myself from having a panic attack. Within minutes we began our descent. The plane dropped much quicker than Kelco's jet, nearly lifting me from my seat. As we approached the ground, my nerves began to fire on all cylinders. I felt as if I was rushing home only to be placed in front of a firing squad. I stared with dread out the window as the ground grew larger and closer with every second.

I never was afraid of heights. It was the hitting the ground part that always bothered me.

THE WELCOME PARTY

The plane glided then bounced down against the pavement of the runway. I scanned the area around the little terminal, searching for sedans with cheap hubcaps or SUVs with dark tinted windows. I didn't see anything out of the ordinary. The plane screeched to a stop, and the pilot duo turned off the engines. I breathed a bit easier, knowing we were safely on the ground and soon I would be out of this filthy airplane. I rushed to call Karen.

"Hello, Steve?" she answered.

"Karen, it's me. I've landed."

"I see your plane."

"Is the coast clear? Wait, you're here? How did you know I'd be here?"

"I started out at Bluegrass, but agents were swarming the place. I just hoped you'd end up here. Seems empty out here."

"Good. We were headed to Bluegrass, but I thought they might be waiting on me there. I'll be right over."

I exited down the plane steps with relief and then turned back toward the plane to see the two supersized twins waving at me from the fuselage. I held a thumbs up and shouted over my shoulder with gratitude, "Great job, guys! Record time!" They smiled and nodded their heads in acknowledgment.

I hurried through the terminal with my roller bag in tow without incident. I made it to the airport's front parking lot. I found Karen standing outside of her car, waiting for me. Beside her, I noticed two people standing with her: my mother and father. *What a reassuring sight. Amid all the chaos my life has become, of course, they are here.* I hurried toward them, hugging them both tightly. "What are you doing here? How'd you know I'd be here?"

My mom observed me with a level of sincerity in her eyes that only a mother can manifest. She replied kindly, "Karen called us. We rushed right over."

My dad placed a supportive hand on my shoulder. "Don't you worry about a thing, son. I'm sure you'll get this mess sorted out. It's probably just a big misunderstanding," he said with conviction.

"I don't have a clue what's going on!" I said, baffled. "Karen, can you fill me in?"

"It's bad, Keller," Karen said, scanning the airport parking lot for any suspicious activity around us. "We need to get you back downtown. Our staff is hiding out at Bob Webb's office. They are holding Grant and Keith for questioning."

"What? Questioning for what?"

Karen grimaced. "We really should get going."

I hugged my parents quickly, grateful for their unconditional support. I knew I had to leave them to go into what felt like an active war zone. I began to step into the front seat of Karen's sedan when she stopped me. She said, "I don't think that's such a good idea, Keller. You should probably hide on the floorboard in the back seat until we get you to Bob Webb's office."

My mouth dropped in shock, but I didn't argue. I opened the back door of the car and crawled onto the floorboard. From the low vantage point, I looked up to the car's interior roof, the gray sky above through the windows, and at my parents' reassuring faces as they briefly watched me through the windows. Their faces grew smaller and then disappeared altogether as Karen smuggled me away.

INTO THE STORM

I projected my voice from the floorboard with as much authority as I could muster. "Okay, Karen, we ain't got much time. I want to know everything you learned from talking with all the employees today."

"Keller, let me tell you. This day will forever be etched in my mind – *what...a...day.*" she said, revving herself up as she continued. "One of our accountants, Joy, got to work early this morning. She was met by Roberta Bottoms, who is the Postal Service Agent leading the raid."

"The Postal Service?"

"Yeah, apparently, she was tearing up the entire control panel that locks all the doors when Joy walked in and tried to stop her. As soon as this happened, Joy was escorted to a cubical, and without explanation, they began questioning her. At the same time this was going on, the agents apprehended Keith, and they were walking back and forth with their guns out as they questioned him. Keith just said they were playing a game of intimidation, like, they actually thrust their guns toward him sometimes as a constant reminder that they had power, you know? He said they wanted him to know they were a force to be reckoned with, and their expectations were not to be dismissed."

"Karen, this is like a bad dream. You're not making any sense. Is it the FBI or the Postal Service? And what would the Postal Service want with us?"

"Keller, I have a lot to tell you, so please don't interrupt."

"By all means, it's just unreal. Please go ahead."

"Keith told me he finally began to understand what this was about when he asked to speak to one of our company attorneys, Scott Brown, who arrives at work just about always at the same time as Keith. They told him, 'We don't know where he is.' Most of the agents that I saw carried two-way radios, and they were on them regularly. Keith said he knew he wasn't getting the truth from them. This Roberta Bottoms, just a nasty woman, Keller, she came in and started trying to intimidate him. She launched into this whole good-cop-bad-cop routine."

"What do you mean?" I asked, just as the car rolled over a bump in the road that tossed me airborne and then back down onto the floorboard.

"Keith said she was in his face saying stuff like, 'Listen here; this is your opportunity to fess up.' Keith told her that there must have been a mistake because we didn't do anything wrong. He also told them that he is a very sick man and asked not to be treated this way."

"And? What did they say?"

"Pssh, typical – not sympathetic at all, not caring that he's a dying man – they just said, 'We know you are, and you should tell us what we want to know.' Keith said they were trying to get him to say that you and Grant Sutherlin had committed mail fraud, with a heavy emphasis on you."

"This is outrageous, Karen – *Mail fraud?*" I said in utter shock.

"Oh, it gets better, Keller. This is a very corrupt bunch. Come to find out, our attorney, Scott Brown, demanded to see Keith at nearly the precise moment Keith asked to speak with Scott because Keith has a right to an attorney before being questioned, but they lied and told him they didn't know where he was! Scott Brown said the agent spoke into his two-way radio, you know, pressing his lips against the mouthpiece so as not to be overheard. Scott couldn't believe what he was witnessing. As the rest of our employees arrived, the officers escorted them upstairs at gunpoint, individually and in small groups, then questioned everyone without explaining why. Some of the employees were told to freeze and put their hands up when they entered the building! They treated us like common criminals! The agents were telling all of us, 'This company needs to be shut down.' That's what they kept telling us!"

I felt terrible to hear our people were treated like that. "Damn, Karen, I'm sorry they put you all through that. They sound like colossal assholes.

"You got that right, Keller, and listen to what another agent said to one of the employees who was already close to tears. He said, 'Unless you talk to us, you're going to jail!' Can you believe that? Do you know anything about this, Keller?"

"This is crazy, Karen! No, you know more than I do. It sounds like we're being hit by the mob or something out of a movie. I hope everyone's okay. I wish I could have been there, but it may have only made things worse."

"Well, I don't know what to say about it either – just an awful day – and I've only told you a fraction of it," she lamented, shaking her head in disbelief.

"This is so bad, Karen. What about you? Did you experience any of this brutality, or were you in the parking garage calling people and doing interviews?"

"Oh yeah, I had to run through the gauntlet too. I decided not to tell the agents that I was your assistant," Karen said, allowing her voice to trail off with the implications of the danger she might have put herself in. She resumed by saying, "Since you were out of town, I knew I was the only one who could take charge until you arrived. I rushed through the interview process with the agents then hurried outside. Of course, the local media was there with their television cameras as the agents took all our company files and records and loaded them onto trucks. That's when I called you."

"Karen, without those records, Kelco is as good as dead," I stated flatly, feeling defeated.

"Keller, the removal of our files has been going on all day. I'm told more than 600 banker boxes were loaded into cargo trucks, one after another. And you're especially not going to like this. An employee offered the agents the keys to unlock the brand-new furniture and filing cabinets to access the records, and they told her they didn't need them. A few minutes later, the agents drilled open the locks to the cabinets and broke open the furniture drawers. They really wanted to cause damage."

"This isn't right. I feel like we should call the police, but they're the one's doing this!"

"Stay down, Keller. We're almost there. You'll be able to see for yourself soon enough."

GROUND ZERO

From my hiding place on Karen's sedan floorboard, I watched the last few strands of light fade in the evening sky; my hope felt dim as well. Karen slowed the car as we entered a parking garage. Blue and red police lights flashed against the cement ceiling of the parking structure. *We're here, I thought.*

"Alright, Keller. I think the coast should be clear. Let's hurry over to Bob Webb's office."

I stepped out of the car and into the strobe of flashing police lights. It felt like something out of a nightmare. Across the street sat Kelco, my business, my life's work. Yellow crime scene tape surrounded our building. Dirty banker boxes filled with our records, our business transactions, lined the streets awaiting pick-up to be hauled away. I had a gut-wrenching pain in my stomach. *Those files are like the lifeblood of this company, and they're bleeding us dry.* Trash and papers littered the street. An expensive Italian leather sofa that I recently purchased for our entrance foyer crudely sat on the sidewalk to prop open the glass doors of the ground floor entrance. A large man who wore bib overalls and boots lounged low on the sofa. He balanced the butt of a shotgun on his right knee.

In disbelief, I said to Karen, "Is this what it has come to in this country? This is a high-end financial operation, and they're throwing our property on the street like this is some kinda' drug bust!" I pointed toward the man on the sofa. "And this guy, he looks like a rogue cowboy from the good ol' boys club. This is how they treat companies?" Karen tugged my elbow, pulling me away from the ledge. "Keller, we need to get inside. That man is the good ol' boys club. His name is Pat Molloy, and I found out this morning that he's the prosecutor on the government's case against us."

"Case against us!" I shouted.

Karen led the way through the parking garage to a connecting entrance to the Frost, Brown, Todd office in the financial building. We entered the office lobby to find what looked like a triage center in a third world country. Dozens of displaced employees sat and stood, scattered around the room looking shell-shocked by what they had just experienced, so much so that no one noticed as I walked into the lobby.

"Well, it looks like a bad day at the office!" I joked awkwardly to announce myself.

Everyone seemed to freeze, and a hush fell inside the room. Grant was the first to notice me. He shouted, "Keller!"

I was at a loss for words. Standing in the presence of all my employees after what they experienced was depressing. I felt the urge toward self-pity and sadness. With nothing more to say or add to change the situation for my employees, or even myself, I gave in to pity. I made eye contact with a few of the women who were in tears. I dropped my head, not wanting anyone to see my struggle against the tears pooling in my eyes. Several of the women embraced me with comforting hugs of support. I scanned the grief-stricken faces around the room, and I sensed they were all looking to me for answers. I didn't have any.

I hugged Keith and Grant. "You guys, alright?"

Grant nodded an affirmation. Keith's gaze seemed far away. "How about you, Keith?" I asked, "you doing okay?"

Keith took a heavy breath and lifted his mouth with effort into a smile. "I've seen better days."

Bob Webb, our newly appointed criminal attorney, approached our circle to join the conversation. He patted me on the back and offered me a hug of support. He said, "Steve, I've been digging to find out all I can. There's not much more we can do today, but we're going to have a fight on our hands. Maybe we should all call it a night and reconvene tomorrow when I'll have more information to share."

"Okay, Bob. I'm just at a loss here. I don't even know what to say."

"I've handled a lot of cases over the years, and I have to admit, this is a first for me too. I don't know what to think about it just yet. Don't worry, though; I'm on it," Bob replied in his most reassuring tone.

"Thanks, Bob. Hi, everyone!" I announced, addressing the room. "It's been a long day. I know it's been a hard day and one that I'm sure we will all never forget. We've done all we can for today, so let's all go home and get some rest. And don't worry; everything is going to be okay. Bob's team is already working on it, and we're going to figure out what's going on here."

"Are we even able to show up for work on Monday?" a voice countered from the crowd.

"Business as usual, guys, okay? Go home and get some rest. Anyone who feels like they need more time off, feel free to take whatever you need. We're here for you, and we'll all get through this."

Everyone slowly dispersed after lingering and chattering. Many of the employees uploaded their horror stories from the day to me before leaving. The head of our thirteen-man IT department named Pat approached me. His hair was disheveled, and he looked like he lost a fight yet still had a spark of mischief in his eyes like he wanted to tell me a secret.

He said, "Steve, do you have a second?"

"Pat, how are you? Of course."

He smiled. "Did you hear what happened?"

"I've heard a lot, but not nearly enough. Tell me everything."

"First of all, these assholes were going to take all of our computer systems with them. I couldn't let that happen, so I agreed to download the system for them."

"Thank God, you did that."

"But get this; while downloading all of our files for them, I noticed Judd Clemmer being way too helpful. Judd was even telling the agents what to read on our database. Steve, I think Judd must be working for the government," Pat explained angrily.

"I'll put someone on him right away, Pat."

"Steve, they didn't stop after downloading our database. They wiped out our database and wanted our backup tapes too. They drilled our safety deposit box at 5/3 Bank. They even took our magnetic computer backup tapes that contain every transaction Kelco's ever logged. This was a raid, Steve...and they're trying to shut us down."

The blood drained from my face. "Pat, no, don't tell me that. Do we have any tapes left?"

"None that I know about," he lamented.

I looked away from Pat thinking, *That's it. That's the end of our business. We can't operate without our files.* I walked away from Pat without saying another word. I slowly ambled out of the attorney's office and entered the parking structure in a daze. The red and blue lights washed over me. I approached the ledge of the structure to observe the destruction of Kelco across the street. The building looked empty, like a river mussel that had been dredged up and hollowed-out for its pearls. The entrance doors were still open, bleeding the last of our files onto the street and into trucks to be carted away.

Someone approached behind me. I didn't react. The person came closer to stand beside me in silence. Without turning to look, I knew Grant was with me. We stared out together over the ledge, not saying a word as we viewed our life's work being destroyed. Something about it felt unclean and just wrong, as if we were watching a bunch of hoodlums spraying graffiti on a Van Gogh.

"Well, Grant, it's hard to believe that this is happening. It feels like I'm watching a bad mob movie," I finally said, breaking the silence between us.

"It's incomprehensible. Who's behind this?" Grant asked.

"I don't know," I said as I allowed the silence to linger as we watched agents heft a load of banker boxes from the street into a truck bed.

Grant looked into my eyes before quickly returning his gaze across the street. He said, "As long as we've known each other, that's the first time I've ever heard you say that."

"Say what?"

"That you don't know something. You always have all the answers. You're always a few steps ahead."

I felt a twinge of resentment toward his statement as I responded, "What are you trying to say, Grant?"

Grant shook his head, dismissing his comment. His gaze drifted off toward nowhere. "It's just, I...I trust you, but...you know...it's nothing. Forget it. It's been a long day," Grant said, then turned and walked away.

"Call me sometime tomorrow, Grant."

"Okay, I will." He shouted over his shoulder.

Grant jumped into his Jeep Cherokee. He revved the engine and punched the gas wildly in anger, speeding through the parking garage.

I didn't blame him. I felt utterly helpless and at the mercy of the powers that be. *Pointing our anger toward the government doesn't do us any good. There's no defending ourselves against this raid.*

"Might as well let it out, Grant," I said aloud to myself. I started the engine in my car. *Just keep driving, I told myself, no matter what.*

KELLER:

In business, perception is not the only thing – it's everything. The negative perception of this well-orchestrated raid on Kelco affected everyone within our business periphery. An immediate and drastic example of such a shift in perception occurred in our banking relationships. The president of our local Central Bank, the branch we used to fulfill our payroll and daily operational costs, had seen the news, and he had personally witnessed the yellow crime scene tape partitioning off Kelco's office building in downtown Lexington. In a knee jerk reaction, and without notice, the bank froze the quarter-million-dollar line of credit we used to float payroll each month, overriding the fact that our line of credit was secured with a three-million-dollar asset in collateral. It didn't matter. The damage was done.

Word of the raid burned through Wall Street like a fire through a dry California forest. In fact, Wall Street knew about the raid before I did. From that moment on, if you wanted to sell a policy, you couldn't. The market became paralyzed. Thousands of innocent people who needed cash to sustain themselves through terminal illness, suddenly found they were without options.

SEEKING SOLITUDE

A gate lifted. I waved cordially to the night security guard on watch as I drove beneath the raised crossbar. The headlights to my Porsche illuminated the dark road ahead. Though worried after the raid, I felt secure and safe, entering the quiet gated community where Tammy had moved. She had only been relocated there for a few weeks. I doubted any potentially prying eyes or ears from the government could have known to follow me there.

I knocked, and soon the door to Tammy's apartment opened. She stood in the doorway, and she looked as beautiful as the day we first met. I could still recall the dress she wore that first night and how she wore her hair tied loosely with chopsticks. Standing there on her doorstep, after so much had happened, I suddenly felt so alone. I felt like a lonely soul standing out in the cold as she and our son lived within this tiny apartment. Tammy observed me with kindness from within the warmth of her new home.

For a moment, I hesitated. *What if she rejects me?*

Tammy opened her mouth to speak, and before her words came out, I rushed forward and embraced her in a hug. She welcomed me instantly, and I knew I was home. She wrapped her arms around me and held me tight. Holding her and being embraced by her overwhelmed me with the comfort that I had been searching for. I finally felt safe to let down my guard. Tears poured from my eyes and ran down my cheeks onto her shoulders.

"I'm...so sorry...Tammy." I said, sniffling between words.

She only held me tighter. Her shoulders shuddered as she cried with me.

"It's okay, Steve. You're home now. It's going to be okay."

"I don't know if it is."

Tammy leaned back within our embrace to look into my eyes. "Everything just feels so out of control. This doesn't seem right," she replied.

I explored the depths of her soft blue eyes, searching for the answers I needed. "I don't know what to do, Tammy. It doesn't make sense to me either. I just don't know anymore."

"You'll find a way, honey. You always do," she said, gently reassuring me.

I shook my head in defiance. "We're done, Tammy. They took our files and all of our backup drives. We can't operate without them. It's over."

"It's all over the news," Tammy lamented.

"Have they given any clues about what the government wants with us?"

Before Tammy could respond, I was distracted by the pitter-patter of footfalls that approached from across the room. Tammy nudged me inside and closed the door behind me, shutting out the cold. My son, Cole, was walking more confidently than he had been when I saw him last. He hurried toward his mom and dad and threw his little arms forward for a hug – my son. I lifted him in my arms and brought him between Tammy and me for a group hug. He grinned with delight, blissfully sheltered from the devastation I had experienced that day. He only cared that his mom and dad were with him, together, and that we all loved each other. I wish life could always be this simple, I thought. The comforting warmth from within their hug was a moment in time that I wanted to last forever, though I knew it couldn't, and I knew it wouldn't. At that moment, the darkness and the cold couldn't get in. That tiny circle of love felt like the only light in the entire universe, and for me, I realized that was enough. It was more than enough.

I sighed as tears rolled down my cheeks and confessed, "I just need some normalcy in my life right now – just something that feels right – and being here with you, with our family, feels more right than anything else in my life."

Fresh tears rolled down Tammy's face as she bit her lip, uncertain. She admitted, "I know this isn't really the time, but we've got some more news. Cole is going to have a little brother or sister soon."

My mouth dropped, speechless.

Tammy smiled and laughed as her tear-filled eyes gleamed with excitement. She said, "I'm pregnant, Steve."

I smiled. New tears fell from my eyes. *I don't know what kind of world this baby will be born into, but I'm going to love this baby and my family with all my heart.*

THE MORNING AFTER

I arrived at the office around nine o'clock Saturday morning. I approached the exterior of the building with trepidation, unsure of what awaited me inside. Part of me wanted to just turn around and leave behind all the grinding I knew awaited me; *a cozy apartment (that no one knows about) with my love, my boy, our growing family is a sweet enough dream...*

The sight at the front of the building severed my daydream, cold on the line. The Italian leather sofa still propped open the entrance doors. The cold morning breeze had carried in the dust and grime from Main Street. Each new gust blew new clouds of debris into the building. *Who knows if any vagrants wandered inside last night? After the raid, though, I doubt there is anything left inside worth stealing.* I shook my head in disgust at the sight. I looked over my shoulders to find myself standing alone on the sidewalk. *Fine, I thought. I'll do it myself.*

I tossed my briefcase, empty as it was, onto the leather sofa's cushions, and then gripped an end with both hands. The other end dragged slowly. The glass and steel entrance door snagged on the sofa. No matter how hard I pulled, the sofa didn't budge. I groaned from the effort, pulling harder, but it refused to move.

"Son of a bitch!" I finally shouted, dropping the end of the sofa.

Breathing hard, I dropped my body down onto the cushions in defeat. The seat and the rest felt comforting. *What's the point anyways?* I considered. *Even if I dragged this thing back inside, they could come back whenever they want and take it all away. Why even bother? Maybe I should just sit down, take a rest, and stop trying so hard.* I stretched my arms overhead and leaned back into the comfort of the cushions. *Yeah, that feels good. Maybe that's what they want from me anyway – to just give up.* I dropped my head back into the cushions and closed my eyes. *Yeah, why not?*

After a moment, I realized I couldn't rest. *What son wants a coward for a father?* My eyes opened to the building's brick exterior that stretched up toward the sky, nine stories tall. Attached to the wall, among the small-town skyline, I saw the bottom of the letters KELCO. *That's my name, I thought with pride. I built this. This building belongs to me because of my hard work and because I didn't give up when things got hard. Those are the accomplishments that withstand the test of time. That's what this country is built on — dreams and relentless perseverance. They can go run themselves out on a rail; fuck quitting.*

I stood from the sofa, rolled up my shirt sleeves with purpose, one side and then the next. Briefcase in hand, I walked around the couch that jutted out toward the street and opened the door as wide as possible, wedging my briefcase under the corner. With the door propped open, I lifted the end of the massive piece of furniture and got mean with it, put some of that West Liberty workhorse to it. The sofa slowly lurched forward; inch by inch, the sofa scraped ahead. I pushed the sofa forward with a heave of finality, and it slid into the entrance lobby. I wiped my brow with the back of a hand and then retrieved my briefcase. The glass entry-door closed gently behind me.

Now, back to business.

I walked through the office in what appeared to be the aftermath of a natural disaster, only nothing felt natural about the man-made destruction. Mud and dirt coated the tile floors and carpeting throughout the office. One by one, I climbed each of the nine stories, surveying the damage. Scraps of paper littered the floor like confetti, years of hard work and effort scattered like garbage from the street. The doors to every file cabinet hung open and empty. *I've never seen anything like this, I thought, as I* observed the destroyed offices.

"This is some shameless shit," I said aloud to myself.

I stepped out of the staircase and into the offices of the ninth floor. The door hung open to Keith's glass-walled office. Papers stacked two feet high rested atop his desk, seemingly the only intact pile of paperwork in the entire office. *Why is this left behind?* I wondered. I flipped through the pages to discover a copy of a portfolio with substantial amounts of data and research on an insurance company called Viaticus. *That's strange.*

Maybe this is some kind of clue?

Within moments Keith entered the office to join me, along with his wife, Susan.

"How you holding up, Steve?" Keith asked.

"Doing okay, buddy. How are you?" I replied, holding his gaze with sincerity.

He knew what I meant; he nodded to my question and said, "I'm hanging in there too."

Susan appeared angry. She said, with pursed lips, "We're just ready to put this whole incident behind us. Aren't we, Keith? You guys aren't doing anything wrong here. Right? So surely they'll figure that out soon."

I shook my head in disgust. "We're not going down without a fight. I can promise you that much."

Keith said, "What do we tell the employees? I spoke with Karen late last night, and she said a few employees are considering whether they should resign. We can't afford to lose anyone right now." Keith's eyebrows lifted his glasses as he looked at me down the bridge of his nose.

I exhaled deeply. "That's the least of our problems. Pat Black told me last night that the federal agents wiped out all of our files."

"We have backup tapes," Keith insisted.

"Not anymore – Pat said they wiped us out."

Keith inhaled sharply through his nose. His body tightened reflexively then he exhaled slowly to relax. After another slow, intentional breath, he said, "Should I call a meeting? We have to tell the employees something. I don't know if we're going to make payroll this month as it is. Central Bank sent notice this morning that they froze our accounts due to the raid."

"Shit! after all the money we've made them – they can't do that!"

"They already have."

"I'll call in some favors. I don't know. We'll figure out something."

The elevator chimed, and the doors opened. Grant emerged from the elevator wearing sweatpants and an overcoat. He ambled toward us with his hands tucked in his jacket pockets, shaking his head at the destruction surrounding him. "Looks like somebody set loose a wild tiger in here," he said, brushing his hair back.

"Tigers surely have more dignity than those bastards, waving their guns in my face," Keith stated.

I put my hand on Keith's shoulder.

"So, catch me up to speed. What did I miss?" Grant asked.

"It's not good," Keith replied solemnly.

"It's bad," I said. "I spoke with Pat Black last night, and he said the agents wiped out all of our files – all of them, including the backups."

"Without those tapes, we have no records," Keith affirmed.

"Without records, we're done. We'll have to start over from scratch," I said, knowing how impossible that would be.

Silence surrounded our small circle as the gravity of the realization hit home. Everything we built together over the past six years had been reduced to rubble and shredded paper in only one devastating day. Without our files, we could not discern one policy from the next within the hundreds of active policies we maintained, each with obligations and premiums to be met to keep in good standing and not lose hundreds of millions of dollars in value for the investors. Without the files, Kelco was dead in the water.

Grant observed us with a curious smirk. He interrupted our pity party by asking, "You mean a tape like this one?" He reached into his overcoat breast pocket and pulled out a backup disk.

"Where did you..." I wondered aloud, unable to form a full sentence.

Grant responded with a smile. "The night before the raid, Shawn – you know, the new IT guy, the computer whiz – he said he decided to do some work late at night and made some system changes. He dropped this tape by my house, and I forgot to bring it in." Grant chuckled.

"That's unbelievable, Grant!" I shouted. "This tape is going to save Kelco! Okay, quick, get me Pat Black. We need copies made of this immediately. Then set a meeting today or tomorrow with Bob Webb—as soon as possible! We need to know whatever he knows. Keith, tell Staci to send everyone home today but to come back on Monday – full staff, all hands on deck. We're back in business!"

DEFENSE

Bob Webb always seemed to possess plenty of energy. He usually wore a smile on his face. His habit of smiling during even the worst situations struck me as odd and a bit unnerving at times, but I was grateful for the dose of optimism his smiling face provided me as I entered Kelco's ninth floor sky-view conference room. Bob was at the helm of the conference table talking animatedly with one hand as he jotted notes with the other. He wore his thick salt and pepper hair brushed back and parted to one side. Long sideburns framed his face to accentuate his strong jawline and amiable nature.

A team of Kelco employees sat huddled around the conference table. Everyone had pens out, writing copious notes as Bob spoke. I recognized Steve Applegate, Jolene Fullerton, Becky Thompson, Lewis Fister, and Grant Sutherlin, all of whom had their eyes trained on Bob. I quickly claimed a chair to join the conversation. Bob looked up from the heated download session and did a double take as he noticed me, saying, "Oh, there you are, Steve. How the hell are ya?"

"That depends on you, Bob," I responded quickly.

"Well, I can tell you that we are out of the blocks and running. Let me inform you of what we have so far. You got a minute?"

"I don't know where else I'd be," I said jokingly. "Bob, you're priority one from this point forward."

"Great. Saddle up then. You're going to want to hear this. We've hired a private investigator and learned some useful information. This is all fresh, but these are my notes so far."

"Okay, Bob, whatever you have, fill me in."

"Two weeks ago, Kelco had some unusual visitors. One of them is a guy named Tim Heath. He's a broker in Atlanta who was on the viatical board with Jolene. He came by the office under the pretense to see Jolene, but she was too busy and pawned him off to Steve Applegate. Tim wanted to see Grant, but Grant didn't have time to come up for air that day and never saw him. Steve Applegate proceeded to tour Tim around the building. The whole time Tim was carrying a briefcase. We think it had a camera in it."

"A camera?" I asked, "what did he hope to record, a video of desks and filing cabinets? I don't get it."

"We think his cell phone acted as a bug, transmitting his conversation to a receiver located at the Radisson Hotel across the street. Tim made a point to meet with Steve Applegate and offered to sell him a bunch of contestable policies. Steve told him that he would look at them, but Kelco doesn't entertain contestable policies under the new regulations. Apparently, the Feds recorded the whole conversation. They gave me a CD that is being included as evidence against Kelco. There's really not much on there of substance. They even recorded a couple of bathroom breaks on the tape."

I scanned the faces seated around the table. "Okay, so what do we have of substance here?"

"What we know so far is that five companies were raided on Friday. A sole proprietor broker located in Cincinnati that Kelco apparently has not dealt with in years and another company located in Ohio who sold policies directly to individuals. As I understand, Kelco had no relationship to this firm whatsoever, as Kelco only sells policies to verified investors and firms. Another firm located in New York called Empire State Viatical was raided, again, no relation. Also, a broker of policies located in Atlanta, Benefits America, owned by Brian Freeman, whom Kelco did deal with, was raided," Bob stated.

"What is the government's case against us?" Grant asked.

"We know Kelco is being charged with mail fraud; the charges allege Kelco engaged in illegal transactions involving contestable policies. As to why Kelco was targeted specifically, we're working on it," Bob said flatly.

"Bob, I need something more concrete than this. This industry has been one big gray area since it started. No one has ever been raided like this. Hell, we helped write the laws! Now our office looks like a bomb went off in here! We need to know what we're up against."

Bob smiled at my side as he searched for a reasonable response. In this instance, his habitual smile didn't feel reassuring; it felt annoying.

Lewis Fister, a trusted accountant, cleared his throat. "Maybe this is politically motivated," he suggested.

Bob scratched his chin. "We're looking into that possibility."

Lewis continued, saying, "Steve, I think this thing started politically, and if it did, it needs to end politically. I have a client whom I think you should contact. His name is Sonny Creed. He's the son of Senator Creed, the Majority Leader of the United States Senate."

"Isn't he from Mississippi?" I asked.

"Yes."

"Lewis, how do you have clients in Mississippi?"

"Oh, Sonny's not in Mississippi. He lives here."

"In Lexington?" I asked, surprised.

"Yes. Sonny is now in the process of forming a lobbying firm with the former United States House member, Larry Hopkins. If you get a hold of Sonny, you've got an intro with his dad, and you may be able to uncover this mess and get someone high enough to see that this whole thing is just wrong."

"Lewis, at this point, I will try anything," I said, dropping my hands open on the conference table.

"Not a bad idea," Bob stated. "It never hurts to make friends in high places, especially with the fight we're about to have on our hands."

"I'll see if he's available to meet with me this week."

My wheels began turning, considering the possibility of reaching out to D.C. through a lobbyist. *This country is founded on the entrepreneurial spirit. If we can get in touch with the right people, they'll help us clear up this mess,* I thought, beginning to feel excited.

Bob interrupted my quickly escalating thoughts as he said, "Oh, you'll find this useful, Steve. The investigator did some digging on your computer department employee, Judd Clemmer. Turns out, the hunch was right. Judd was paid six thousand dollars by the Feds to spy and steal information from the company before the raid. Apparently, his lifestyle involves illicit drug use and a tangled, strange relationship with his wife. He owns a three hundred-thousand-dollar piece of land on a twenty-five-thousand-dollar salary. You might want to address his current relationship with Kelco."

"I'll do that immediately."

Bob nodded his head with finality. "Okay, gang, I'd say we all have our work cut out for us, and it being a Sunday, what do you say we circle back when we make more headway?"

Bob and I stood from the table to firmly shake hands. I addressed the employees at the table by saying, "Thank you all for coming. See you back here bright and early for tomorrow's meeting."

EARLY TO RISE

I entered the offices of Kelco early on Monday morning, ready to seize the day. A sense of urgency and a readiness to join the fight propelled my steps as I walked each of the nine Kelco office building floors with a Polaroid camera in hand, snapping pictures of the destruction. Papers littered the floor where my steps fell. *Click*. I snapped a picture. The machine within the camera whirred, and a picture ejected from the camera, slowly developing in my opposite hand as I continued. I entered an office to find desk drawers busted open, seemingly by a crowbar. Click. Glass was shattered on the floor. *Click*.

Floor after floor, I observed the destruction. As I continued snapping pictures, I found myself asking, *How? Why?* Without any clear answers, I grew angry at the feeling of injustice that rose within me. The click of the camera became almost hypnotic, rousing the fight within me.

A few minutes after nine o'clock, I made my way to the fifth floor, the only floor large enough to accommodate our entire staff in one large room. Nearly one hundred Kelco employees stood gathered around the room, waiting to begin the meeting that I had called to start the day.

"Good morning," I addressed them all loudly, projecting my voice as I walked through the crowd toward the room's front, "I hope everyone was able to get some rest this weekend after the events from last week." A few heads nodded in agreement, and a few low murmurs rippled through the room in response.

I reached the front of the room and addressed the crowd in front of me as a few employees stood behind me. "Now, I'm just as upset about all of this as you are. Never in a million years could I imagine that something like this could happen in America., the freest country in the world! This sort of treatment shouldn't happen in this country. It's not right! We *didn't deserve* this – you didn't deserve this! And I'm here to tell you that we are not going to allow it! We're going to fight!" I announced as I observed the faces of my employees throughout the room. Every one of them is counting on me.

A woman's voice from the middle of the crowd broke the silence. She said, "What's going on, Steve? Why did we get raided?"

I searched the room and recognized the voice as Paula Abner's, one of the first employees hired on with Kelco in the early days. I responded, "We don't know! I know we all want answers. We just don't know yet, but we're working on it. I can promise you that much. We've hired private investigators. Bob Webb and his team are working around the clock to get to the bottom of all this. We're even looking into taking our own action in D.C. What we do know is this: the raid almost shut us down. The government tried to wipe our database and put us out of business, but we're not going down without a fight! We rebooted our systems, and as of today, Kelco is officially back in business!" I shouted, clapping along with my announcement. A few employees began to clap, and then a few more until the energy started to rise.

"I can assure you that Kelco is here to stay. We have done nothing wrong. I promise you that we will fight to prove it and we won't give up. Look around you. For those who have been with us from the very beginning, look at what we've built together," I said, gesturing to the massive nine-story building where nearly one hundred of us were assembled. "We've accomplished something incredible together. Each of you deserves to be proud of what you do, and we're just getting started!" I cheered loudly. Claps and cheers rippled through the crowd with growing excitement.

"Now, I know what we all went through last week was traumatic. If anyone needs support, we've brought on two psychologists who are available to you. There is a sign-up sheet at the back of the room, or you can see Staci to let her know. Also, my door is always open. I'm here for you, and I will try to help in any way I can."

I paused, allowing the crowd's mood to shift, then continued in a more ominous tone, "We are learning new information every day, and I promise you we will find out exactly what is going on here. We know the Feds hired spies to record conversations with Kelco staff, and we even know that some of our very own Kelco employees have been working with the Feds. Yeah...they've been selling information... trying to sell us all out."

I turned to the employees who stood behind me. Judd Clemmer stood among them, doughy faced with long surfer-looking hair. He watched, wide-eyed as I approached him. I quickly aimed the Polaroid camera. Click. I snapped his picture. The film scrolled from the camera and began developing in my hand.

"What did you do that for?" Judd exclaimed.

I stared at Judd as I shook the picture in my hand. "I'll give you one guess, Judd."

"I don't know! Why? Do you think I'm working with the Feds?"

I stepped closer to Judd, still shaking the picture. "You're damn right, I do. I know you are."

I turned my back on him to address the rest of the employees. "Judd here chose to accept six thousand dollars from the government to help them with the raid last week, knowing we didn't break any laws. He risked the job and the livelihood of every one of us in this room, all for his own benefit.

I turned to Judd and handed him the now developed Polaroid photo of his own face. "Here, Judd, this is so you'll always remember the look on your face when you got fired."

Judd's jaw dropped. Hushed murmurs and chuckles rolled through the crowd of employees.

"You can't just fire me like that!" Judd shouted.

"I just did! Goodbye, Judd!"

Red-faced and flushed, he refused to move.

"Judd, don't make this awkward. I'll call security if necessary."

KELLER:

If you wanted to sell a viatical policy that week, you were out of luck. The entire market was shut down. Wall Street completely closed every Life Settlement funding deal, trying to figure out how Kelco could be the subject of such an assault by the government. The most proactive regulatory reform proponent in the industry had just been the subject of the most publicized raid in this industry's history. None of it made sense. Wall Street was asking what they had missed. Everybody wanted answers, including us. Never having a complaint filed with the Better Business Bureau or the Department of Insurance or with the consumer protectionist for the industry, we felt desperate, with nowhere to turn. It felt bleak.

BANKING ON A COMEBACK

"As soon as I know something, I will let you know," I said, speaking into the phone receiver while sitting at my desk. My ear felt hot and irritated from overuse. Bankers and lenders had been calling me non-stop all day. One by one, I did my best to reassure them that Kelco was still in business. "Listen, we're working on it. In the meanwhile, how about this? I will work on liquidating policies to pay your loans back."

"Keller, we're not a large bank. We have a significant portion of our assets tied up with you. We need answers." John Walters, of the local First Security Bank of Kentucky, insisted.

"When Bob Webb comes up for air, you're welcome to talk to Bob as well. Now, I have to get back to a horde of unanswered phone calls. Listen, John, I will let you know something as soon as we do, okay? Have a good day," I stated, hanging up the phone.

I shook my head, grateful to be off the phone. The intercom buzzed, followed by Staci's voice as she said, "Steve, your twelve o'clock is here. Sonny Creed is in the lobby for you."

I pressed the intercom button, "Thanks, Staci. I'll be right down."

How about that? I thought with amusement. *The Senate majority leader's son is here to see me. Maybe now I can get some serious assistance.*

I met Sonny on the third floor, our reception area. He stood about six feet and several inches tall, lean with handsome features, maybe early thirties. *He's younger than I expected. He sort of looks like the actor Rob Lowe.* Sonny flashed an infectious smile and reached out his hand to greet me, oozing political charisma.

"Sonny, I'm Steve Keller. Thank you for coming over. This is Staci, our receptionist."

"Hello," Staci offered, blushing. She quickly extended her hand toward Sonny, looking at him with puppy dog eyes.

That's good, I thought as Sonny shook her hand. *He needs to put a face to the victims of this raid. That could help us.* After a few more minutes lingering in the lobby with Staci, I toured Sonny around the entire office and showed him how we operate our business. The destruction from the raid was mostly clean now, although the aftershock still remained within every employee's mind, we chatted with as we walked. I led Sonny to the ninth floor. We ended the tour in my office, where we stopped to chat. I offered Sonny the couch and turned around an armchair to face where he sat.

"So, Sonny, how in the world did you end up in Lexington, Kentucky?" I asked.

"My godfather, Troy Anders, started investing in Domino's Pizza in the Virginia, D.C., area years ago. He has around fifty of them now. He offered to help me out and partner with him on a few franchises. I looked around the country, and I noticed there were not any around Lexington. I came here to check out the town and fell in love with this place. I put one restaurant downtown by the University of Kentucky, one in Frankfort, and another just outside of town."

"How are those working out for you?" I asked.

"It's not like it used to be. We've had theft problems and management problems. I'm trying to sell the one in Frankfort. The one close by is okay," Sonny stated without amusement.

After enough small talk and pleasantries, I decided to change the subject. "My accountant, Lewis Fister, said you are setting up a lobbying firm?"

"Yes, I'm currently in the process now. I brought on an older gentleman as a partner to balance out my age. He's a former House Representative, a Kentuckian too. You might know him, Larry Hopkins. It's not that I need Larry, but given his experience and gray hair, he has his purpose."

"No, I don't know him. I understand that all too well, though," I replied earnestly as my thoughts flashed back to the early days of Kelco.

"What is it you guys are looking for?" Sonny sked.

I leaned forward to the edge of my chair and spoke with fervor, saying, "Sonny, we have not broken one insurance law. Hell, I wrote the law for this state and hired a lobbyist to get it passed. There is something wrong here, and it's not with Kelco. We have credit lines arranged with over eighty banks, many of which have been keeping a close eye on our business practices for several years now. We maintain an A rating with both Moody's and Standard and Poor's, the world's largest rating agencies, and you know how rigorous their ratings are."

Sonny scratched his chin, considering my words. "How can I help?" he asked bluntly.

"Look, with all of this bureaucratic red tape around Kelco now, the banks are freezing our accounts and threatening to dry up our credit lines. They're all looking for answers. I can't function in New York until I get these people off our ass," I said, letting my words trail off, hoping Sonny would pick up my line of thought.

Sonny paused and glanced out the window behind me. Finally, he said, "That's a big ask, Steve."

"Well, that's why I'm bringing in the big guns," I said, raising my eyebrows in Sonny's direction. "I figure hiring you and your lobby firm, of course, is a direct line to your dad."

Sonny rocked back on the couch as if my words struck too close to home. "That's an even bigger ask, Steve," Sonny said with a laugh and a Hollywood smile.

"The only thing I'm really asking for is answers."

Sonny shifted his position on the couch and began using his hands to animate his words. He said, "This is a nuanced business, you know? I'll have to get my partner involved, and we will need to do our due diligence and research."

I interrupted Sonny. "Just tell me this; can you set a meeting for me with your dad?"

Sonny grinned, "I like to believe anything is possible, given the right circumstances."

I stood from my seat with a laugh, going along with Sonny's playful attitude. "I'll be in D.C. in a few weeks. How about a meeting then?"

Sonny rose from the couch. "I'll talk things over with Larry. Hey, do you mind if we check on my car? I just bought this new BMW 5 Series, got it loaded with the racing package, and I parked it out front. I don't want a ticket. You need to see this car anyway. You seem like a guy who appreciates cars."

Feeling frustrated and without answers, only more questions, I relented. "Sure, let's go."

We exited the front entryway to Kelco's building to emerge on Main Street. Sonny's new car stood out like a diamond among pebbles alongside the older, less expensive cars that lined the street. Sonny waltzed toward the parking meter, speaking over his shoulder. "What do you think?"

"It looks fast. Do you ever open it up?" I said, unable to deny my admiration for the car.

Sonny seemed satisfied by the meter and slowed down his pace. With a grin, he said, "Every chance I get."

"When did you get it?"

Sonny leaned back against the passenger door. "Last month," he stated as he glanced inside the window of the car. "I'll probably trade it in for something else in a week or two."

My face contorted with confusion. "Why? I thought you just bought it."

Sonny nodded nonchalantly. "I trade my cars out at least every few months. This is my eighth car this year," he said, beaming with pride. "You want to take it for a spin?"

"As much as I want to, I have to put out these forest fires. I better get back to work," I said, resenting Sonny's ability to be so carefree on a workday. I wished I had such freedoms. Our lives felt worlds apart. Sonny's father sat in the second most powerful seat in the world as Senate Majority Leader. My father, as successful as he was in my eyes, was a small business owner of a salvage company in Eastern Kentucky. Unlike some people, I have to work for everything I have, Sonny, I thought as he stepped forward to shake my hand.

"I think you can make a real difference, Sonny," I said, shaking his hand firmly.

"I'll do what I can. Our minimum retainer fee is ten thousand per month. Is that doable?" he asked politely.

I smiled at him through clenched teeth and a tightened jaw. "Whatever it takes to make this thing go away."

"Great, we'll do what we can for you," Sonny said as he ambled around the front of his shiny new car, glistening in the glow of early afternoon. He opened the driver's door, and I projected my voice to catch his attention before he slipped inside, saying, "So what do you say? Can you get me that meeting with your dad in a couple weeks?"

Sonny smirked, flashing a few teeth. "Hey, anything's possible." He waved a hand in my direction and then slid into the driver's seat. The engine quickly roared to life with unbridled power. *Imagine the power at his disposal with only the slightest touch of the gas pedal,* I thought as I grinned at him. I stepped inside the doors of Kelco to return to the endless onslaught of phone calls that awaited as I heard Sonny rev the engine like a hot rod on the starter block as he sped away. My jaw remained clenched long after he was gone.

FIRES ON THE MOUNTAIN

Date: September 2001

Karen met me in the Kelco hallway, and together we entered the glass conference room. While choosing seats around the conference table, we heard Staci's voice through the intercom as she said, "Steve, I've got Ruppert, Arthur Anderson and Viaticus on line one holding for you, and Keith is on the line remotely."

"Okay, thank you, Staci." I hit the call button, and instantly the group was live.

"Hey guys, it's Steve and Keith."

"Hello, we've got Dave Harris and Ruppert Harrison with Arthur Anderson; and John Banks and Gary Chodes with Viaticus.

"Hey, guys!" Keith and I each said in turn.

"Well, gentlemen, you've certainly had an interesting go at it," Ruppert offered with a chuckle, which I assumed was due to his sense of irony at his own mundane expression to describe such a monumental crisis that financially affected us all.

"Yes, you could say that," I replied dryly.

"Steve, this is John Banks."

"Hi, John," I replied.

"It's just awful what has happened. I'm extremely sympathetic to your situation, and I mean that in all sincerity."

"I appreciate that, John."

"Steve, the deal you constructed to buy out Viaticus is spectacular. I gathered this group together to salvage your efforts. We would very much like to discuss this in person with you as soon as possible. Can you meet us in a couple of days in New York?"

"I think we can do that, John," I said as I scanned through a calendar at my desk. We needed to meet with AON anyway. We had a lot of damage control on Wall Street to perform.

"Perfect. Let's meet at Arthur Anderson's office."

"How about the Marriott at the World Trade Center?" I asked.

"Okay, we can do that. We will call you Friday morning," John replied. "Hang in there, fellas."

"Oh, wait, hang on. I'll be in D.C. through the tenth and return on the eleventh. Can we hold off until the following week?"

"The sooner, the better," John stated.

"Okay, guys, see you next week," I stated, ending the conference call and remaining on the line to talk with Keith.

"Keith, how you doing, buddy?"

"I'm okay, Keller," he said in a weak and battered tone.

"If you need to take some time…"

Keith interjected, saying, "I'm fine, Keller. I can handle it."

"Okay, I got you – just making sure. Then let's plan to fly in there Monday morning and meet with AON and as many people as we can schedule."

"I'll call Wendy and schedule the day," Keith affirmed.

"Good. Bob Webb is due any minute to interview folks and get a handle on the events that led up to the raid. We're running blind here. We need to know what caused the raid."

"And who was behind it," Keith said resolutely.

"Great. Whatever you come up with, let me know. I'm hoping I can find some answers on the Hill."

KING OF THE HILL

Tammy and I had belonged to the Young Presidents Organization for the past several years. This was the most powerful organization in the world for entrepreneurs under fifty years old. We were scheduled to attend a four-day event in Washington, D.C., with the YPO group and also the group for the Presidents over fifty, the World Presidents Organization. I was looking for publicity with my peers, politicians, anyone who would open an ear.

The YPO group had serious pull. We arranged a meeting over the four days with most of the Cabinet members for President Bush. During Clinton's reign, he showed up to talk to the group. President Bush had not been present; he was campaigning for financial reform in swing states. Tammy and I stayed at The Four Seasons, where many other YPO members stayed as well. There was also a king from some small, obscure country, with enough security around to quickly become annoying to the other guests. Depending on the king's itinerary, coming or going from the hotel, everybody would have to park a block away and walk to the hotel. Sometimes the lobby would be shut down for this person. The nuisance grew tiring after a couple of days.

The weekend contained black-tie parties at various political locations in D.C. We had dinner in embassies and one in the State Department building, where we met with high-level diplomats and other YPO members. There was always some agenda, landing us in front of influential political figures who were usually off-limits to the general public. But these forums were canned productions. It was one-way communication. They were talking to the group, taking very few questions, if any at all. There was hardly any opportunity for us to talk to these individuals about our situation.

We toured government facilities as part of the agenda. On one particular day, three large commercial buses pulled up to our hotel and began to load all the YPO members from The Four Seasons. The buses went to three other hotels loading up the rest of the YPO guests, taking the group to the CIA facilities for an all-day tour and meetings with the CIA's Director. As the buses pulled into the private compound, traveling through these beautiful, winding grounds, I started thinking that Tammy and I may not make it into the facility. *We're never going to pass the identity check,* I feared. We were under the microscope of the Postal Service and the FBI. *How embarrassing this will be if we get turned away at the security checkpoint.*

"Tam, we may not get through," I whispered as we sat side by side on the bus, peering through the window.

"Wouldn't that be embarrassing."

"That's what I was just thinking. I'd never live it down with this bunch."

All three buses pulled up to a small smoked glass building. Everybody was to go in and present their IDs for a security check. Once in the building, there was a large gift shop and some other novelties to see. This was just a preliminary post before we journeyed on to the CIA Headquarters. Tammy and I waited until after everyone checked in at the security desk. After waiting on all three buses of people, we then approached the check-in desk and presented our passports. A lady took them from us and began to type the information into the computer.

We stood there breathless, not saying a word, desperately trying to read the lady's face to see if she was going to give us that glance of threatened panic or puzzlement, wondering how such ordinary-looking people could be tagged with such a horrendous accusation. I was prepared for the worst reaction possible, and that's when the woman handed us our passports with a gentle smile. "Enjoy your visit" was all she said.

I hesitated to accept the passports. Tammy grabbed them quickly and shoved me forward, getting us out of there. How bizarre. *A week after the raid, I passed security clearance for the White House a week after the raid, and I had also been cleared to tour the CIA Headquarters for an audience with the Director of the CIA?* It was all hard to believe.

After our CIA tour, the buses were forced to stop a block from our hotel. We deboarded the bus and proceeded to walk to the hotel in the chilling winter air. *All because some king wis staying at the hotel from some dusty country.*

I grabbed my cell phone and began to dial a number, hoping that shiny nepo-child would finally come through for us. So far, my patient pleas in D.C. had gone to voicemail.

At this point, my call felt like a last grab for a life preserver.

"Hello, Sonny speaking," a voice responded through the phone.

"Sonny, this is Steve Keller. Tammy and I are in D.C., where we are just wrapping up a four-day weekend with the Young Presidents Organization. I know this is short notice, but is there any way you could arrange for me to meet your father?"

"There is a chance. I will have to call him and see. I'll call you back in a few," Sonny stated.

"Okay, great! Goodbye."

Tammy looked at me after having listened to the conversation. "Do you think we'll get to see him?"

"We'll see in a few minutes. We need to contact somebody up here."

We hung around the hotel, waiting on a callback. In about an hour, Sonny called. I answered the phone on the first ring.

"Hello, Steve speaking."

"Sorry about taking so long to call you back. Look, my father is in a Budget Committee meeting with all the Committee members at his office. Where are you now?"

"I'm sitting at the hotel, The Four Seasons."

"I know exactly where that is. Can you leave right now and get to the Capitol?"

"Yes!"

"Okay. Enter the side door to the Senate section. When you get there, find a cop at the Capitol. Tell him you have an appointment at the Majority Leader's office. When you get to the office, ask for Jaclyn. Tell her I sent you there to meet my father. She will take it from there."

"Okay, Sonny, we're on our way. Keep your cell phone close just in case. Thank you."

"Get going now! You don't have much time. Bye."

I hung up the phone and looked at Tammy. "We're in! Grab your coat. We've got to go now!"

Luckily the king had already left the building, allowing us to quickly flag a cab outside the hotel. Within minutes we were at the Capitol trying to figure out where to find Senator Creed's office. We saw a long visitor line streaming from behind the building that contained hundreds of people waiting to tour the Capitol. Our cabbie drove as close as he could to the side of the building before letting us out. In a fast run-walk, I pulled Tammy, scurrying to a security guard at an entranceway that we guessed went to the Senate side.

"Excuse me, sir, we have an appointment with Senator Creed. Could you direct us to his office?"

"Yes, it's the next door down. I'll have a guard escort you." This was unbelievably good fortune. We were going to make it there in ample time.

As we entered the Capitol, I thought about how sparsely populated it seemed, having seen the long tourism line. We turned the corner and were now heading down the hallway to the Senate office and the balcony's location for the Senate Floor. We began to see people again – not tourists but pages, Senate staff, representatives from varying organizations, all sitting around the hallways on benches. The place was bustling with everybody trying to fill their own agendas.

"Here, you are, Mr. and Mrs. Keller," the guard stated.

"Thank you, sir."

A young attractive brunette woman approached us. "Can I help you?"

"Yes, I'm Steve Keller, and this is my wife, Tammy. Sonny told us to look up Jaclyn here for an appointment with Senator Creed."

"Oh, yes, Mr. Keller, come on back here." I walked into this giant, antique-filled room. It was the waiting room for Senator Creed's office. Tammy and I watched as a procession of famous career Senators walked past, all of whom we had only seen on television but distinctly recognized. One by one, they passed us to attend a meeting, entering a door behind where we stood in the large waiting room.

"Jaclyn, this is Mr. Keller and his wife. Sonny sent them here to meet Senator Creed," the brunette woman announced.

"Hi, Mr. Keller, yes, Sonny called me earlier. How's Sonny getting along in Kentucky?"

"Oh, he seems to be doing fine."

"Please wait here. I've had to juggle some folks around for you, and I'm going to head Senator Creed off before he enters that room in the back."

"Okay, Jaclyn. We really appreciate this."

The parade of every significant Republican Senator continued. In about fifteen minutes, Jaclyn came to us. "Okay, Mr. and Mrs. Keller, right this way. He only has a few minutes."

Tammy and I followed Jaclyn around the waiting room toward the room where the Senators had gone. Before arriving at the room, we turned left and were facing two large mahogany doors.

Jaclyn opened the door and entered.

The room was very spacious with a grand mahogany desk, red carpet, and ornate furniture. The room epitomized the term 'stately.' There were a couple of chairs in front of Senator Creed's desk. To my left was a small leather couch where Tammy sat. I sat in the leather chair to the left of the Senator's desk. We both sat, not saying a word, waiting for one of the most powerful persons on Capitol Hill. This is just too surreal. I don't even feel nervous.

After about five minutes, the side doors opened from yet another room attached to the office. With every hair sprayed perfectly into place, just as I had seen him hundreds of times on television, Senator Creed's smiling face led his way into the room. After the greetings were out of the way, the Senator took his seat behind the antique desk. He had an uncanny ability to instantly make you feel right at home as if Tammy and I had known him our entire lives.

"Hello, Steve, Tammy, a pleasure to meet you both. So, Steve, what's on your mind?" The Senator asked with a natural southern charm.

"Well, Senator, I think we both know why I'm here. I don't really feel at liberty to talk about the case, but I will tell you that this should not happen in America," I stated.

The Senator leaned over his desk, replacing his smile with a tone of seriousness. His eyes suddenly became penetrating. My feeling of comfort was being challenged. "I'm going to tell you the exact same thing that I told Bill Gates sitting in that same chair, not even thirty days ago, Steve."

The Senator's tone reminded me of a stern lecture that a kid would have received from a father figure. He said, "I told him, Bill, just because you're from Seattle, Washington, do you not think everyone in D.C. knows who you are? That awareness helps, but it's a matter of relationships, to oil the wheels so to speak. Now, Bill is represented by some 50 lobbyists on Capitol Hill."

"I can see how that could be effective. My pockets aren't as deep as Bill Gates, but I'm starting to see how things work around here," I replied, heavily implying the deal I negotiated with the lobbying firm run by his son, Sonny, to represent Kelco.

"Have you heard of the Singing Senators?" he commented.

"I can't say that I have."

"We happen to be a barbershop quartet. We practice just down the hall here."

"Care to sing a few bars?" I joked.

The Senator smiled softly. "Let's just say, Attorney General Bodine and I go way back. I'll have a talk with him a see if he'll look into your situation."

"Thank you, sir. That would be such a relief."

The Senator suddenly shifted his weight, adjusting uncomfortably in his chair, seeming to distance himself in the small space between us. He said, "Well, listen, I've got to get back to this budget meeting." The Senator withdrew a notepad from within a desk drawer and began writing while he said, "In the meantime, here is the name and number of the person you need to talk with. He's an attorney with experience in these matters." He tore loose the page from his notebook and handed it to me across his desk.

"James Doran?" I asked, reading aloud from the note.

"You hire him, and he will get you sorted out. Tell him I sent you his way." The Senator stood up and made his way around his desk to Tammy. "Jaclyn!" the Senator yelled.

The door opened, and Jaclyn peeped in. "Yes, Senator?"

"Can you bring the photographer in here?"

"Certainly."

As if the man had been waiting outside the door, a photographer suddenly stepped into the office.

"Yes, Senator, you requested some shots?"

"Yes, let's get a couple of pictures before I have to go to my meeting. Tammy, stand beside me, so you make me look better. Steve, you sure know how to pick 'em," Senator Creed said in his charming southern drawl.

I stood on one side of the Senator, and Tammy stood on the other. We posed for a few photos before the Senator was forced to leave.

"Thank you for seeing us, Senator," Tammy and I both said sincerely.

"Don't mention it. I will see you later, perhaps in Kentucky."

"That would be great!" I replied.

"Goodbye." the Senator said and then disappeared into the room where all the senior Senators had convened.

As we left Senator Creed's office, making our way through the packed waiting room, I overheard Jaclyn on the phone, scheduling the remainder of the Senator's day. She said, "Sir, I'm sorry, but the Senator just got pulled into an emergency meeting. He will not be able to see the king today. I understand you've been waiting, but you need to reschedule. I'm sorry."

I couldn't contain a laugh. Make me park two blocks down the street again. I thought in amusement. *I just bumped your entire meeting. How do you like that inconvenience, your highness?*

KELLER:

Politics can make you king for a day...or kick you to the curb just as quickly. After the meeting, I felt a sense of accomplishment...maybe even a sense of power, not because our meeting bumped the king's meeting but because we made headway with the Senator. It felt like a significant achievement. I now had a dialogue. However, his message was very unsettling. I certainly couldn't keep up with the spending power of Bill Gates. I hoped his cryptic message would make more sense to me later on. For now, we had achieved our goal of meeting with the Senator, plus bumped a King. It was a good day.

THE DAY THE TOWERS FELL

Behind the wheel of my Porsche 911, I drove the downtown streets of Lexington. For some reason, stillness hung in the morning air – an eerie quiet. The roads seemed deserted. Something seemed amiss. Then again, maybe I was just tired. I had been in Washington D.C. the night prior, still processing the meaning of the conversation with Senator Creed. As I drove to work, I felt assured that hiring Sonny's lobbying firm to gain his father's influence was the right move to solve our legal problem, but I was weary. I felt battered, like a fighter on the ropes, clinging to any signs of potential relief from the incessant pressure Kelco was experiencing after the raid.

I arrived in front of Kelco's nine-story headquarters, still standing tall amidst the adversity. I admired what we built and took a sudden pause to appreciate our achievement as I slowly pulled into the parking garage. I hoped that I could do the same and be a pillar of strength for the employees and for myself to keep pushing forward each day. After leaving the parking structure to walk across the street to the front entrance of the Kelco building, I noticed a man waving a large American flag. He was dressed in a leather jacket with patches of P.O.W. and other emblems boldly expressing that he was a Vietnam veteran, the first time I had ever seen such a display in front of our building. Cars honked their horns as they passed by.

Grant hurried toward me as soon as I stepped off the elevator to the ninth-floor lobby. "Have you heard?" he asked frantically.

"I leard what?" I responded, and after having experienced a federal raid, a million potential dangers bounced around my mind.

"The World Trade Center just got hit by a plane," Grant exclaimed.

"A plane? How could that happen?"

"Not sure. It's bad though. Reports are saying maybe it was terrorists. Nobody really knows."

I stood shell-shocked by the information, unsure what to say or how to respond.

"Were any of our people hurt?" I asked.

"We don't know yet. After the second plane hit, the towers collapsed."

Grant's words snapped me back to reality as he said, "We got a hold of Wendy White, and she was stuck in traffic, thank God. She is fine. She said the 93rd floor was hit hard. She's afraid there are no survivors."

My heart sank. *That's the floor Mike Lomax and his entire team occupy. The team we work with.* A stark reality pierced my thoughts, *If the raid didn't happen, there's a high likelihood that we would have been there...* "Have you tried Mike?" I asked as the faces of so many friends and colleagues flashed through my mind.

"I can't get a hold of him. Everyone's trying to call him. Jim Braughtigan's afraid he was in the building...I just had dinner with Mike and his new wife."

"Let's get a hold of all of our people; I want to confirm they are all okay!" I paused for a minute and thought about Tammy and Cole. "Wow, we could have been there," I stated, feeling a sudden urge to go home. I hurried through the building and told the staff to wrap up for the day and go home if they wished.

I drove home in disbelief, wondering how a building that stood so lofty and immovable, a pillar of the global financial system, could crumble in a matter of minutes. I was horrified, thinking of the devastation of lives; I couldn't stop thinking about my wife and young son. *How could someone, anyone, choose such violence and destruction with complete disregard for the lives damaged in the process?* It felt cold and calculated and callous, void of all empathy. My mind then drifted again to feeling sorrow for the guys we had worked with on the 93rd floor, three days per week for several years. Those men were now among the missing...so young.

I felt helpless, powerless in the situation, and I hated the feeling. I was as clueless as the rest of the world until my phone range. It was Sonny, shouting, "Steve, all hell has broken loose! Have you heard?" I could hear loud, frantic voices yelling in the background on the other end of the phone.

"Yes, I'm aware. Who is behind this?" I shouted over the chaos blaring through the other end of the phone.

"We're trying to find out now. We don't know who is behind this and if they will try to kill our families. We don't know what any of this all means. Listen, I'm in a car with my dad and two Senators. I have to go. We are being taken to a bunker."

Overlapping voices shouted in the background. I heard whom I believed to be Senator Creed and what sounded like Senator John McCain. *Whoa, if they're scared, this attack is the real deal.* I heard one of the voices shout, "Someone is damn well going to pay! I can assure you of that!"

Sonny shouted to me over the voices in the background, saying, "Steve, got to go. I don't know when I will be able to contact you again. If this thing gets really bad, will you secure my wife and kids? There's a chance I can't make it back into town in time. Just give them a place to hide out, until this all calms down. Who knows how far these terrorists will go."

"Consider it done. Remember, I am from Eastern Kentucky where everyone knows one another, and we all own a bunch of guns. I can hide them there. I am standing by. Just try and keep me posted – if you can.

The call ended, and suddenly I sat again in silence, alone. I stopped my car at a streetlight and stared at a man across the street who leisurely strolled with his dog on a leash, presumably unaware that our country was under attack.

I wondered how many people were oblivious to the events unfolding around them. While our nation's congressmen were being shuttled to a bunker, fearing Armageddon, this man and his dog enjoyed a leisurely stroll.

The light turned green, and I remained stopped at the light. The wind ceased, and the trees stood still. I now looked at the trees in a different light. I stepped out of the car, not caring about the concept of traffic regulations. I did something that I had not done for as long as I could remember since the raid happened: I slowed down for a moment and took in my surroundings. I noticed that the trees slightly swayed in a rhythmic motion along with the wind. Something in the air felt different. I recognized that it may never feel the way it once did again.

KELLER:

One's beliefs, built over years of understanding, can be wiped clean when devastating events hit home, or when events affect those we love and care about most. It can forever change one's perspective in the flash of a second. It makes one look at the world in a whole different light. In that moment of reflection, life shifted into a different light. The things I once chased with passion, the magazine covers, the handshakes in the boardrooms, the battles to prove who was right, suddenly felt hollow. My face on the cover of Forbes meant nothing compared to watching Cole chase his dream of becoming a pilot. The hunger for revenge against the agents who dismantled Kelco quieted down, replaced by the simple hope of seeing my people back on their feet, working again, no longer carrying the weight of that raid. It wasn't about winning anymore. It was about redirecting that same determination, reshaping it into something meaningful, something that wasn't built on anger but in rebuilding, on purpose.

FIGHTING FROM THE ASHES

I sat at the Kelco conference table with Grant sitting by my side, a chair empty at my other side where Keith would usually sit in attendance; he was still enduring intensive chemotherapy treatments in Oklahoma. Keith sat in with us by conference call. I sorely missed his in-person presence, especially given the magnitude of the upcoming meeting with James Doran, the attorney recommended by Senator Creed.

As I checked my watch, growing impatient, in walked James Doran. He strolled into the conference room, chest and belly first like an English Bulldog, with the jowls to match. We quickly shook hands, and he flopped into a chair, ready to get down to brass tacks. Speaking slowly with a thick Boston accent, he said, "Mister Keller! I had a good look at y' file. Sounds like your company got itself a cancer – good thing you brought in a surgeon. I'm gonna go in there, and I'm gonna cut it out. You know? I'm gonna put my entire team on it. That's 19 of us. Lots of man-hours if you want it done right. You know? But this is what I do, and I guarantee you that these problems will be long gone by the time we're done."

Keith's voice projected from the conference call speakers on the table, saying, "Mr. Doran, that sounds too good to be true.

"It is, and you'll see that reflected in my rates," James Doran said with unflinching assuredness.

"How much we talking?" I asked.

"Put me on retainer for half a mil, and I'll do my best to make this swift and simple. I don't see this going any more than a million. Is that doable?"

I turned to Grant, and he looked as shocked as I felt. Keith said nothing on the phone. *It doesn't matter what it costs,* I though. "One million and you guarantee you'll make all of this go away?"

"Y' got that right. This whole thing will be nothing but a bad dream when I'm done here."

Just then, a knock on the conference room door interrupted us. Staci entered the room with a look of determination. She made quick eye contact with me, insistent.

I said, "James, hang on a sec. Staci?"

"Hi, sorry," Staci said, looking at James and then urgently back to me, "Steve, you really need to take this call."

"Okay, James, are we squared away here?"

"Don't you worry. This is what I do, Mr. Keller. You're in good hands here – the best."

His words felt both disconcerting and reassuring at the same time. I said, "Okay, I'm trusting you on this. If the Senate Majority Leader recommends you, well, then I just got to roll with it. I sure hope you're worth the price tag."

"Don't y' worry; you'll realize I was worth every penny – twice as much even. I'm going to jam this motion so far down the throats of this Podunk court, they won't know what hit 'em."

This 'Podunk' town he's talking about is my home. Despite his off-putting demeanor and condescending insults, I knew I needed his help. In response, I only said, "Okay, we're counting on you."

I hurried into the hallway, where Staci said, "A woman insists on talking to you. She won't take no for an answer."

"Who is it?"

"Gloria Wolk – do you know her?" Staci asked.

"Really? Not personally. Okay, I'll take it in my office."

"Line two."

I walked with quick steps to the elevator and then to my office, where I closed the door, ensuring the call's privacy. I knew Gloria Wolk to be a no-non-sense insurance industry watchdog. She was responsible for numerous arti-cles challenging various public officials and industry executives. She was a stickler for the letter of the law practices. The industry at large benefited from her watchful eye, but she was tenaciously outspoken when she noticed foul play. You didn't want to be on the wrong side of an argument against her. I took a quick deep breath sitting behind my desk and pushed the blinking light for line two. "Hi, this is Steve."

"Steve Keller. Gloria Wolk here. I have someone on the line that you need to talk to – right now."

"What is this pertaining to?"

"I'll let him explain that before he changes his mind."

"Okay, then, put him through."

My mind reeled with possibilities. After the past few months of dire circumstances at Kelco, my mind tended to race to several worst-case scenarios. Suddenly I heard a deep male voice with a strong southern drawl. The voice said, "Mr. Keller?"

"Yes, who am I speaking with?" I said, pushing back any hint of anxiety in my voice.

"Hi there. This is Dale Barron. I was recently with the Texas Insurance Commission Fraud Department."

I held my breath, waiting to hear his next words. I couldn't bear any more bad news.

He continued, saying, "Gloria suggested I call you, because well, you see…I, uh…I have some information that I think you'll want."

"I'm listening."

"Well, you see, I'm no longer with the fraud department. I'm working private practice now, and I can't divulge this information without some form of payment in return."

"So, you want me to pay you. And why would I do that?"

"Do you know about the conference that was held in Carmel, Indiana?"

"What about it?" I bluffed, pretending to know what he referred to.

"Then you know about Operation Clean Sheet? And Barbara Farrington? Convera Financial? Or the group of insurance underwriters that worked with government agencies to organize the federal raid on your industry?"

I didn't respond. My mind raced with unanswered questions that I wanted to ask, but I couldn't let on that I had no idea what he was talking about. My confusion was interrupted by a deep chuckle on the other end of the phone.

"Mr. Keller, I assure you; you're going to want the information I have for you. Write me a check for ten thousand dollars to cover my consulting fees, and I'll send you a package with everything you need to know."

"How can I trust your information?"

"Because, well, before I went private, I was the lead speaker at this conference on behalf of Convera Financial and Barbara Farrington and company for Operation Clean Sheet."

ASSEMBLING THE COMEBACK

The next day, an overnight from Dale Baron arrived at Kelco's headquarters. Waiting on the package's arrival reminded me of when Grant and I waited with anticipation for a FedEx package, years prior. Back then, we waited for a check from our first sale that funded the start of Kelco. This time, we waited to find out who was attempting to destroy the company we built together.

The contents of the package sat atop the conference room table. I sat at the head of the table as Grant sat by my side. Keith's in-person presence was sorely missed as he endured intensive chemotherapy treatments in a clinic in Nebraska. He attended remotely, patched in on the conference call from his treatment center. Our team of attorneys sat gathered around the table: Bob Webb, our lead attorney; Chris Burnside, a fiery redhead with strong opinions; Keith's personal attorney, Kent Westbury, who remotely represented Keith's interests; and Jack Smith, an attorney we were contemplating hiring because of his close personal ties with the local prosecutor who had it out for us, Pat Malloy. Our lobbyist team also sat in attendance: Sonny Creed and his business partner, Larry Hopkins. Larry was a large-framed man who wore his gray hair parted to one side, and his designer glasses gave him a distinguished look. Larry possessed ample experience, having served fourteen years in public service as a member of Kentucky's U.S. House of Representatives; he knew his way around Washington, D.C.

The contents of the package looked to be about three inches thick. While the conference phone rang on the table, I flipped through the documents, which seemed to be a who's who of the viatical industry. A list, pages long, named affiliated brokers and agents. Insurance brokers were listed with the number of policies produced by each insurance agent and bought or sold by each broker, arranged alphabetically. I stopped on the K's, where a vast section was devoted to

Kelco. A picture of our building was prominently displayed, along with pages and pages that disclosed our interactions with other viatical companies and agents in the insurance industry.

Connected to each transaction were names listed. Names I had never heard of along with policies transacted by brokers through Kelco. The document was titled as a Convera Financial Insurance Seminar.

The phone rang from the conference call speaker atop the conference table, then a familiar deep southern voice entered the room.

"Hello, Dale Barron here, did my package make it?" Dale said in his good ol' boy southern drawl. To me, his voice resembled a hint of the old western movie star, John Wayne

"Dale, it's Steve Keller, Keith Drach, and Grant Sutherlin. We also have our legal team here."

"Did my package make it?" Dale restated.

"We have it right here."

"And what do you think?" Dale asked.

"It looks like some kinda' hit list," I stated.

Dale laughed. "Well, something close – what you have there is the training manual that was used to train the Postal Service on how to raid you guys."

"Who trained them?" I asked.

"Convera Finanical Insurance and other companies – I was brought in as an adviser."

Keith's voice interjected on the call, saying, "I'm sorry, but you will have to explain further. This is unbelievable."

"Here's the deal, fellas. There were two meetings. The first meeting was attended by some fifty insurance companies, all held in Carmel, Indiana, at Convera Financial's headquarters. The second meeting was nothing but a coverup of the first meeting. Convera Financial sent out invitations for a four-day seminar to postal service agents from every state. They flew 'em in there and put 'em up in hotels. Barbara Farrington, the lead attorney for Convera Financial, well, she stepped in after the other fella got his head chopped off by a helicopter. She was running the show there at the—"

I interrupted and asked, "Dale, excuse me, but did you say he had his head chopped off?"

Dale responded, "Yes, sir, sure did. The pilots told them to follow a strict path to enter and exit the helicopter, but I guess these guys were above instructions and decided to follow their own rules. That didn't work out too well for the CFO who was six foot ten, or so."

My jaw nearly hung down on the conference table as I noticed everyone in attendance was equally shocked by Dale's words.

He didn't skip a beat. He continued, "You see, Barbara Farrington was brought on by the big wig over there to solve their problem of paying out on so many policies. That's when she called me up about this whole, 'Operation Clean Sheet' – figured she could kill two birds with one stone if she could drum up a conspiracy between the viatical brokers' industry and the agents who supply the policies. All she had to do was entice the Postal Service to pursue charges."

"Why the Postal Service? Why not the FBI?" Grant asked.

"Oh, Barbara went to D.C. to entice the FBI. She talked to an Agent Walsh there. He told her that he didn't see the illegal activity, and he was not going to pursue this. He flat turned her down, but that didn't stop old Barb. She went to the lowest rung of law enforcement, the Postal Service, to do her bidding."

"I thought all they policed were pipe bombs and pornography," I stated.

"Not necessarily. They can engage anything transmitted through the mail or via wire transmission."

"Dale, Sonny Creed, here – excuse me, but how do you know all of this anyway?" Sonny asked.

"Because I was one of the keynote speakers for the Postal Service meeting I've described. You see, gentlemen, I worked as the head of the Fraud Department in the Texas Department of Insurance. I brought the first prosecution in this industry, taking down Southwest Viatical. You guys bought policies from that firm."

"Yes, Hoyt and that bunch," Grant exclaimed.

"Recently, Southwest was recruiting AIDS patients through an insurance broker who was a Southwest affiliate," Dale stated.

"That was one reason we stopped dealing with that firm a long time ago," I said.

"Yes, I know. Well, that scheme is the one that Barbara Farrington had painted and sold to the Postal Service. She led the group to believe that every company in the industry was involved with this type of activity, yours included."

"They believed that the whole industry could be part of a conspiracy?" Keith asked, incredulously.

"Far-fetched, I know, but the Postal Service bought it, hook line and sinker," Dale stated.

"Dale, we know there are bad actors in this market, but Kelco is the country's most licensed firm. We try to offer regulation for every state. I have three full-time attorneys who focus on this endeavor. That's certainly not something a corrupt firm would do, so I have to ask you: why the raid on Kelco?"

"Several reasons – my guess is that you own a lot of policies in the Convera Financial family of companies, policies that Convera Financial would rather not payout," Dale stated.

"Dale, why are you divulging all of this to us?" Keith asked.

"Simple – I left the Insurance Department and went into private practice. I expected that the government would hire me to lead the investigations. This never happened. They decided they didn't need me. When I first got involved with this meeting, I thought there might be a conspiracy between the agents and companies like yours, but the only conspiracy I see here is what happened at Convera Financial headquarters." Dale explained.

Jack Smith said, "Why do you call it, 'Operation Clean Sheet?' What's that about?"

"That's a term Barbara came up with to define when an insured, lies on an application about their health or says they didn't smoke cigarettes when they did, for example, and then obtain a policy based on that lie," Dale explained.

"This has been going on for years, well before the evolution of the viatical and Life Settlement industry," Jack exclaimed.

"There's no question about that," Dale replied.

"That's backward," I exclaimed. "The fiduciary responsibility falls on the agents and the underwriters! Why the hell would they raid us?"

Jack continued, "So let me get this straight, Mr. Barron. You're telling us that this whole Convera Financial meeting was one elaborate plan to eradicate the viatical industry?"

"Yes, sir, I experienced it firsthand and was brought in to help them do just that," Dale replied.

"Incredible!" Jack said, leaning back, his hand-drawn to his chin as silence overcame everyone around the conference table.

"Dale, you have blown us away here. This has been truly incredible. We'll get to work on all you've shared with us. Thank you, Dale, for everything," Bob Webb stated.

"Yes, thank you, Dale," I added, "We'll be in touch."

"It's my pleasure. I hope it helps you out. Goodbye." Dale replied.

Keith, Grant, and I were all smiles as everyone sat around the table, looking at one another, waiting for someone to break the silence.

Larry Hopkins, who had been soaking everything up, finally decided to do so. He said, "Well, gentlemen! I don't know about the rest of you, but after having just witnessed this conversation, I'm behind Kelco — all the way."

Sonny looked around and stated, "There's no question. That was powerful."

"Steve!" Chris shouted, nearly startling everyone. He said, "I have the absolute perfect guy to put on the Convera Financial trail. His name is Don Finch, an investigator right there in Carmel. I heard about that helicopter incident. This guy, Don Finch, just spent the past two years representing Dauphin Helicopters, the company that Convera Financial sued after the accident."

"Chris, call the guy and get him on board. Have him gather all the information he can: everything...anything at all," I stated.

FOUL PLAY

I liked Bob Webb for many reasons. He was impulsive and shot from the hip – a straight-shooter, always pulling the trigger first and asking questions later. He struck me as the type of person who would find some way to achieve whatever he attempted.

After our conference call with Dale Barron, Bob went on a mission of his own, determined to find answers. Several days after we had last met, Bob came storming onto the ninth floor, almost running into my office. He panted, out of breath, beaming from ear to ear, with his briefcase in hand. He nearly shouted, "Steve, I had to come to see you right away. This thing just keeps growing tentacles. I found something in conjunction with what Dale Barron laid out for us."

I sat bolt upright in my chair, eager to hear more. I said, "Bob, slow down. Take a seat."

Bob didn't bother with the pleasantries. He barreled forward, bombarding me with information. "Yeah, yeah, listen, while I was talking to those jackasses from Lincoln Life, I managed to go through a box of their files. When I started, they tried to stop me. They claimed that they had 'already been looked at by Chris Burnside.' I told them, 'That's great, but I hadn't gone through them myself yet,' so while they were talking, trying to rush me out of there, I managed to find this."

Bob pulled a letter out of his briefcase and handed it to me. I observed the letter, noticing it was drafted on the official letterhead from Convera Financial Insurance, signed by Barbara Farrington: addressed to Lincoln Life.

We believe that our agents and other agents in the insurance industry are taking advantage of the industry's underwriting. We believe agents are selling policies to people afflicted with AIDS and then selling the policies to viatical companies. If you detect any unusual patterns within your sales force, please compile names and

*forward me the activity at the above address. We are currently orga-
nizing a meeting with the Postal Service. We believe this is a unique
opportunity for us to create a partnership with the government on
this matter. Thank you for your cooperation.*

*Sincerely,
Barbara J. Farrington.*

"Partnership with the government! For Christ's sake, Bob, is this
for real?" I asked.

Bob then stated, "Steve, I saw this letter and just about fell over.
Can you believe this? 'Partnership with the government'...to take out
their competitor! Barbara didn't even try to hide it! Of course, she never thought we would be going through Lincoln Life's files."

"And they let you have this, Bob?" I asked.

"No, they most certainly didn't. They told me I couldn't have any
documents from their office, so I stole it," Bob laughed. "I couldn't let
the most important paper in this entire case out of my reach."

I laughed with excitement at the gall of this attorney to be so bold,
again making sure he got the job done, no matter the risk. I started to
ask, "How did you get it out?" then stopped myself by saying, "Never
mind – it's not important. This is gold, Bob!" I exclaimed.

"It's just unbelievable! I have to meet with Don Finch and try and
get a handle on Barbara Farrington. He says he's uncovering a trea-
sure-trove of information on her. We're going to subpoena her for a
deposition."

"The sooner, the better," I stated.

"Hey, how's Keith doing?" Bob asked.

"He's going through pure hell with chemo treatments in Nebraska.
It sounds worse than the disease," I replied.

"Give him my best. I've got to get back to Louisville. I just had to
show this to you in person."

"You did well, Bob. We need to sue Convera Financial," I stated.

KELLER:

We did sue Convera Financial and made the case open to the public.

While Kelco was fighting to keep our business and our livelihoods, Keith was fighting for his life. The Nebraska facility was killing every cancerous cell in his body but wiping out his entire immune system in the process. They would then cleanse his blood, separate the stem cells, and then perform a blood transfusion and stem cell replacement.

The treatment Keith had received at the local University of Kentucky hospital was just a dress rehearsal compared to what he was going through in Nebraska. The doctors administered what was called a blast chemo, or 'Beam.' In six days, Keith received chemo treatments thirty times greater than what he had received in over three weeks during previous treatments. The doctors prescribed OxyContin to counteract the pain. Keith described the pain he experienced when swallowing liquids or any food as feeling like swallowing razor blades. His weight dropped from 235 pounds down to 193.

While Keith was going through the most excruciating pain of his life, Pat Molloy, the rogue prosecutor pursuing charges against Kelco, dared to call Keith's lawyer, Kent Westberry. Molloy asked if Keith would accept a deal in exchange for testifying against Grant and me. Kent Westbury conveyed the offer to Keith, and in a graveled voice, Keith stated, "Under no circumstances. Such a deal would give people the impression that something illegal was done, and we didn't break a law. We didn't do anything wrong. Tell Pat, thanks, but no thanks. I'm standing on my principles."

Like the rest of us, Keith had no idea how corrupt a system we were dealing with.

THE ROOT OF THE RAID

A month later, on December 1st, Keith entered the ninth floor with fewer files in his office and a lot less hair. Keith's blood transfusion and stem cell implants had been successful. If ever there was a star patient from the Nebraska hospital, that honor would go to Keith. His presence immediately gave everyone in our office an uplifting feeling of hope. We all felt a sense that if Keith could survive his battle against cancer, we could handle the damage from Convera Financials' petty, foul play. Grant and I had been doing everything we could to keep the ship afloat, but it was getting harder by the day.

I was grateful for Keith's steadying presence in my office as Keith and I met with Don Finch, who sat across from me.

"So, Don, what can you tell us about Convera Financial?" I asked.

"More than you're going to believe. Steve, this company is morally dysfunctional. I've never seen anything like it."

"How so?" I asked.

"Keller, I know this company like the back of my hand. I just completed the investigation of a helicopter company in the death of their lead attorney, Lyle Ensor."

"Dale Baron mentioned that — seems bizarre, to say the least!"

"The case unveiled how ruthless their people truly are. After first investigating them, I was bothered to the point where I had trouble sleeping."

"Goodness, Don. You want some water?" I asked.

"Please."

I poured Don a glass from a nearby pitcher of ice water.

"Are you okay going forward for us on this case?" I asked as I handed him the glass of water.

"I'm too involved now. I've already talked to people on your behalf. I know who I can approach and whom I cannot. Let me introduce you to what we are dealing with. I will start by giving you a background of this company, and then I will take you behind the scenes of what I found out over the past two years."

"Okay, let's roll," I said, settling down into my chair.

"Let's start with the beginning. Scott. Halberg founded Convera Financial in 1979, originally called Security National of Indiana. Halberg grew the company exceptionally fast by acquiring other insurance companies. It first merged with Consolidated National Life and changed its name to Convera Financial. By 1985, Convera Financial went public on this fast-track growth and was valued at one hundred million. Two years later, they built an ostentatious new headquarters in Carmel, Indiana.

"Halberg kept acquiring companies aggressively. In 1990, he acquired at least seven, and after this, he acquired at least nine more over the next decade. This resulted in massive growth. However, these acquisitions were not a healthy long-term business model.

Halberg was a raider. When he took over a company, he gutted the staff, reduced the operating costs, and sucked the reserves out, transferring them to the parent company. What was left behind was usually discarded. Halberg then started acquiring high profile entities found outside the insurance industry. He acquired an interest in a casino, bought a NASCAR racing team, and paid ninety-five million dollars for the naming rights to the new Indiana Pacers basketball arena at that time, designating it the Convera Financial Field House. Halberg's money machine grew to another level. In 1997 he was one of the highest-paid CEOs in America with a $119.4 million compensation package. The following year he just missed being named one of the four hundred wealthiest Americans by Forbes. As his uncontrollable greed grew, his mental state and actions started raising eyebrows." Don took a breath.

"What do you mean?" I asked.

"He became eccentric, I mean...weird. He would fly in a helicopter daily to and from work. He became paranoid. He thought people were out to steal his fortune. He began hiring deputized police to work for him, personally. He had more police working directly for him than all of Marion County, Indiana," Don stated, almost fearful of sharing the story.

"Why did they need that many police?" Keith asked.

"You tell me...The other employees at Convera Financial called them spooks. Halberg never went anywhere without his head spooks. He had a whole entourage."

"What was he so afraid of?" I wondered aloud.

"Lord knows...actions he took against others, I can only assume. Why else?" Don asked.

"I couldn't think of any other reason. I certainly don't feel the need for such protection." I stated.

"In 1998, after Convera Financials' corporate attorney had a fatal accident in one of Halberg's helicopters, Barbara Farrington came on board. This same year Convera Financial purchased a company located in Arizona, called Greentree Financial Corporation, a mobile home lender that was promptly renamed Convera Financial Finance. Greentree was the largest mobile home financier in the country.

"The acquisition cost was around six billion dollars. The acquisition was termed a 'Fatal Decision' by the *Indianapolis Star*. Seems to me, when Halberg's corporate attorney got killed, that is when he really started down a rogue criminal path," Don continued.

"How so?" Keith asked.

"He started becoming desperate. You see, the insurance companies do minimal underwriting on their policies, as you know."

"Yeah, we were aware of that," I replied.

"Well, Convera Financial did hardly any underwriting on the insurance companies they purchased, so when the policies started coming due and the viatical companies were being paid out in record levels due to the increase in AIDS-related deaths, it was depleting Halberg's cash reserves. He then instructed Barbara Farrington to orchestrate a means to eradicate the problem. That's when she came up with *Operation Clean Sheet*."

"So, this was the cause for the prior meeting held at Convera Financial, the one Dale Barron described?" I asked.

"This was when at least fifty companies got together to come up with a scheme to take you out," Don stated.

"They didn't want to pay out the policy benefits..." I mused.

"Bingo. While all of this was taking place, the dam in Halberg's operation began to crack. The Indianapolis Star reported on it, and I think they were right on with their prediction. See, Greentree's mortgage payments were lagging behind big time with their borrowers. This meant that if these payments were seriously late, Greentree's bond ratings would drop. A lot of mutual fund companies would be prohibited from investing in the company. Halberg and his middle management had borrowed six hundred million dollars to purchase stock options in Convera Financial. If Greentree crashed, everything the group mortgaged would be forfeited to the banks.

"Halberg became desperate and took desperate actions. At certain times of the month, Halberg and his chief financial officer would fly out to Greentree over the weekends when all the employees were gone. They would personally zero out the account to make them appear like all the mortgages had been paid on time."

"They were cooking the books. How long did this go on?" Keith asked.

"It was months until they got caught! Convera Financials' stock shot down from fifty-eight per share to five. It dropped instantly after they got caught."

"Did they go to jail?"

"No! they were all fired. The entire senior management team was let go, middle management, and all the spooks."

"And nobody was charged with fraud?" I asked again.

"Nobody! Convera Financial sued Halberg personally for damages, but that was the only recourse."

"I guess he was above the law," I stated.

"Speaking of above the law, Barbara Farrington became just as obsessed with Operation Clean Sheet as Halberg was with Greentree. At first, Barbara was strictly investigating Convera Financials' internal agents. She then became preoccupied with the viatical settlement companies and the impact eradicating their industry could have on the company's bottom line. She traveled to D.C. and met with the FBI to pitch Convera Financials' plan to get some kind of official investigation launched."

"Is that where it started?" Keith asked.

"No, the FBI declined, stating they didn't see any evidence of fraud or wrongdoing."

"So how did they make this happen?" Keith asked.

"The spooks – these people's backgrounds were from all walks of law enforcement – CIA, FBI, Postal Service, NSA – you name it. Convera Financial even sponsored an annual golf tournament for law officials. Their charity donated money to build facilities in their communities, expecting political favors in return. We are talking millions and millions of dollars being donated to keep these people in his pocket," Don stated.

"No wonder no one went to jail," I observed.

"Yep! A whole new connotation to insurance." Keith stated, raising his eyebrows in my direction.

With that little look, Keith made me feel like he was fully back in the saddle and fighting by my side again. It gave me confidence and reminded me how much I had missed him.

"This established association with the law enforcement agencies is exactly how they managed to call the dogs in for the raid. Their spooks pressed a local Postal Service Agent out of Indianapolis named Greg Barriault to launch an investigation. They worked so closely with the agency that Convera Financial invited at least one Postal Service Agent from each state to their headquarters for a four-day conference, essentially to sell them a bill of goods that never existed and train them how to raid your company."

"And they hired Dale Barron to walk them through it," I stated.

"They did. Steve, I know you're already aware of the letter Bob discovered, but in short, the invitations announced the conference as an unprecedented opportunity for the insurance industry to partner with the Government. This is why I knew I had to learn more about Farrington."

"What did you find out?" I asked eagerly.

"Farrington basically wrote the entire search warrant used during the raid on Kelco and the rest of the viatical companies. When Roberta Bottoms, the head investigator for the U.S. Postal Service, was ready to take the search warrant affidavit to the Judge for signature, she approached Barbara to sign it on three different occasions, but for some strange reason, Barbara refused all three times...So Roberta signed it without her. And that's where you are today. I'm not sure Barbara ever intended to take it this far," Don stated frankly.

"Do you think others urged Convera Financial to use their law enforcement structure to attack Kelco?" Keith asked.

"It's highly possible. They were not working alone. I'm sure your non-compete contracts with most of Wall Street were a factor. Other companies may have wanted to enter the market, but you were standing in the way."

"Any ideas?" I asked.

"Did you know that Ray Yonkers was two blocks down from Kelco the morning of the raid?" Don announced.

"What? The head spook? How do you..." I stated, trailing off as Don interrupted.

"Steve, this is what I do."

"Wow, these are some bold sons of bitches!" I exclaimed.

"This is an unsettling group," Don agreed.

"What's the status of Halberg now?" I asked.

"He's hanging out in his palace-like estate with Toni Rae," Don replied.

"Who is Toni Rae?" I asked.

"Oh, it gets better. Back in the late '90s, Halberg threw a party for his son, who was turning 21. Toni Rae, a stripper at the time, popped out of a cake. Halberg Sr., being the scumbag that he is, ended up marrying the poor girl then sent her to 'finishing school' to learn to fit in with the social elites that he catered to," Don stated.

"Don, you said you spoke with Barbara Farrington. Where is she? Is she willing to sign an affidavit, attesting to all of this?"

"I'm not sure. One of my contacts, Tracy Ruple, who was given a job at the Postal Service after the mass exodus, thinks she might be working for an insurance company in Ohio. I will continue to mine my sources and see if she or anyone else is willing to come forward on this. As I get more and trust me, there will be more, I will call you."

"Don, I cannot tell you how elated I am that you're on this case. I need to get to the source – Farrington!"

I shouldn't have been surprised by anything after discovering the scheme responsible for the Kelco raid, but nothing could have prepared me for the call I received several days later from one of our attorneys, Chris Burnside, about what happened when he found Farrington.

THE FARRINGTON ENCOUNTER

Late Monday morning the following week, while in my office at Kelco, I received a phone call that dynamited my mountain. My pit bull of an attorney, Chris Burnside, had employed every trick in the book to somehow locate Barbara Farrington. The last I had heard, Chris and the private investigator, Norman Wilson, had been tracking her down in Ohio after a subpoena had been granted for her deposition. It was around 11:00 o'clock when my desk phone rang, followed by Karen's voice, telling me to pick up. She said, "It's Chris Burnside. He says it's an emergency!"

I clicked the speakerphone button and said, "Hello, Chris, it's Steve."

"Thank God you're there," Chris stated, sounding out of breath.

I rose up onto the edge of my seat. "What's the matter, Chris? Where are you?"

"I'm in Carmel, sitting in a car with Norman Wilson, outside of Barbara Farrington's condo."

"I thought Barbara was in Ohio," I replied.

"She is...kinda'."

"I don't understand."

"Norm and I were in Ohio last week. Barbara is working for another insurance company here in Cincinnati – Greater American Life of Ohio. It's owned by Carl Lender, who owns Chiquita Banana. But get this: Barbara has been living out of hotel rooms since she moved to Cincinnati. She changes rooms or hotels every day. It's like she is hiding from someone. That's why no one could find her. Apparently, she's selling her condo in Carmel to raise money before going completely off the map."

"So, you think she will show up at her condo?"

"She already has. Norm and I posed as a buyer for her condo and arranged for her realtor to have Barbara meet us there for a tour."

My jaw nearly dropped to the floor. "Chris, that's ingenious."

"What's better...she actually showed up! It was an early morning appointment. She walked us through her condo and started talking about the kitchen cabinets and appliances when I stopped her. I said, Barbara, we're not here to buy your condo, but we are here to serve you a subpoena for your deposition."

"What did she say then?" I asked.

"Steve, it's hard to describe the look and reaction. Her hands began to shake as she held the papers. Tears started to swell in her eyes. A look of anguish and panic spread across her face...I wasn't ready for such a reaction."

"What did you do?"

"Oh, it gets worse. She let out a blood-curdling scream and started shaking her head, screaming, 'You can't do this! I can't be deposed. The Big C will kill me. They will kill me. I will do anything you request but not this. You don't understand. They will kill me!'"

"The Big C will kill me? Who is the Big C?" I stated.

"Steve, this woman broke down, her knees grew weak, and she fell over the kitchen countertop. I had never seen anything like this, especially from another attorney."

"So, what happened next?"

"Well, I told her to try and calm down, that I would reconsider the subpoena, if she would sign an affidavit stating, among other things, that she knew of no wrongdoing by Kelco and that we were not involved in any conspiracies with insurance agents. She said she could agree to that. I scheduled a time for us to meet next week in Ohio."

"That's great news, Chris. When you get back, I will tell you about the conversation I had with Don Finch. Barbara has good cause to be scared."

"Barbara acted like she either knew something horrible or had seen something bad firsthand," Chris affirmed.

"Chris, Norm – great work, guys! We'll talk more soon when we're not on the phone."

"Thanks. I'm heading back now. Goodbye, Steve."

I hung up the phone and thought about Barbara's response. *Bar-*

bara must have firsthand experience with something awful that happened while she was at Convera Financial. She knew enough to make her go into hysterics, just at the thought of sharing the truth about Convera Financial. The Convera Financial story just kept unraveling. I could not imagine having an employee ever thinking that Kelco would put them in harm's way. That should never happen. I began to understand that we were not dealing with an ordinary insurance company. We were dealing with a Mafia-style outfit, strong-arming a multi-billion-dollar industry, using Federal law enforcement as their personal hit-squad, and it was all being orchestrated by someone who seemed to be a sociopath.

Great...this is what we're up against, I thought, leaning back in my chair.

Several days later, our fears became a reality.

KELLER:

During those two years of battle, my entire world had been slipping away a little bit at a time, like a fighter's consciousness who's been eating punches for too many rounds. On July 11, 2002, an indictment was finally served, and it felt like a country haymaker, dropping me and Kelco to the bloody mat.

Grant, Keith, and I, along with Kelco and our broker company, Genesis, were the indictment subjects. Of course, we knew the government's theory, that we bought policies under two years old, focusing on policyholders who had lied on their applications, and this would be the thrust of their argument against us. The government used Barbara Farrington's term for this activity, Clean Sheeting. To this day, Clean Sheeting is included in neither a state nor federal statute. Legally, it does not exist; it was not and still, to present day, is not law. However, in black and white, Clean Sheeting was listed among the charges filed in the indictment against Kelco. However, the government didn't stop there. It was apparent to all of the industry's insiders and those advising me that the indictment had been drafted based on James Doran's premature motion the motion that cost Kelco one million dollars for the D.C. attorney to file after Senator Creed insisted that I hire Doran. During that frantic time, it never once occurred to me that perhaps Doran's motion might have been a deliberate effort to sabotage us from the inside out. We were "paying to play," but if Senator Creed was being paid by the insurance companies to set us up, then we couldn't compete against their deeper pockets.

Found in the indictment, were fabricated scenarios that we knew were preposterous, but the general public would find disturbing. The most egregious spin on the indictment that never would have found its way into the charges had it not been for Doran's premature motion was a term listed as "blood-swapping." The indictment actually stated that Kelco helped individuals swap tainted blood for clean blood to qualify for and obtain policies that required blood tests. It was a shock factor to give the public pause and paint us in the worst light possible. Until James Doran's motion, we suspected there were bad actors in the industry engaging in this type of fraud, but we never transacted policies under those terms and absolutely never would have coerced potential policyholders under any circumstances. We didn't need to. After the creation of the Life Settlements market, Kelco was processing more policies than we could handle.

One of three people listed on the indictment, who supposedly engaged in such practices, was a licensed phlebotomist who had performed blood tests years before doing business with Kelco. I believe many people would think if information like this came from the government, there was likely some truth in it; most believe in the old adage, "Where's there's smoke, there's fire." I can believe these scam-artists committed fraud, but Kelco had never even met them. I was beginning to see that, just because we were engaged with the justice system, it didn't mean it was about the truth. Ronald Reagan once said, "The nine most terrifying words in the English language are, 'I'm from the government, and I'm here to help,'"; they felt true to me then.

As I combed through the indictment, I encountered a lot of confidential informants. These were mostly people who had sold policies all over the country and had been indicted of blatantly criminal acts unrelated to Kelco; now, in exchange for a reduced sentence, they were manufacturing falsehoods against us. I didn't know it then, but I understand now that this type of coercion of defendants, turning them into false-witnesses, amounts to a government-sanctioned form of blackmail – again, not justice.

Listed in the indictment were some 48 counts. All of them dealt with buying and selling contestable policies where someone lied on the application. As I read through the indictment, I became more perplexed. Wayne Holcombe, our attorney who developed our business model, not only advised us on each transaction, but also performed the due diligence, the quality control, operations on every policy. With his law firm acting as a guardrail to prevent foul play and ensure the legality and morality of every transaction that Kelco participated in, what could possibly go so wrong? I had personally sponsored and co-written the insurance laws for the state of Kentucky. I knew for a fact that we didn't break any insurance laws. I was legally licensed in thirty-eight states.

Before Convera Financial and Barbara Farrington's hit job, Kelco never had one complaint filed anywhere in the thirty-eight states in which we were licensed. The indictment didn't make sense. At the time, I had no understanding of Federal law or how government agencies operate. I never saw it as necessary because the insurance industry was, and still is to this day, not under the jurisdiction of federal law — only state law. As I held this indictment, I asked myself, *Okay, you got indicated. Now what? This is no more than a formal accusation that I have to disprove in court.*

It broke my heart, but I started the first round of layoffs right after receiving the indictment. For two years after the raid, it had been a miracle that we could continue doing any business in the industry. Now, with the indictment in hand, I knew it would be impossible.

I called my little group of "core" Kelco employees into my office, including Paula Abner, Rene Smith, and Becky Thompson. They already knew what this was about. I respected these people, and I knew they deserved my candor. Paula and Becky had been with me since the early days at the Office Suites. Rene Smith had come aboard later but had heard all the old stories. We all shared stories from our history together. In this setting, instead of crying, we spent the time laughing. We were living for the moment, reflecting on our past experiences. There had been so many great, crazy times. We were a family more than a company, but now we had to separate. All my resources would be needed to assemble a legal squadron for battle in court. It was our only hope in defending our freedom and the company; it was our only chance at putting the pieces and the family back together again.

GATEKEEPERS

I walked through the United States Capitol Building halls with Keith and Bob Webb, insistent on meeting with Senator Creed. Walking through the grand hallways, I hoped to, by chance, see the Senator as we were led by a staffer to a meeting room. My calls to meet with the Senator had been mostly ignored. However, his son, Sonny, and his mentor, Troy Anders, agreed to meet with us. I watched as a procession of Congressmen filed out of a room, passing by our group. I scanned the recognizable faces but didn't see Senator Creed.

We entered a well-appointed meeting room with crisp, bright white walls, adorned with portraits of statesmen past. Sonny, tall, handsome and as nauseatingly charismatic as always, greeted us warmly with a smile as we entered the room, saying, "Keller! so good to see you! And, Keith, I'm happy to see you're doing well. You look great. And you must be the Bob Webb I've heard so much about. Gentlemen, this is Troy Anders."

Troy Anders, heavyset, in his early sixties, and aware of his presence within the room, was the head of the GOP war chest and an important behind-the-scenes figure within the Republican Party. He stood from a chair within the sitting area to greet us with handshakes. He said, "The Kelco team – Sonny filled me in. Please, take a seat."

Our team from Kelco sat on a long couch across from Sonny and Troy, who each sat in armchairs. I kicked off the conversation. "Thank you for meeting with us. I got to say; it's tougher to get a meeting here than it is to sit down with the Pope," I joked.

We all shared a laugh as Sonny said, "Sorry about that, new protocols. Things have been locked down here after 9/11."

"Sonny, I was hoping to meet with your dad. He hasn't been returning my calls. What's the deal?"

Sonny started to respond, but Troy interjected before he could speak, saying, "What is it that you need, Mr. Keller?"

"Well, I'm sure Sonny told you. We got indicted last week, and the Senator assured us it was already taken care of—"

Troy interrupted before I could say more, asserting, "There are no guarantees in life. I highly doubt he assured you anything. The nature of this work in DC is precarious, especially lobbies, as I hope you can respect."

"Mr. Anders, sir, with all due respect, I've already paid over a million dollars to make this thing go away, plus your monthly lobbying fees, and all I've got for it is an indictment that's buried me deeper in the hole I was already in. I can't even get a meeting with the Senator for Christ's sake."

Troy Anders sat back in his seat and shot out a taunting laugh, responding, "That's the nature of this business, Mr. Keller. Haven't you learned your lesson yet?"

I sat forward in my seat as I said, "And what lesson might that be?"

"Here in DC, you got to pay to play."

I sat quietly for a moment, seething with silent indignation. *What the fuck is he talking about? I've already paid and can't afford to pay a damn dime more. With the indictment, this fucking guy well knows we're hanging on by a thread. Hell fire! I wish I could take these D.C. gatekeeping playboys out back behind the wreck yard in West Liberty.* After collecting my thoughts, I said, "I want to talk to the Senator. Sonny, can you get me a meeting with your dad?"

"That's going to be tough. His schedule is packed solid. That's why we're here."

"I'm only paying you because you promised access to your dad and he had me hire this buffoon, James Doran, who basically wrote the government's indictment! He got me into this mess, and I just want to talk to him about what happened."

"If he's booked, he's booked," Troy said.

"How much is it going to cost?" I asked.

Sonny and Troy looked to each other, considering. I looked to Keith and Bob Webb, knowing I said the magic words.

POLO AND POLITICS

The sound of horse hooves thundered from the polo fields as I watched Sonny and his team as they competed against a visiting team at the Lexington Horse Park. Horse riders wearing heavy jackets to shield them from the brisk autumn air swung mallets at a ball atop the grass, clacking the ball toward a goal on either side of the field. Tammy and I, along with Cole, sat beside Senator Creed and his wife in a private box beneath the announcers' stand. Sonny had been able to convince his dad to allow me to tag along for the game. As the game proceeded, I tried at every opportune moment to turn the conversation toward Kelco and my impending trial date. Mostly, my attempts were ignored. The Senator was a master at steering the conversation back toward lighter, more superficial topics.

As the buzzer sounded, signaling half-time, Senator Creed excused himself, making his way out from our private box onto the field to keep with tradition in joining the crowd to stomp the divots made during the match to prepare the field for the second half. I joined the Senator, feeling confident that, being away from our wives, I could strike up the conversation about Kelco again.

I said, "Senator, I really need to talk with you."

"Okay, what can I do for you?" he said over his shoulder as he kept his attention focused on the field ahead and down onto the divots in the ground.

"I've been trying reach you to talk about Kelco. Finally, I got through to Sonny and Troy about what's happening…"

"And what did they say?" he interjected.

"Well, they said I should have learned my lesson by now – that I should have known that I've got to pay to play."

My comment seemed to vanish into thin air between me and the Senator like the steam from my breath in the cold afternoon air. He continued walking as if I hadn't said anything at all.

I followed after him, insistent, saying, "It's not right! We got indicted! I'm supposed to appear in court next month!"

"I'm sorry to hear that, Mr. Keller, but I'm at a loss here. I'm not sure what you want me to do about it," he said as he trudged forward on the field.

I began stomping the divots alongside the Senator, refusing to walk behind him, forcing him to face me as we both trudged forward. As I stomped hard on a divot, flattening the earth beneath me, I said, "You said you would fix this! I want you to get the Feds off my back!"

The Senator suddenly stopped walking. He turned and faced me on the open field and looked at me with eyes colder than the chill in the air, saying, "I think you're mistaken here, Mr. Keller. That is not how this arrangement works."

"I was promised that all of this would go away. I've paid well over a million dollars to your son, for access to you, and to James Doran, who filed a motion that dug the hole the government is now trying to bury me in. I want you to keep your word and do something about it!" I demanded.

He exhaled before speaking, and the smoke rising his lips hung in the distance between us as he said, "Let me make this point very clear. I don't work for you. You're lucky I even took the time to meet with you." He looked over his shoulders and then said, "You have no idea what you're up against." As if he had said too much, the Senator shook his head, looked away from me, and continued trudging forward on the field.

"What does that mean?" I asked, catching up to walk alongside him.

He said, "Let me tell you a story about someone I know. He's a good man, honest, hardworking. He was my driver for a time. In this line of work, Mr. Keller, sometimes we have to make sacrifices – tough choices. I'm sure, as a businessman, you understand this.

"I'm not sure I follow," I said, stomping a divot into the ground, growing angrier by the second.

"Sometimes, things happen beyond our control, or we get caught up in things that are just over our heads. Do you understand? That's what happened with the young man – circumstances beyond his control – and he found himself in legal trouble. He was facing years of incarceration. Now, he had the opportunity to talk and share some damaging information about me in exchange for a reduced sentence." The Senator paused for a moment, making direct eye contact with me to say, "He has a wife and kids, Mr. Keller – a family man. You know what this man did?"

I shook my head, *No*, gridlocked in eye contact.

The Senator said, "He did the time and kept his mouth shut. I owe my whole career to this man. I suggest you do the same."

His words impacted me, stopping me cold. I stood there, stunned for a moment as he continued walking ahead. Over his shoulder, he said, "This will be the last I'll hear about this issue. I suggest you enjoy the day and enjoy your time with your family."

WE PLEAD...YOUR HONOR

The day I feared most finally came. Keith, Grant, and I stood alongside Bob Webb behind the defendant's bench in Federal court before Judge Karl Forester. As I stood before the Judge, I wondered, *Why am I being tried Federally, when the states govern the insurance industry? Hell, I co-wrote the laws that govern thirty-eight states where I'm licensed. Surely the Judge will see that and dismiss this whole misunderstanding.*

Judge Forester began with the court's procedural formalities and then asked the Prosecution and Defense to state our cases. The government, led by prosecutor Pat Malloy, who had overseen the Kelco raid with a shotgun slung over his shoulder like some frontier sheriff, tendered his theory of what Kelco was doing wrong. In his gruff, aging, thick southern accent, he claimed, "Your Honor, we are here today for the crimes that have been committed by Kelco and its executive officers. We've built a case against them, which details their extensive use of financial tools, such as trusts, to make it very difficult for anyone to understand their fraudulent business's inner workings."

The Judge replied, "Mr. Malloy, if that's all you have, the use of trusts, that's certainly a legal structure, and I will end this right here."

Pat Malloy scrambled for words, saying, "Yes, of course, there's more – much more. Kelco is guilty of Clean Sheeting, buying policies under two years old where the policyholder has committed fraud. Furthermore, Your Honor, we got testimonies of policyholders who were HIV positive and knowingly engaged in illegal blood-swapping, at the behest of Kelco, to fraudulently obtain life insurance policies that, upon underwriting by insurers, were then bought by Kelco and sold again on the open market."

What? That's outrageous! blood-swapping? I leaned toward Bob Webb and nudged him with my elbow, saying, "That's not right. How can they even claim that?"

Bob looked to me sternly as he gestured with a hand for me to calm down. He looked enraged, and I trusted he would make our defense clear when given a chance to speak. Pat Malloy finished his opening arguments, alleging accusations that named me, Keith, Grant, Kelco, and Genesis, our subsidiary company.

The Judge turned to the four of us who stood behind the Defense table. He said, "Thank you, Prosecution. Defense, how do you plead?"

As Bob stood from his chair to address the Judge, Grant, Keith, and I all looked to one another, sharing a surreal moment. We maintained a look of hope as we each turned toward the Judge with a unified expression of solidarity, *We didn't break a law.*

Bob announced, "Your Honor, I'd like to start by saying the Prosecution's case is not based on law. We are here because a small but growing company has challenged the bottom line of an industry that has governed itself for far too long and has attempted to manufacture laws when no laws have been voted upon by our people's representatives. Kelco and its executives have played by the rules and followed the laws that are in place. Therefore, the Defense, pleads not guilty, Your Honor."

"Defendants hereby enter a plea of not guilty," the Judge announced then banged his gavel. "Counsel, you will each be notified for scheduling of the trial date."

"Your Honor?" Bob interjected, "before we convene, I feel it important to make clear that I will no longer represent the defendants through trial and will be recusing myself from the case."

I couldn't believe my ears. I stared at Bob in confusion.

"Understood. Defense, you will have thirty days to replace your counsel. Court is adjourned."

Shortly thereafter, Keith, Grant, Bob, and I left the Federal court building to make the trek back to the Kelco building. I didn't know what to say to Bob, and I think we were at a loss for words. Bob started to cross the street, veering off from our group toward his office.

I then asked him, "Say, Bob, what was that back there? You're not going to represent us at trial? I don't understand. We need you through this."

"Well, Steve, we haven't entered into an agreement about this," Bob replied.

"Look, Bob, I have paid your firm over one point two million dollars over the past two years. We're quickly running out of money. I need a flat fee from you to continue," I said.

"Steve, I don't know if I can do that."

"Well, Bob, there's no way I can afford to continue with you. I have no choice. I cannot continue an open meter with limited funds. We have no more business now. We're dying in the water here," I pleaded.

"I understand, but I don't think my firm will allow me to continue on a flat fee."

"Well, Bob, that's a problem. You let me know if something can be done."

KELLER:

Being inside the Federal Court system felt like playing a new board game for the first time, without limitations. Every time I would advance to a new space, someone would tell me a new rule. It reminded me of being a kid, playing games with other kids who made up the rules as they went to ensure only they could win. The subjects of the indictment were me, Keith, Grant, Kelco, and Genesis. Each of these entities had to have separate representation, meaning I had to hire five attorneys for a criminal trial. With no cash flow and very few policies now held in reserve, it was going to take everything we had. Anything other than a flat fee for the trial was out of the question. I began to think that perhaps the case was beyond Bob's ability. Maybe that's why he had the deer in the headlights look in the courtroom. Something had to be resolved and soon. We were going to trial against some of the best fiction writers our country possessed, who were writing chapters of false accusations, and after the Prosecution's claims during the arraignment, I expected they would also be writing the lines for the witnesses.

ASSEMBLING THE CAST

Preparing for a Federal Court trial was like two theatrical troupes competing for the best act on Broadway. If by chance, somewhere in the mix, the truth accidentally surfaced, the Government's side would lose. It proved challenging to assemble a respectable white-collar defense team on a limited budget. To generate funds for the attorneys, Grant and I sold, in desperation, policies that Kelco owned. The Government attorneys were in full stride, running around the country, threatening would-be witnesses unless they recited the provided script. Apparently, the Government's rehearsal had already been in full swing for the past two years.

Now they were in dress rehearsal while we were busy trying to find our directors. I retained my in-house attorneys, Scott Brown and Ron Kreiter, and a young employee, Adam Neel, who seemed close to having a photographic memory. We set up a war room on the seventh and ninth floors. I then hired two local attorneys, Burl McCoy, who was primarily a criminal drug attorney, and Jim Shuffett, an older attorney, who spent most of his time on the golf course, often with the court's officers.

Several months passed, and the void of a lead attorney still persisted. I interviewed a couple of law firms in Washington, D.C. Both meetings ended in frustration. A senior partner from Bob Webb's firm recommended I hire an attorney located in Nashville, named Jim Neal. The court had begun to pressure us to name an attorney, the Prosecution wanting to know who their sparring partner was going to be. With the pressure of the trial looming, Grant began to act frantic because he didn't yet have an attorney to represent him. His parents were insistent on supporting him through this process, so I promised all of them I would hire an attorney for him before I did so for myself. Therefore, Grant and I traveled to Nashville in the hopes that Mr. Neal would fit that bill. Mr. Neal offered his firm, but not his services, saying as we began to leave, "Boys, before you go, I'm going to give you some free advice. While you can, put some money aside for your families just in case things go badly. You can take that advice or not, but you're in one helluva treacherous game," Mr. Neal warned.

Shortly thereafter, we found Grant's attorney right under our noses. John Cline had tried a recent case with Bob Webb. We found John Cline to be one of the most talented, underrated, reasonably priced attorneys out of the whole group. Hiring John Cline still left me without an attorney representing me. The court was beside themselves now. While the Feds were steadily rehearsing with their play roster of witnesses, we still needed to figure out who these characters were. We only knew the names of the witnesses from having transacted their insurance policies. Burl McCoy suggested a private investigator. Jim Starks had been a state police officer, retiring at a young age and starting a private investigation firm, working for Burl's clients primarily. We took Burl's advice. Our other private investigator, Don Finch, was making significant progress at Convera Financial. He located an ex-coworker, Tracy Ruple, whom he had known from their days together at CNA Insurance.

When speaking to Tracy, I asked, "So, Tracy, what do you know about Barbara Farrington and Operation *Clean Sheet*?"

"I worked directly with Barbara. Barbara took full credit for creating Operation Clean Sheet. I remember mentioning something to Barbara about the Life Settlement market."

"What was her response?" Don asked.

"Barbara said she was well aware of that market but that they were doing that business properly. She said, 'We can't go there,'" Tracy replied, adding, "You're aware that Convera Financial drafted the indictment for Kelco, aren't you?"

"We are. That explains the indictment for *Clean Sheeting*, a term made up by Barbara. It's not even a statutory crime." I told her.

"You've got it. Roberta Bottoms, the postal inspector, tried on three different occasions to get Barbara to sign the indictment. She refused all three times."

"Who signed it?" Don asked.

"Bottoms," Tracy replied.

Don Finch flew to Florida to meet with a retired senior manager from Convera Financial.

Don had gotten to know this guy well during the Dauphin Helicopter investigation. It quickly became apparent that this guy knew all too well of the corporate attack on Kelco.

Don asked him, "Are you aware Kelco has sued Convera Financial for malicious business tort interference for one billion dollars?"

"Sure am. I don't know why Mr. Keller didn't sue them earlier. What Convera Financial did to Kelco was criminal!" He proclaimed.

Even though time was not on our side in obtaining legal counsel, our private investigators were mining boatloads of data to prove what really happened. We were just at the edge of the frame yet already uncovering a disturbing image inside this frame being placed around us to put all of us in prison and all Life Settlements companies like us out of business.

The Feds were way ahead of us, story composed, and cast assembled.

The latest intel made known to us was that an attorney, Robin Gwynn, who worked for Ron Kreiter while at the Department of Insurance in Kentucky, had now been appointed to Assistant United States Attorney. Since insurance cases were never heard at the Federal level unless they involved the Securities and Exchange Commission, the prosecutors were just as ignorant about the subject matter and legality in our industry as my criminal attorneys. A glaring hypocrisy came to light while awaiting trial and assembling our team. The Prosecution prevented me from hiring an attorney recommended by our in-house legal expert, Ron Kreiter, but the court took no exception to the fact that the lead prosecutor, Pat Malloy, was married to Jeanie Malloy, a Kelco employee of many years. Despite my insistence on a double standard, the show continued onward, and the closer we came to the actual trial date, the Government's obligation to follow the rules seemed to matter less and less.

While waiting, we received reports that the Feds were making their rounds all around our small town. One-stop they made was to visit Lewis Fister's office, our longstanding accountant.

Lewis called us after the visit to share the encounter.

"Are you guys there?" Lewis asked.

"Yes, Lewis. You've got Keith, Grant, and me on speaker," I stated.

"I just had the strangest meeting. The FBI sent a girl over here who was a forensic accountant. She wanted to see the books. As you know Steve, we've been using an off-the-shelf accounting program, Peachtree Accounting Software, for years," Lewis stated.

"Okay," I replied.

"Well, when you first bring the program up, it has two tutorial programs to teach you how to use it. One is called Big Green Garden Supplies, and the other is Toolbox Construction."

"Okay, I'm with you," I replied.

"Well, I left the woman alone with the program for about an hour. There's certainly nothing to hide, so I didn't care what she looked at. In about an hour or so, she came into my office, ecstatic, saying, 'I got them now. I know what they are doing, using dummy employees to launder money. There must be ninety fake employees in Big Green Garden Supplies alone. I'm taking them down and you along with them.'"

"Oh my God, Lewis," Grant stated.

"What did you say?" I asked.

"I looked at this woman while trying to keep from bursting out, laughing right in her face. I was in shock, thinking, at first, it was a joke, but then I could tell this woman was dead serious."

"So, what did you say?" Keith asked.

"Well, I looked at her and said, 'You have got to be kidding me. Lady, those are tutorial programs that are on every copy of Peachtree Software in the country.'"

"What did she say?" I asked, no longer able to contain the laughter.

"She told me that I better be telling her the truth. Keller, it's just absurd. This is the group investigating your company?" Lewis asked.

"Wow, Lewis, let's hope that is emblematic of the competence we can expect in this trial. I'm sure our attorneys will appreciate that one," I said, ending the call.

Over the next week, the court increased its pressure on us to name our lead defense attorney. It seemed the prosecutors were worried that, if we had to postpone the trial, some of the statutes of limitations on the witnesses' charges would run out. If this happened, then the prosecutors' leverage would cease to exist. Then, the scumbag U. S. Attorneys might risk the possibility of telling the truth. Such an event would blow the Government's case wide open.

It was Keith's brother-in-law who recommended our lead attorney. Keith and I flew to Chicago to meet Bob Tarun, who was with the law firm of Winston and Strawn. Bob's office was located in the heart of the city in an impressive building that housed hundreds of attorneys. Bob was wrapping up a conversation with some clients while walking to the nondescript lobby on his floor to meet us. Approaching us was a six-foot-two, pepper-haired attorney. His hair was cropped over his ears, parted on the side. He wore a blue-and-white-striped, seersucker suit, white bucks, and a yellow bow tie. The attire was quite a contrast to the mid-western persona.

"Gentlemen, I'm Bob Tarun. Let's go back to the conference room. Now, Keith, you're Marvin Nunley's brother-in-law?" Bob Tarun asked.

"Yes, Marvin is married to my sister, Gloria," Keith replied.

"I tried a huge civil case with Marvin," Bob stated.

"That's what I understand," Keith replied.

"I understand you have been the subject of a government raid?"

"Mr. Tarun, we are looking for a lead attorney to head our case in trial. We have not broken a law, and we're not about to plead out. I'm just letting you know where we stand," Keith stated.

"I'm glad to hear that. I honestly think I was born to do what I do. I love trials. If you're not going to trial, I'm probably not your man. I love a fight. I love what I do," Bob rattled off.

"That's encouraging to hear. Most attorneys these days don't know what a courtroom looks like. Everyone pleads out. That's why the Feds have a 97% success rate," I stated.

"That's very true. Speaking of courtrooms, let's take a walk."

We walked to the elevator and exited two floors up. Bob opened the two large wooden panel doors like he was unveiling a surprise gift for us, exposing a complete replica of a courtroom.

"This is our training courtroom. We hold mock trials with a full jury to gather different responses on different arguments," Bob explained.

"Where do all of these people come from?" I asked.

"Oh, we hire them. We have people who do this on the side."

I immediately thought that we could really get up to speed with this setup.

Bob was agreeable to a flat fee, and with the dog and pony show the Government was hosting, we now had ourselves a lead attorney who was ready to take on a trial. We just needed information about the witnesses the Government planned to call to the stand against us.

SETTING THE STAGE

When Pat Malloy listed "blood-swapping" as one of the charges alleged against us, I was shocked; to me, the idea was outrageous. As a company, Kelco processed thousands of policies each year. Taking on the risk of seeking out and acquiring a handful of fraudulent policies through blood-swapping, likely a negligible percentage of our total business, was preposterous. I had heard of such practices within the dreg of companies in the industry, but I made sure that Kelco never engaged in such unnecessary scamming.

Though it seemed preposterous to us, we understood the government's angle, and our only defense against their litany of ingenuine testimonies was to uncover each witness's truth and the leverage the prosecutors were exploiting to elicit their cooperation. Our two private investigators, Don Finch and Jim Starks, proved to be our most valuable team members for this discovery.

While in my office, I called Jim Starks while he was out on the road acquiring evidence for our defense. He answered after a few rings and said, "Keller, I'm seriously thinking about charging you more money."

"What's going on, Jim?" I asked.

"Man, you talk about a weird group. I just met with the Reverend."

"You mean, Chuck Cole?" I asked, shocked.

"Sure do. We met in this old house. I guess that's where they congregate when bringing in new members to his church. I met an insurance guy there, Steven Steirs. Apparently, the Reverend would bring people there to meet Steirs to get insurance on the AIDS patients. He would then sell the policy to anyone in the industry. The insurance agent, Steirs, said he didn't know what the Reverend did with the policy after it had been written, and I think he's telling the truth." Jim said.

"Were they blood-swapping to get the approvals?"

"He didn't mention it, but I think so. Keller, I got to say, you guys dealt with some really sick characters."

"So does American Express," I replied.

"Excuse me?" Jim exclaimed.

"American Express and Kelco deal with thousands of people. The Federal Government selected the bottom of the barrel scumbags for testimonies to make us look bad. The same people dealt with American Express. If someone makes an illegal transaction with an American Express card, does that make American Express a criminal enterprise? No, people commit fraud, but if we didn't participate or even know it was going on, how can the government charge us for that?" I asked.

"I see your point. I will say this. The Feds did a good job of recruiting lowlifes to testify. All of their testimonies are from people who are already facing their own criminal charges. I bet you they're cutting deals to lower their own sentences if they say what the Feds want to hear about Kelco."

"They can't do that!"

"Of course they can, and they wouldn't be the first batch of criminals ever to tell lies. This Fuller character is even worse than the Reverend."

"What did you find out?" I asked.

"I'm not finished yet, but I did track down an investor who bought a two-million-dollar policy from a guy who was Fuller's partner. Apparently, Fuller worked as a phlebotomist for a firm here in Atlanta. This firm performed 'medicals,' basically blood tests, for insurance companies. It seems Fuller switched his partner's blood for healthy blood for the two-million-dollar policy."

"When was this done?" I asked.

"Before Fuller was aware of Kelco, and we can prove that," Jim stated.

"Well, that blows the theory that Kelco orchestrated and taught him to switch blood."

"Yes, Fuller already had this swapping business perfected way before he ever met Kelco."

"What happened with that policy?" I asked.

"Well, the partner died, and the insurance company performed an investigation because they didn't want to cough up the two million bucks. Fuller's scheme got exposed, and this whole activity fell on the firm's shoulders where he was employed."

"Were they sued?" I asked.

"I don't think so. However, Fuller was immediately fired, and I believe he might have been sued personally. The company apparently uncovered a lot of problems. The president of the firm was extremely nervous about my presence there, asking questions and all."

"You went to that company?" I exclaimed.

"Oh yeah. There is a lot more that went on there, more than you can imagine. I believe the owner is afraid that, if Fuller's activity is found out, it could shut down his company. What insurance company would use a medical underwriting firm with a rogue guy like Fuller, who was doing God knows what, swapping blood to get approvals?"

"Did you talk to Fuller?"

"I did. I went to his house. His driveway was full of old cars, an old Mercedes two-seater, an old Corolla, a 1980's Crown Vic...stuff like that. I got the license numbers and ran the plates. They're Fuller's."

"Was he home?" I asked.

"Another guy answered the door and lied to me at first. When I told him I would keep coming back until I talked to him, Fuller finally appeared."

"What did he look like?" I asked.

"He was really short, about five feet tall, a black guy, kind of balding on top, and he wore large frame glasses."

"Was he talkative at all?"

"He was, said he met a black guy who worked for Genesis a couple of years ago at an AIDS fair in Atlanta."

"Genesis was our acquisition arm. We had an office in Buckhead before we shut it down and moved to Kentucky. The guy he met is Sonny Collins."

"The football player from U.K.?"

"Yeah, that's him. He still holds the rushing record here. Sonny was working for Genesis, trying to acquire AIDS policies in Atlanta."

"I've pretty much got enough on this slimeball, Fuller. It seems he has some twenty different credit cards illegally under different social security numbers. He's still an active insurance agent, even after the blow-up at his old office. It's unbelievable!" Jim exclaimed.

"What's the game plan from here, Jim?" I asked.

"I'm going to New York to see the two other blood swappers. I may come back to Atlanta, but I want to go ahead and knock this out."

"You know where to find me, Jim. I'll keep my cell on 24-7 for you. Be safe," I said, ending the call.

Almost immediately after I hung up with Jim, my office phone began to ring. "Hello, Steve speaking," I answered.

"Steve, it's Sonny," Sonny Creed announced.

This fucking guy. I restrained my tone, "Hey, Sonny. What's going on?"

"There's an investigative reporter from the Washington Post who's doing a story on Senators and their children acting as lobbyists in D. C. This report is out to do harm. I need for you to deny our affiliation with everything that is going on, you understand?" Sonny said.

I felt disappointed and annoyed by the request; I thought, *Why the hell would I want to protect this spoiled nepotism brat?* However, I tried to be practical, to move past this man-child and shield myself from any additional heat, so I said, "Look, Sonny, don't worry about it. We'll keep it quiet on this end."

"Man, I really appreciate it. This guy is a pain in the ass."

"I can relate," I replied.

"Thanks, Steve. Goodbye."

I immediately called Ron Kreiter and conveyed the conversation to Ron to be prepared for the *Post's* calls. Within a few hours, the *Post* called, and Ron, who took the call, denied anything being done by Sonny on our behalf. At least that wasn't a lie because, in truth, the Creeds hadn't done anything to help our cause, despite paying them more than a million dollars in fees.

Several days later, Jim Starks called again. I opened the conversation saying, "How's it going, Jim? Did you find Ricketts?"

"I did, but I found his mother first. She was a nice enough lady. She doesn't think much of her son. Apparently, Ricketts adopted a teen-age girl who had AIDS. He sold an insurance policy on the girl and took the girl to Disneyland, but his mother says he spent most of the money on himself. Get this, his mother said she would testify against him. She said, 'He is one big, fat liar, and what he is doing is not right.' She then told me where Ricketts lived. I went to visit him, as well."

"How'd that go?" I asked.

"Ricketts seemed scared to death. I asked him about his relation-ship with Kelco, and he said he really didn't know anybody there. He said he sold some policies through another viatical firm and thinks Kelco bought them secondhand. Ricketts said he dealt with a lot of viatical firms. This guy is really sick, by the way. He claims he's a he-mophiliac. He contracted AIDS through a needle."

"What about his relationship to the other blood swapper, Carmine Carpinone?" I asked.

"He said he doesn't know him. He said it's possible that Carmine may have called him by phone; he's not sure. He didn't know Jeff Full-er. He said the Feds have been to visit him a lot."

"In conjunction with?" I asked.

"He mentioned some other companies, primarily, but I think they may have mentioned Kelco at one of the many interviews. This guy is really out of his mind. He was all over the board – seemed crazy to me. I also think this Carmine Carpinone guy is a loose cannon," Jim stated.

"What do you mean?" I asked.

"He sued his in-laws for a million dollars after falling off their roof that he offered to fix. He's been caught up on charges of insurance fraud, theft, and several other misdemeanors. He is a walking lawsuit waiting to happen."

"Did you talk to him?"

"Yeah, he's a weird-looking fellow."

"How so?"

"Well, for one thing, he looks like he had to cut a hair transplant short. He has plugs in the very front of his head, but nothing on top or in the back."

"Did he offer much information to you?"

"Not much. Of course, he may have been lying. He doesn't know Fuller. He claims to have called Ricketts once but never indicated that there was any business between the two. He verified that he sold policies to Kelco, and he usually talked with Grant about these transactions. He has never met anybody from Kelco."

"How do you feel about the meeting overall?" I asked.

"After I was finished, I felt like I needed to take a shower. This guy was slimy. He will say whatever the Feds want him to say, especially if they have a pending charge hanging over him to bargain with," Jim replied.

"Well, at least we know what we're dealing with."

"Yeah, a bunch of sick bastards," Jim replied.

"You've got that right. You coming back here anytime soon?"

"Heading that way as we speak. My son's got a regional wrestling meet this weekend. I will see you on Monday."

"Jim, great job. Travel safe. Good-bye."

Aside from everything we had done in preparing for this trial, Jim Starks proved to be the most beneficial asset on our team. What Jim was bringing to the table were facts, the truth. Without Jim, we would have never known what we were up against. The more data Jim gathered, the more confident I felt. He already had enough data to vindicate us, and he wasn't even halfway through his list. When it came time for the trial to begin – *The United States of America Vs. Stephen Keller, Grant Sutherlin, Keith Drach, Kelco, and Genesis Mutual* – I felt ready...well, as ready as you can ever be to defend yourself against the might of the most powerful litigative entity in the world.

LET THE SHOW BEGIN

The day of the big show in court finally arrived, and the government playwrights called their first witnesses. I stood alongside Grant and Keith with our team of attorneys, ready to face anything the Government brought forward against us. I had a feeling the Feds lined up their reptile testifiers in descending order, from slimiest to least slimy. The benches within the courtroom behind us were packed with Kelco employees and our families, anxious to defend our livelihoods and integrity.

I couldn't stop looking toward my family, thinking my son needed a dad he could look up to, my wife needed a husband she could count on, my newborn daughter, Sydney, needed a father who would protect her.

A barking bailiff cut through my thoughts, announcing, "The first witness called is Carmine Carpinone, Your Honor."

Two courtroom doors swung open, and the bailiff escorted one of the strangest looking characters I had ever seen.

Carmine wore a tapered suit that seemed to change colors, shifting between green to a turquoise blue as he walked to the witness stand. His hair plugs were grown out and combed from front to back, stopping halfway across his head, exposing his bald scalp. His suit was so tight it restricted the movement of his arms as he walked. His upper torso was grossly out of proportion from his frail lower body, and the tight taper of his suit accentuated the contrast. He wore what looked to be high heel Victoria Secret suede boots, with fur around the top cuffs with his pants tucked into the boots to cap off the look. He reminded me of a character straight out of a Saturday Night Live skit. I watched as the jurors reacted to him, clasping their mouths, or ducking to hide behind other jurors seated on the front row. *I hope the jury recognizes the sleaziness of these characters*, I thought.

While on the stand, Carpinone admitted to lying in front of the

Grand Jury during his testimony. I wanted him charged with perjury and kicked out of the courtroom, but the Judge just let the incident ride and simply said, "Well, don't do that again, Mr. Carpinone."

The Judge's inaction became an embedded concern in my mind as the days of the trial dragged on. If he didn't take exception to the witnesses' lies, I believed it would be impossible to receive a fair hearing. The slow, arduous process of the trial created painfully long, strenuous days. A repetitive theme emerged. The scumbags all got up and recited a well-rehearsed theme, saying, "I sold life insurance policies that I acquired by lying about policy applicants' illnesses on the insurance application."

Our stance in defense was that we had not known that they lied and that the insurance companies chose not to perform any underwriting investigation, which was their responsibility, and when those companies entered into a contract with each of these scumbags, the scum became their burden, not Kelco's. Under the well-defined insurance law, before the new concept of *clean sheeting*, which had yet to become law, a policy under two years old could be contested. The insurance company decided to keep it or not. No law existed at the Department of Insurance that prevented Kelco from trading in such policies.

After several more policy sellers testified, stating the same prescribed theme, it was time for the five-foot-tall phlebotomist from Atlanta, Jeffery Fuller, to enter the witness stand. Jeffery began his testimony by attempting to implicate us in a blood-swapping scheme, for which he had already personally been charged with fraud. With the information that Jim Starks had dredged up, our attorney team discredited him during the cross-examination by producing a paper trail of over ten thousand lies. Fuller admitted to selling some three hundred million dollars in face value of policies while carrying out this scam. He admitted to using twenty different social security numbers and admitted to not paying his taxes for several years.

Given all the facts our team produced of Fuller's personal unlawful activity, it seemed evident that the Government had no interest in pursuing Fuller's admitted illegal acts. It became clear to me that Kelco was the sole target in the Government's crosshairs. Our attorney team informed me that the statute of limitations had been allowed to run out on Fuller's actions because of his agreement to testify against Kelco. Even more disturbing, colleagues from the Life Settlements industry, Phil Loy and Brian Freeman, informed me during the trial that charges had been filed against Fuller for sexual assault where he would perform rectal exams on the policy applicants. Hundreds of claims in Atlanta had been filed against him. News outlets were plastering his picture across televisions and daily papers in Atlanta during our trial, yet his testimony was allowed by the Judge, without exception. As if this trail wasn't corrupt enough, Jim Starks discovered that one of the Lexington prosecutors had contacted an Assistant U.S. Attorney in Atlanta and negotiated a deal to hold off placing further charges against Fuller until after the Kelco trial concluded, intending not to interfere with the state's witness deal that had already been struck to reduce Fuller's upcoming sentence in exchange for his testimony against Kelco. During cross-examination, Fuller admitted that he met with the Feds approximately fifty times to prepare his testimony. While on the stand, his script had been well-rehearsed, and he tried his best to implicate Grant and me in conversations about blood-swapping activities on policies. I never knew Jeffrey Fuller, and I would never knowingly have a business relationship with this toad. Our team knew his entire testimony was a lie but proving that was difficult while the jury listened to him drag our names through his muck.

Over the following weeks, as the trial dragged on, more witnesses from Kelco were called. Ex-employees were called. Some were disgruntled employees who had been fired, and they seemed to utilize the trial as their chance to impose vengeance. Other employees called to the stand, who had been with the company for the longest, accounted for the truth, thankfully. One woman, Ann Dileo, who after her employment at Kelco later went on to become the CEO of Alpha Capital, told the court that her attorneys in New York had said to her that Kelco and the industry at large was a legal and legitimate business. Before her testimony, Ann had pled guilty to personal fraud charges brought against her, and we learned that she was a member of the Witness Security Program and had testified in some five different trials on behalf of federal prosecutors. During each previous trial, she had followed a predictable script that the U. S. Attorneys provided her that day. In return, Ann not only got out of jail early but also avoided altogether her previous penalty of paying restitution.

Alpha Capital was set up to trade in contestable policies. Kelco represented a small fraction of the policies Alpha bought and resold to individual investors. The relationship with Dileo had been formally dissolved some two years before the Government's raid. However, our past business relationship, considering her admission of fraud, reflected negatively during our trial.

I was no attorney, but it seemed logical that our defense team of attorneys should have called witnesses to the stand who played an integral role in Kelco's business transactions. I asked Bob Tarun why he refused to call our Pittsburgh attorney, Wayne Holcombe, to testify. Bob responded, "Wayne was not on the front end of the transactions." In my opinion, Bob's response was ridiculous. Wayne had handled each transaction and even advised us about which policies to stay away from due to the potential risk of a policy being contested by insurers. Wayne not only gave legal advice to Kelco but also performed our back-office operations. I understood that one cannot be convicted of a federal law if that person was given advice from an attorney and then carried out the actions according to the legal instructions. In legal terms, it was called mens rea which determines the defendant's mindset and whether a defendant knowingly or willingly committed illegal activity. Of the thousands of policies transacted by Kelco, every transaction was thoroughly evaluated for legality through Wayne Holcombe's attorney firm based in Pittsburgh.

Even more frustrating was the fact that Bob Tarun decided to call only three witnesses in our defense, Ron Kreiter, who knew better than anyone how diligently we had attempted to follow the law; Michelle Kuykendall, one of Kelco's earliest hires during the days when Grant and I were first building the business; and Mitchell Cain, the Head of Facilities at Kelco. While Mitchell could attest to how he was treated the day of the raid, there was absolutely no link between the issues in question at the trial and Mitchell's role within the company. Also not called were the private investigators from Lexington or Carmel, Indiana. None of the investment banks were called, such as Lloyds of London, to testify to the validity of the transactions. No one from the Insurance Department was called; George Nichols was not called, none of the other buyers of contestable policies, nor any other insurance companies. We could have called a hundred people, but our lead defense attorney, Bob Tarun, chose to call only three.

As the trial trudged on, my fears grew; I didn't know what to do to clear my name. The sheer volume of the Government's case against us felt like a mountain of rubble, and we were living under it, trying to catch a breath. They piled on for weeks, and on a meager budget, our defense team of attorneys seemed buried too, defenseless and eager for the trial to come to an end. As the trial finally neared its end, my worst fears were realized.

AN UNEXPECTED VISIT

It felt like dynamite going off right next to our ears the morning the swamp boss paid us a visit. After a recess for lunch, the attorneys, family, and friends looked out the windows toward the street and noticed a shocking sight for the small city of Lexington. A Secret Service motorcade had parked in front of the District Court building, lining the entire street, with police cars blocking the road and officers rerouting traffic. Secret Service agents with coiled wires dangling from their ears, wearing dark suits and sunglasses, stood guarding the courthouse steps. My attorneys notified me that the United States Attorney General, Virgil Bodine, had called a special recess to speak with our Judge privately in chambers before delivering the jury instructions for deliberation on our verdict in the following days. We were not the only ones to witness this spectacle. The entire jury was at recess for lunch, surely taking in the same scene, and we all witnessed the government's might in clear view.

My mind flashed back to the conversation in the hallowed halls when Senator Creed told me about the Singing Senators and his close ties to the U.S. Attorney General Virgil Bodine. My heart fell to my feet. After my final conversation with the Senator and his son, I knew Virgil Bodine was not making an appearance on my behalf. I then remembered with precision the words Jerry Wendorf of ATLAS GLOBAL said to me after I rejected his offer to buy out Kelco: "Do you have any idea how big we are, young man? You're about to find out." I reflected on Senator Creed's words when he told me about his driver: "He did the time and kept his mouth shut. I suggest you do the same." The "pay to play" meeting in D.C. came to mind, and I could see Troy Anders's smiling, predatory face as he said, "Have you learned your lesson yet, Steve?"

Staring dumbfounded at the Secret Service motorcade, as U.S. Attorney General Bodine met with the Judge privately, I knew the verdict of our trial had already been decided.

During the final days, I focused on the demeanor of Judge Forester after the visit with Bodine. He seemed more severe and callous toward the defense. It seemed like a chain reaction began to unfold in the courtroom. First, a woman seated on the jury whom our defense team felt was sure to be siding with us suddenly became ill. The Judge insisted that she be replaced with a reserve juror, an alternate. A single woman who worked at the Equine Research Center, Ms. Leer, stood up from the court bench and walked toward the jury box, passing Roberta Bottoms.

I watched her literally wink at Roberta Bottoms, the Postal Service's lead agent, driving the indictment and federal charges against us. I suddenly felt sick to my stomach.

After the Bodine visit, we felt tied to the tracks as a 130-car train came barreling our way; it seemed that anytime the Prosecution couldn't produce solid evidence, some was provided or made up. I felt like I was experiencing a terrifying show, like something at a three-ring circus, only Grant, Keith, and I were the lions in the cage and couldn't stop the show. Finally, as the trial came to an end, the Judge issued the jury instructions, over fifty pages of instructions to consider while in deliberation.

After two days of deliberations, the jury returned a verdict to the Judge. He asked Grant, Keith, and I to approach the bench. He then announced loudly so that our families and everyone sitting within the courtroom could clearly hear the verdict. He said, "The jury finds Kelco, Genesis Life, Stephen Keller, Grant Sutherlin, and Keith Drach...*guilty.*" *My legs suddenly felt weak. The Judge continued speaking, and it seemed like I heard his words underwater, unable to clearly focus. The next words I could comprehend were "conspiracy to commit mail fraud." Mail fraud? I am being found guilty of mail fraud? No insurance laws were ever discussed in this trial courtroom. How can this be? A company that dealt solely in the business of insurance, regulated by state law, without any violation of federal law presented in court, has been found guilty of conspiracy to commit mail fraud?*

In my shocked state, I heard the Judge say, "Mr. Keller, the Court sentences you to serve a term of no less than one hundred and sixty-eight months in Federal Incarceration."

I nearly dropped to the floor, stunned. It felt like a slow-moving nightmare, unreal, yet I couldn't wake up. I turned my head to meet my father's heartbroken gaze. He slowly shook his head in disbelief. His image mirrored the shock I was experiencing internally. It broke me to see my father witness his son's life collapse in front of his eyes. How helpless he must have felt. As a father myself, I felt a deep pang of guilt about my own children. Who would protect them? Would Tammy have to raise them on her own? This isn't right. This can't be possible.

The Judge continued, addressing Grant, "Mr. Sutherlin, the Court sentences you to serve a term of no less than one hundred fifty-one months."

I tried to make eye contact with Grant, but he wouldn't meet my gaze. Seeing him receive such an outrageous sentence crushed me. Before Kelco was even a real business, he had been my first hire, back when he was only eighteen as an intern. Over the ten years since we first met, I had watched him grow up, and he had become my best friend, my best man at my wedding. Together, along with our gray-haired CFO, Keith, we built Kelco from the ground up and revolutionized an industry.

In the courtroom, at that moment, it felt like I was dragging him underground with me. I knew exactly where his parents were sitting; I could not look at them, especially after witnessing my father's reaction. I felt helpless and so sorry that I could not have done more. None of us deserved this. It wasn't right, but there wasn't a damn thing we could do about it. Not anymore. But I couldn't help feeling that I had failed him.

The Judge addressed Keith next, saying, "Mr. Drach, the jury recognizes your lack of involvement with the sellers of policies and, therefore, offer a reduction in the counts of which you have been found guilty. The Court sentences you to serve a term of no less than seventy-eight months."

The Judge then banged the gavel, issuing our sentences into law. Before dismissing the court, he announced, "It is the Court's decision that the sentences shall be postponed until pending appeals are heard by the Sixth Circuit Appellate Court."

The Judge then left the courtroom, and I sat heavily in a chair behind the defense table. I looked over to the gallery in the courtroom and found Tammy. Tears streaked her face as she was being hugged and consoled by her mom and my family members, as her world as she knew it ended. I dropped my head, unsure of what else to convey other than utter shock, disappointment, and shame for putting them in this position. I had done my best, but that didn't matter. I failed them too.

KELLER:

Looking back, I didn't know enough then. I was like a deer in the headlights, staring into the unstoppable locomotive that had been barreling toward us. During the entire trial, there was no mention of the McCarran Ferguson Act, that states, "A company dealing in the business of insurance, and regulated as such, shall be shielded from the Federal Commerce clauses, thus giving jurisdiction to the states, where the states regulate and possess laws for the business of insurance." This is a Federal Act. The bottom line is that this case should have never been brought forth in federal court because all the laws and regulations reside in the states, not the Federal Government. I did not know the laws that could have defended me while standing before Judge Forester. Even more troublesome was that none of my criminal defense attorneys seemed to know anything about insurance law or the McCarran Ferguson Act either.

After our conviction and sentencing, a prosecutor from Washington, D.C., who had joined the Prosecution table mid-trial, Karen Taylor, revealed her real role in our trial. She was known as "The Forfeiture Queen." Her task was to force the forfeiture of our assets and facilitate the seizure for the Government. I had no idea how this process worked. I didn't know that a jury could decide on the forfeiture of assets. I didn't know that one could request a separate hearing and that my wife could contest assets owned by joint custody, and I'm astounded that my attorneys didn't know either. Ms. Taylor used the conspiracy to commit mail fraud conviction as grounds to charge us with money laundering. This enabled her to take our property, cash, and any accounts we had in the banks: everything. I didn't even consider such a possibility at the time. I later learned that this saddling of one conviction to make a claim for another is a trick the federal system uses to seize assets, a practice that amounts to billions seized each year, filling the government coffers. The explanation used to substantiate the money-laundering charges against us was that if you placed one dollar that came from fraudulent practices into a bank account that held one hundred million dollars, it was then impossible to determine and differentiate the single fraudulent dollar. Therefore, the Government was justified in taking every dollar.

What I had accumulated in eight years, my home, my cars, my bank accounts, my private jet, my business, and every policy owned by the company of Kelco became the property of the United States Government, including the contestable policies the Prosecution claimed were fraudulent. Those same "fraudulent" policies were later listed on the insurance policy market and sold. Who bought the majority of Kelco's policies? our competitors, most notably the competitor who attempted to buy out Kelco and had been rejected — Atlas Global.

PART FOUR
ON A WING AND A PRAYER

A NEW WORLD

The decision to run had been made in the dark hours between midnight and dawn, when fear outweighs reason and survival trumps everything else. Now, as the plane touched down on the runway in Panama City with a jolt that sent my stomach lurching, I wondered if I'd traded one prison for another. Through the window, I watched uniformed guards carrying rifles and machine guns, their military emblems glinting in the tropical sun. Military vehicles with official insignia patrolled the tarmac. The sight would have rattled me more if I hadn't already witnessed similar displays during my travels through South America and Europe. Those cold, callous greetings had become familiar territory. However, this time was different. This time, I wasn't Stephen Keller, CEO of Kelco, traveling on business. This time...I was a fugitive.

My focus shifted to the next hurdle: Customs. *One step at a time*, I told myself, *just like closing a deal, one step at a time.*

We filed off the packed jet and entered what looked like a mid-sized regional airport back home. The modern interior struck me as a sharp contrast to the military muscling we'd witnessed minutes earlier. Moving with the flow of foot traffic toward baggage claim, I kept pace with the crowd, my mind racing through contingencies. *What if they have our names? What if the Feds already reached out to their authorities? What if this is all a trap?*

Eight toll booth structures spread across the walkway ahead, Immigration agents frantically processing a crowd that belonged in LaGuardia, not Panama. We approached the booth directly ahead. A woman leaned down from her side window to retrieve our single passport. Spanish words flew from the booth like rapid gunfire.

A man behind me, looking more American than Panamanian, detected our struggle with the language. "She wants to know if you have any birth certificates or any other papers for the rest of the group," he translated.

We handed over Cole's birth certificate and mine. Sydney stared at the agent from my arms, her eyes wide with curiosity. *My little girl has no idea we're running for our lives.* The thought broke my heart.

The man interrupted my thoughts when he engaged the agent in animated dialogue and then turned to us, explaining, "She's asking if the baby has any papers."

"No, we don't have any for her," I replied, trying to keep my voice steady.

People piled up behind us like timber jamming a narrow stretch of river. The agent looked perplexed, exhaled dramatically while rolling her eyes, then stamped our papers with resignation. *"Bienvenidos a Panamá."*

Maybe we'd gotten lucky with that particular agent. Maybe the masses pressing behind us had forced her hand. I didn't question why — another bullet dodged; another level cleared in this game of survival. In business, you take the wins when they come, no matter how small; in my post-business state, I would take any victory at all.

Tammy had taken over carrying Sydney as I held Cole's hand, navigating the large walkway toward baggage claim. The native tongue created a constant buzz around us. Cole looked up at me with that innocent clarity only children possess. "Daddy, we're in the Spanish world now!"

I laughed at my four-year-old's blunt assessment, though the words carried more weight than he could know. The kid nailed it. "Yes Cole, we are definitely in the Spanish world."

The carousel spit out our luggage, piece by piece. I stacked smaller suitcases atop the larger wheeled ones, securing everything with elastic bands. At that moment, our entire life reduced to what we could carry, I became convinced that wheeled suitcases ranked among the twentieth century's greatest inventions. As I turned to pull our worldly possessions toward the exit, an older Hispanic gentleman in a three-piece suit materialized before me. He looked out of place among the airport staff.

"Buenas tardes."

"Hello," I responded, my pulse quickening.

"I'm Señor Contreras with Customs. I need to check your baggage. Do you have your declaration form?"

"Yes, sir." I handed it over.

"Please follow me."

Tammy tapped my shoulder as we walked, whispering, "What did you declare?"

"Don't worry – all of it." No room for problems in this country. The last thing we needed was to get caught in a lie over money.

We stopped at what resembled a grocery store checkout stand. The man examined the declaration card without questioning the figure. He must have thought it was a misprint. *Or maybe he just doesn't care.*

His stoic demeanor offered nothing; I volunteered nothing. In negotiations, sometimes silence is your best friend.

"Well, Mr. Keller, you and your family enjoy Panama. Everything is in order here."

"Thank you." We grabbed our bags and headed for the taxi stand.

"Where to?" a cabbie shouted.

"We need to find a hotel. Do you know of any decent hotels in the city?"

"Yes. But it's going to be difficult to find a room with the Centennial."

"The what?"

"It's Panama's Centennial celebration for liberating ourselves from Colombia."

Nobody told me about a celebration! My mind flashed to all the planning, all the preparation, and somehow, we'd missed this crucial detail. "Look, it's late, we've had a long day. I'll tip you well if you can find us a room."

The humidity hit like a physical force, even at eight o'clock at night. The cab looked like Toyota's first attempt at automobile manufacturing – no shocks, no radio, no air. We tried two hotels – both full. Sweat beads covered our faces. Sydney started wailing when we stopped at the third nondescript hotel. This time I accompanied the cabbie, hoping to persuade the clerk. In business, sometimes you have to show up in person to close the deal.

The woman called a resort outside the city. "Yes, the Gamboa Resort has a room for you. It's a little pricey and a bit of a drive," the cabbie relayed.

"Is it a good place?" I asked.

"Oh, yes, sir, very good place," the cabbie stated.

"How far away?"

"Maybe a half an hour."

"Let's go."

Nice became relative. My worst fear was no place to stay, especially with two kids. We'd gone from a mansion in Kentucky to searching for any roof over our heads. As we drove through Panama City, people and cars jammed every inch of space. In certain parts, the city resembled Times Square with its neon lighting, a compact mass of land projecting the image of a major metropolis. However, in the turn-of-a-corner, we would confront evident poverty, people living in shacks. Nonetheless, in this particular part of the capital, affluence reigned. Mercedes and Lexus SUVs appeared as common as any other car. We even passed a Ferrari dealership. *Money flows here, I thought, just like home...just have to figure out how to tap into it.*

The less affluent relied on public transportation: art deco school buses painted in individual Latino abstracts. Some sported chrome wheels and pipes running upward like Mack trucks. Most had musical horns as cacophonic as the traffic itself. Some buses displayed airbrushed murals of famous people. They'd become Panama City's trademark. I even spotted one parked in an office building's entrance-way.

The traffic combined New-York attitude, demolition-derby mayhem, and Indy-500 speed. Lanes seemed to exist as mere suggestions, just a little paint to add atmosphere. Without question, this town possessed some of the world's best drivers. I couldn't imagine such chaos in the States. Our cabbie navigated unfazed, slipping between bumpers, crossing multiple "lanes," exiting onto a road leading away from the city.

The neon lights and constant horn blowing faded behind us. The farther we drove, the darker it grew. Within minutes, I could no longer detect houses or buildings, only pitch darkness. Twenty minutes passed. We came to a red light attached to a standalone pole. Fifty feet behind the light sat a red and white wooden bridge on pontoons, floating on water. The narrow bridge allowed only one-way traffic. The light changed to green and the cabbie crossed. The rumbling wood beneath our tires sounded like a Jenga tower tumbling down. Abruptly the clanking ceased as we transitioned onto the smoothest blacktop I'd experienced since leaving the States.

Within a hundred yards, the driver turned right and began climbing a sizable, precipitous hillside. The well-maintained road wound back and forth, reducing the grade. Someone spent money on this road, someone with influence. At the top, the hill leveled off. Two-story, block-constructed former U.S. military houses sat fifty yards from the road. The manicured grounds looked inviting, even in the darkness. Screen doors indicated no air conditioning, but at this point, a bed and roof looked like paradise.

"Señor Keller, these houses used to be your military houses. I think you can rent them now."

"Is this the hotel?"

"No, but part of the hotel."

Another quarter mile and I began seeing the silhouette of a giant grass hut against backlighting. The cabbie followed the light, driving beneath the large structure. A bellman approached and opened our doors. I stepped out and could hardly believe my eyes. The reception desk sat fifty feet away. Behind it, a huge aquarium displayed giant multi-colored fish patrolling their domain. The enormous lobby wound around to our right, out of view. Bamboo tables dotted the marble floor. Tropical flower arrangements adorned every surface. This place rivaled the hotels we'd left in Cancun.

"Hola! Welcome to The Rain Forest," the desk clerk announced.

From CEO to fugitive in one plane ride, I thought as I signed the register. But at least we're safe...for now.

FIRST CONTACT

Between the weight of the exhaustion and relief of the air conditioning, we slept soundly. For the first time in weeks, I didn't wake up in a cold sweat, wondering, *Is today the day they'll come for me.* Curiosity about our new surroundings caused us all to wake early. As we walked from our room to the dining hall along the suspended walkway wrapping around the hotel's exterior, the view stopped us in our tracks.

"Tammy! We're in Jurassic Park!" I exclaimed.

We looked straight down from our vantage point and saw vast green hues of rain forest stretching as far as the eye could see. Rivers and large bodies of water dotted the landscape miles away. Continuing around the balcony, we spotted a pool resting at a lip on the mountain, some two hundred yards below. We soon realized we were staying in one humongous resort, occupying hundreds of acres in the rain forest. Two miles away sat the Gamboa Restaurant, where boat tours explored the Panama Canal. Behind the main hotel, a world-renowned lepidopterist had set up shop to study the multitude of butterflies. Tours showcased different species in a controlled environment. Other tours featured wildlife from monkeys to boa constrictors.

This is what money buys in Panama, I thought. Isolation, beauty, and most importantly, anonymity.

I found a payphone in the lobby and pulled out the business card David Vonn had given me months ago at a conference. Back then, I was Stephen Keller, CEO of Kelco, and he was trying to sell me on investing in Panamanian teak forests. Now I was calling him as a desperate man looking for any port in a storm.

"Robert Cunningham please. This is Steve Keller."

"One minute."

"Steve, how are you?"

"Fantastic! I'm now in your beautiful country. We're staying at the Gamboa Resort." I tried to keep my voice light, casual.

"Really? That's a nice resort."

"I'm impressed," I stated.

"Let's get together."

"The sooner the better," I replied.

"You want to come to our office?"

"I'm without a car. It would be easier if you came here. That way you could meet my wife and kids."

"I gotta tell you, Steve, I first thought you were some kind of lunatic. I thought this was a joke. You're serious, aren't you?"

"Unfortunately, very serious, Robert, we need help."

"How about eight o'clock tonight?"

"Perfect. I will meet you at the bar area located in front of the stairs behind the reception desk."

"Yes, I know where it is."

"The President of our company might want to join us. He's a great guy. His name is David Vonn. He's very interested in your story."

"That's perfect. I'm interested in what you guys have put together here. You never know what might come of all this." *Always leave the door open for opportunity, I thought, even when you're running for your life.*

"That's true. We'll see you at eight. Goodbye."

It was the first family dinner outing we'd experienced in months without looking over our shoulders. Even the kids showed excitement dressing in their finer casual clothes. After dinner, Tammy and I took the kids to a game room filled with coin-operated games and kiddie rides.

I asked her, "Tammy, at 8:30, will you bring the kids to the patio area in front of the stairs? I think it will become real to these guys that we are a normal family involved in a not so normal circumstance."

"I totally agree. If I can drag them away from the games, we'll be there around that time," Tammy replied, half-jokingly.

I waited at an open table closest to the stairs, offering the best view of the lobby. My mind raced through how much to tell them, what to hold back. In any negotiation, information is power. Give too much away, you lose leverage. Give too little, you lose trust.

Moments later two men walked in together, looking either lost or searching for somebody. One stood over six feet with thick brown hair parted on the side. The other was five-eleven, an older gentleman, balding on top with salt and pepper hair around the sides and back. Both wore jackets and casual button-up shirts with nice slacks. The tall one spotted me by my red polo shirt, which stood out by design. *Always make it easy for the deal to find you.*

"Are you Steve?"

I recognized his voice. "You must be Robert."

The man's face lit up with laughter as we shook hands. "You're finally here. Welcome to Panama!"

"It's good to be here."

"Steve, this is Mr. Vonn, the President of Rain Forest LTD."

"Call me David."

"Thanks for coming, David."

We sat down and for the first time, I began telling our story to a third party — not the whole story, of course — just enough to make them understand the seriousness of our situation without scaring them off. It was like pitching a deal where the product was our survival.

Tammy's timing proved perfect, as always. The elevator doors opened behind our table and Tammy emerged holding both children's hands.

"Sorry we're late. We had to ride the elevator a couple of times. The glass elevator offered too great of a view to ask them to leave sooner," Tammy stated sarcastically.

"You're right on time." I gave Tammy a hug and picked up Sydney. "This is my wife, Tammy, my daughter, Sydney, and my son, Cole."

Cole stuck out his hand to shake with Robert. His boldness surprised both men, and they chuckled in response. *That's my boy, I thought, already knows how to work a room.*

"Well, you certainly are a handsome family," Robert commented.

"How do you like Panama so far?" David asked.

"So far, so good. We've only seen the city driving through it. *This place is great*," Tammy said.

"I've lived here for over ten years now, and I still love it. The people are great," David responded.

"Yes, the people have been really nice to us," Tammy replied.

"We're going to get something worked out for you."

"That would be great. We're on our own here and we need a Visa," I stated, testing the waters.

"Right now, I've got to get these two to bed. Steve, will you be long?" Tammy asked.

"No, I'll be with you shortly," I replied.

"Okay. Goodbye. Nice to meet you."

"Same to you," the two men replied.

After thirty minutes, the two seemed satisfied we were a real family. We had our first contact. They didn't promise anything concrete, but they didn't run away either. In business, sometimes that's all you need to start building something.

My phone rang early the next morning. "Hello."

"Yes, Mr. Keller. This is the front desk. I wanted to let you know that we have two large groups arriving here in two days. The hotel will need every room. I have a reservation for you downtown. I'm sorry about this," the hotel clerk stated.

"No problem. We thank you for your assistance," I responded. Paradise is always temporary, I thought.

I wasn't ready to move from Gamboa, but I never would be. Any move meant a downgrade. For the next two days we lived like they were our last on earth. We packed in as much with the kids as possible. On the last day, we left our bags at the bell stand and took a trolley to the resort's remote restaurant by the Canal tours. After a fresh seafood lunch, I ventured over to the small, open-bow boats.

"How much are the tours?" I asked a boat captain.

The man looked at my family and smiled. "For you, ten dollars."

"Kids, let's go tour the Panama Canal!"

After securing life vests on everyone, we were soon speeding past giant ships that seemed to crawl along the Canal. Our little boat looked like a gnat beside the large vessels. As we traveled across this vast, man-made phenomenon, this miracle of engineering, it seemed impossible that humans had achieved this. The Canal had many coves and areas accessible only by boat. We ventured into a few, gliding across the glass-smooth surface.

"If you have time, señor, I can take you to Monkey Island."

"What is Monkey Island?"

"When the Canal was flooded, several mountains became isolated. One mountain contained monkeys. They are still there, trapped by the water."

"Let's go!"

In moments, we found ourselves in a large cove that seemed to stretch for miles. The captain stopped at an island, formerly a mountain, and coasted the boat as close as possible to the trees hanging over the water. He began pulling fruit from the trees.

"Is this Monkey Island?"

"No, this is the fruit that they like," he said, grabbing a large green growth from a tree. "We take the fruit over to their island to bring in the monkeys."

After collecting sufficient fruit, he sped off to an island located less than a minute away. As we approached the giant mountain that shot straight up almost out of sight, the captain killed the engine and coasted to a tree reaching down to meet the water. The captain grabbed a branch and started making a sucking sound through puckered lips, like blowing kisses.

He held a piece of fruit in the air. A large, dark-colored monkey with a white stripe down his long tail and a white face seemed to jump from the mountain's pinnacle to the captain's tree. He picked the fruit from the captain's hand and began devouring it like he'd just come off a restricted diet. Soon Cole was managing the feeding. I held Sydney in a bear hug while she reached out for the monkey to join the action. I placed in her hand a piece of the elongated fruit that resembled a pepper. She stuck out her hand with the fruit to feed the monkey, watching intently with her big blue eyes, working her pacifier overtime. The monkey came nearer and took the fruit from her hand, Sydney's eyes never leaving him.

The monkey's interpretation of Sydney's pacifier chewing was apparently offensive. Within milliseconds, the monkey turned violent. He showed razor-sharp teeth the size of a medium dog's and wound up his free hand like he was going to throw a punch. He swung his arm toward Sydney's face. I pulled Sydney away to dodge the monkey's hand. His claws missed her face but landed on her nylon vest, ripping it open with the razor-sharp claws. The monkey let out a shrill scream at Sydney. I freed my right arm, preparing to punch the monkey if he made another move toward us. In his fury, he decided to scurry back up the tree. Sydney and I had enough of monkeys.

"Let's get out of here!" I shouted. "We're in the rain forest, not the zoo."

Even paradise has its dangers, I thought as we sped away. Just when you think you're safe, something comes out of nowhere to remind you that you're not.

CONCRETE JUNGLE

A cab dropped us off at a busy hotel at the corner of a congested intersection. The building was old but still in demand from transient business traffic. The small lobby had only one clerk catering to the constant flow. We got a room I seriously doubted would have been rented had the hotel not experienced overflow capacity. The large room consisted of two attached bedrooms with a small kitchen and washroom. It also had an old, decorative bricked balcony. An antiquated television set occupied one room. The carpet, bedspreads and pictures on the wall looked at least twenty years old. Coming from the Gamboa Resort, this place had the feel of a cage in a concrete jungle. From penthouse to crack house, I thought. The trajectory of my life is looking grim.

Our room sat on the eighth story. The balcony off the front entrance overlooked a restaurant. Trees and umbrellas were visible on the ground floor. Noise from the restaurant traveled up to our room like the receiving end of a megaphone.

Packing and unpacking luggage had become a tedium for both of us. Tonight was no exception. We only unpacked some of the luggage. Maybe it was our subconscious desire to leave this particular cage. Never get too comfortable, I thought. *Always be ready to run.*

Leaving would have to wait. We needed diapers and other supplies, available only at the grocery store one block away. People crawled the downtown area like ants at a picnic. I carried Sydney in her backpack and Tammy carried Cole. We managed to reach a two-lane road that looked to be one of the main arteries downtown. People lined both sides of the street, three or four deep. We could see the grocery store on the other side. It was a good-sized store, larger than most of our supermarkets but smaller than our mega-marts. We darted across the parade line and made it to the store. Guards stood in front brandishing AK-47s. The overthrow of Noriega had extinguished the previous small military presence and created a robust, frankly, intimidating industry: Private Security Service. Every business seemed to retain such services. Ironically, the presence of uniformed men brandishing guns surprisingly brought a sense of calm and safety I hadn't experienced in large U.S. cities. No one was going to get out of hand with these guys present. Armed guards at grocery stores, this is what happens when the system breaks down, when trust evaporates. Disillusioned as I was with home and our overwhelming corruption, I thought, *Maybe we're not so different after all.*

Leaving the grocery store, we noticed what looked like a carnival atop an adjacent parking garage. Four stories high, a Ferris wheel lit up and attracted the children's attention.

"We'll try this tomorrow," I suggested.

We made it back to our cage in the concrete jungle and unloaded the kids and groceries. It felt like we were living in the antithesis of the Gamboa Resort. The horns blowing, the restaurant's clinking of dishes and loud conversations from patrons below made for a restless night. We were infinitely more comfortable in the rain forest than this concrete jungle we now inhabited.

The next day we did what anybody on the run would do without a car. We rode the Ferris wheel. Sometimes the best *reconnaissance comes from unexpected places.* When the Ferris wheel reached its peak, you could see a vast swath of the city. We rode it five or six times, taking in our surroundings. The kids loved it. It felt like the only way we could gather our bearings and see the city without transportation.

From up high, I felt myself surveying Panama City, defaulting to my CEO tendencies. I could see the flow of commerce, the patterns of wealth, the places where deals were made. Even as a fugitive, I couldn't stop thinking business.

Living in the concrete jungle for a week, we began to feel cagey or somewhat peaky, like a camper who's been bit by mosquitoes too many times, perhaps early-onset malaria. The noise level seemed to intensify daily as more people gathered in the city, as more parades passed through. People flew in from other countries and drove in from all regions throughout Panama.

I made a call to the only contact we had.

"Robert Cunningham speaking."

"Robert, Steve Keller. Where can we go to get the hell out of this city, and particularly, this hotel? We are feeling rattled."

"There is a resort about forty minutes away where a lot of the city folks go called Corona."

"Like the beer?"

"Exactly. It's on a beach. They have an old golf course, pool area and some other stuff. Right now, the rooms are half price because everybody is coming to the city for this weekend's celebration."

"That's perfect. Fifty percent off to boot? We're there. Call me on the cell phone if you need me. I'll be back when all these people leave."

"They should be gone in one more week. I'll find somewhere more manageable for you to go when you come back."

"Okay, Robert. That sounds great. I'll talk to you later."

Tammy and I walked across the street from the hotel to a car rental business. Tammy had a credit card, but I knew if we used it the Feds would track us as quickly as the card was swiped. *Every transaction leaves a trail. Every piece of plastic is a breadcrumb leading back to you.*

We walked into the chained-off lot containing various cars and selected a Ford Bronco.

"Hola, may I help you?" a dark-haired man asked.

"Yes. I need to rent a car for a week."

"No problem. Do you have a license and credit card?"

"A United States license and we'd rather pay cash."

"Okay. But I have to keep the credit card, you understand."

"Look. I have a problem with the credit card company. Here's a hundred-dollar bill. Do not run that credit card. Do we understand each other?"

" Sí, señor!"

"I will pay cash when I return. Do we have a deal?"

"Yes, sir," he said as we shook hands.

Everything has a price in Panama, I mused. just like back home.

You just have to know how to negotiate.

Soon we were parking the truck on the curb of our cagey hotel. I loaded the truck while Tammy watched the kids. Tammy had to drive. I couldn't risk a small traffic violation revealing my status. Tammy attacked the traffic like a pro. Soon, we escaped the city and reached a remote area offering us a piece of sanity.

We spent the week in the Corona area. Since we had a car, we ventured out to see the countryside. We toured a development of houses in the mountains. The area was beautiful and diverse. The Corona resort resembled a rustic country club, no one lived out here to work. I had to get back to the city and get established. We couldn't just keep floating from hotel to hotel. The one thing we missed from our previous life was some semblance of routine. Even when running, I needed something to run to.

FINDING OUR FEET

In a week, Robert managed to locate a private hotel set up more like an apartment. It was a standalone building owned by a local family. The owner's daughter had recently divorced and was now calling the hotel home. She had a son Cole's age. The woman became good friends with us, particularly with Tammy, and I was happy for her to have a friend she could confide in about her current situation.

The hotel had a pool area on the roof. We would often hang out with the newly divorced woman, Selene, and our children would play together. It was here I met a good friend of hers, Manuel Sanchez. Manuel was a ship captain whose job was escorting massive ships through the Panama Canal. The Panama Canal employed nine thousand people. The ship captains occupied the top rung of the ladder. Their income averaged around three hundred thousand a year. On top of this, Manuel's wife was a doctor.

I was looking for a business opportunity. Manuel was looking for a venture that would increase his wealth and ultimate retirement. He was infatuated with business, and business was my favorite topic. I found my predicament the ultimate test for an entrepreneur. *Dropped in the middle of a country where I know no one; I don't speak the language; and no one can know my background. Can I still make it? Can I still build something from nothing?*

I constantly studied the culture and evaluated the opportunities in this small, tropical country. I learned more about the teak lumber business from Manuel than from the reforestation company. Manuel had been investing in forestland in Northern Panama for years. The reforestation companies were all good sources of supply. I was ready to purchase teak cutting and molding machinery from Taiwan. I was pleased at how much cheaper these were than I'd imagined.

The plan was simple enough. A worldwide shortage of teak existed. The forests of Central and South America had long since lost most of their teak trees. Burma had been virtually clear-cut of the valuable timber, and other

Asian countries were cracking down. Teak remained available from Panamanian forests with more harvestable over the next decade. The thing to do was position the new company as the source for quality teak planking for yachts. I didn't know if I would get rich selling teak to opulent yachtsmen, but no doubt a good living existed there. The investor-base all guided ships through the Canal. It made sense to me. *Find a need and fill it, I thought, Business 101, whether you're a CEO or a fugitive.*

But before pursuing this, I had to find a way to set up shop for my family. Rome wasn't built in a day, but living out of hotels with a family was getting old. While sitting beside the pool, my phone rang. The ID registered David Vonn. I hit the send button.

"Hello."

"Hello, Steven?"

"Yes, David."

"Are you busy right now?"

"I'm sitting at the pool at the moment, watching our kids."

"I want to bring you to our office. Can you be ready in, say, thirty minutes?"

"Is this formal?"

"I would wear a sports coat," he replied.

"Okay. I'll see you in thirty minutes. Goodbye."

"Who was that?" Tammy asked.

"David. He wants me to go to his office. He's got something cooking. He asked me to wear a sports coat."

"Okay. Take your phone."

"As always." I gave Tammy a kiss and waved at the kids. They were too busy splashing around with their new friend to pay much attention.

I waited in the small lobby for the large Land Cruiser to pull up. From private jets to borrowed rides, I thought, nonetheless, a deal is a deal, no matter how you get there.

Within fifteen minutes, we arrived at David's office. He introduced me to some of the workers there. Most of the staff had gone for the day or traveled to a remote location. David began pulling out large schematics of professionally drawn maps displaying thousands of acres of teak forests for which Reforestation LTD was responsible.

"Mr. Keller, the reason I brought you here is to show you our operation. We have been extremely successful. I have forty-eight full-time employees at this office. We have over three hundred maintaining the teak plantation."

"Where is this area located on the map?" I asked.

"Right next to Colombia. I travel there by helicopter. The reason I brought you here today is I'm afraid that this company is growing beyond my ability to manage alone. I wanted to see if you would be interested in becoming the President of Operations."

Even in exile, opportunity can find you if you're open to it, I thought. "I'm still getting a handle on this industry, and I've got a lot more to learn. But if you will work with me, yes, I'm very interested," especially since this was my first and only job offer.

"Well then, I have to talk to my investors. They all live in Europe. I will talk to them next week."

"That sounds great. Where's Robert?" I asked.

"He flew some investors to see the operations in the area I just showed you near Colombia."

"Do you do that often?" I asked.

"Yes. If investors want to see the product, we take them into the jungle," David stated. "Hey Steve, why don't we all go to dinner tonight? Bring Tammy, and I will bring my girlfriend, Cecillia."

"I'll have to see if I can get a babysitter tonight. I think the girl whose dad owns the hotel will watch our kids. She has a nanny living with her as well."

"You know, Steven, speaking of Robert, I'm a little worried about him."

"What do you mean?"

"We've been out of touch with him since... three days ago." David placed his hand on his chin and stared at the ground.

"Has this happened before?"

"Not for this long. Between you and me, Steve, I'm worried."

"Well, maybe he just had mechanical trouble. Try not to think the worst."

"Yes, you're right. I'll be by to pick you up with Cecillia, around eight. Call me if you have a problem with the babysitter."

"Okay, and David — thank you."

Something's wrong, I thought as I left. In business, when communication stops, it's never good.

WHEN THE SKY FALLS

Tammy and I secured a babysitter. Selene's nanny was more than glad to look after the kids. In fact, she had a small party planned for the three. Cole loved going there due to the many toys Selene's son possessed. At 7:30 the phone rang. The phone registered David.

"Hello, David, Steve here."

"This is Cecillia, David's girlfriend." She sounded frantic. I could tell from her voice she was troubled. "David can't make it tonight. He just got a call. Robert's helicopter crashed in the jungle. David flew out there to look for him," Cecillia stated in a distressed voice.

My stomach dropped. "How many were on the helicopter?"

"Six, including the pilot."

"Please call me the minute you know something."

"Okay, Mr. Keller, I will. Goodbye."

Days passed after that call without new information regarding the accident. The waiting reminded me of those days after the raid, not knowing what would happen next or who would potentially turn on us. On Monday evening, my phone rang. It was David.

"Hello, Steve here."

"Steven, this is David."

"David, what's happened?"

"We found Robert. He's alive. I'm at the St. Marie Hospital with him. Why don't you come down here? I need to talk to you."

"I'll be right there. Goodbye."

Hurriedly, I said, "Tammy, they found Robert. He's at the hospital. It sounds bad. David wants me to go there now."

"I'm going with you," Tammy replied.

"Okay. Selene asked if Cole could come up and play with her son. I'll ask if she wouldn't mind for her nanny to watch Sydney."

"Make the call and let's go."

I arrived at the hospital, apprehensive about what I was walking into. The smell of disinfectant and fear hung in the air, I found David talking with two other gentlemen dressed in suits. There were others waiting to see Robert as well. David had his back to us but noticed everyone glancing at us when we walked in the room. He turned his head and caught a glimpse out of the corner of his eye, stopping dead in his thought, his finger frozen pointing at the two suits. Slowly, he turned around and smiled as if he'd just seen his long-lost friend.

"Steve and Tammy, thanks for coming. Robert's doing okay, but he is really lucky."

"What about the rest of them?"

"They were not so lucky."

"All of them?"

"Yes, I'm afraid so – no survivors."

Five people dead, I thought. I couldn't help but think about their families, perhaps thinking through all of the anxiety I was feeling for the family I'd dragged down into exile with me. Somehow, I also jumped to thinking about all the families we had tried to help with our viatical policies. *Just like with the policies we traded, these victims are just numbers until you know them, until you see the faces.*

David introduced us to some of Robert's family. While we made small talk, David leaned over and said under his breath, "Steven, can I see you for a minute?"

We walked over to the other side of the room where no one was sitting.

"This event is the worst thing that's ever happened to me and this company. I'm... I'm... I don't know what to do!"

I recognized the panic in his eyes. The same look I'd had when the Feds raided Kelco – when the world collapses and you don't know which way is up.

"What are you talking about, David?"

"One of the women on that helicopter is from Texas. She worked for a newspaper. Her family is well off. I have already had attorneys calling the office."

"Where were the rest of the people from?"

"Another woman and two men were from Europe. The pilot was

from here."

"What have you told the attorneys?"

"Nothing – I haven't taken their calls."

"That's good, but you have to confront them soon," I responded.

"I'm scared," David declared.

I can empathize, I thought. "Was this your helicopter?"

"Yes."

"Okay. Get a hold of your attorneys and draft a suit against the helicopter company. Next, I want you to call the attorneys and tell them everything. Invite them into the lawsuit. If they are with you, they can't be against you. In America we say a good offense is the best defense. If you don't do this, they are going to eat you alive. The American legal system is brutal."

"That's one hell of an idea. I'm following you."

"Hey guys, get over here." He motioned for the two men in the suits. "This is Mr. Keller. He's the man I have told you about. Hopefully, he will be on board soon."

"Nice to meet you. I'm George and this is Ortega. We are David's business partners."

I reiterated the plan I had just conveyed to David. The two listened intently, nodding their heads up and down. I finished, explaining, "Control the narrative, or it controls you."

A nurse emerged from the ICU ward. "Is there a Mr. Keller here?"

I stopped the conversation and turned to the lady, surprised.

"Yes, I'm Steve," I replied.

"Robert would like to see you," the lady responded.

I went back to where Robert's bed was located. It was a giant hallway with curtains separating the few patients in ICU. My mind expected the worst. All in all, the picture wasn't nearly as bad as the horror I'd painted in my mind. One eye was badly bruised. The black, yellowish tint ran down his right cheek. His left leg was elevated in a harness and both arms were bound with enormous wraps.

"Robert, you look like you had a rough night!" I stated jokingly, trying to lighten the mood.

Robert's head turned to meet me. "Steve, I'm screwed up my friend.

I think my back is shot. I feel like every bone in my body is busted."

"You are lucky to have made it. What the hell happened?"

"I cannot tell you. I was unconscious for days, lying across a tree in the jungle. By the grace of God, David found me, or I would still be out there. I don't remember going down. One minute I'm talking to the clients, the next moment I'm here, screwed up. I don't even know if I can walk again. Those poor people...They were a nice group. I had known that pilot for years."

"Robert, I'm here for you if you need me. When you get out, I can help you."

"Screw it. I'm finished. I'm moving to Europe when I'm able, physically. I'm finished." He turned his head and stared at the wall. He took a deep breath. "Oh, that even hurts. I must have broken every fucking bone in my body."

"Thank you, Robert, for all your help. Just know if you need anything, I'm a phone call away."

"Listen pal, here's what you do. You enjoy that family and your wife. Enjoy every minute like it's your last. Don't miss a moment with them. Your family is your heartbeat. Don't miss a beat! You hear me?"

"I do, Robert." I replied. Perhaps because I did not know this man particularly well, perhaps because I knew I had been called in more to protect his business interests than as a friend, his words struck a nerve; it seemed personally important to him that he impart this wisdom on me. *A man lying broken in a hospital bed, telling me what I should have known all along, I thought. Maybe that's what it takes; maybe you have to lose everything to understand what really matters. I sure hope that's not true.*

"Sir, I'm going to have to ask you to leave," the nurse stated. "He needs rest."

"Take care of yourself, Steve."

"Robert, thanks for everything. I'm here for you."

"Goodbye."

A NEW PERSPECTIVE

Over the next couple of weeks, David was scrambling. Articles surfaced about the crash in small blogs of European newspapers. David needed me more than ever. No CEO is ever prepared for such pandemonium. There was never a college class for crisis management. If a CEO makes it through such a fire and lives another day, only then will such a person truly be able to meet adversity without a flinch. I had stood in those flames, and now I was watching David smoldering in a similar fire. But given my current situation, I couldn't save him.

Too many eyes focused on his company after the crash. I had to remain invisible. My association with David could ratchet the flames even higher. News media could really have a field day learning about my association with a firm that would soon be the focus of a tragic accident. The story would be spun a thousand ways before printing. By the time the article would be ready for press, I could imagine I would be listed as the one flying the helicopter. *Not a good look for me or for David's company.*

Panama had two seasons: rainy and not so rainy. In the wintertime, it rained harder in one day than most states in the U.S. would experience in a season. The good thing about the rain was that it would usually come in the morning and finish before noon. David didn't want to lose me, but his firm was under the microscope. He couldn't bring me into his operation at this time.

I was housed in a vacant bottom floor of a two-story building down the street from David's office. CAT5 cables had been run into the building from David's office to hook up my computer. I spent my days in the vacant room where one desk with my computer was all that sat in the large empty space. I tried to go online and entice people to invest in the Reforestation program. I approached expatriates and Europeans but to no avail.

Most buildings in Panama had bars over the windows. This building was no exception. This particular morning, I looked through the windows, wondering if the bars were a premonition of my future lot in life. *Was this my future view?* I stepped back and asked myself where I was now. *What's the difference? I'm looking through this view now.*

I couldn't get anything going business-wise from a hole in the wall with a computer. Who was I kidding? All I was doing was going through hollow motions, a semblance of my former life. David's problems weren't going to resolve themselves anytime soon. I had been through that exercise of futile optimism. I rode that optimism into the ground with Kelco. I had to find a way to survive, and I couldn't begin to throw a life vest to David when I was already lost at sea. I gazed out through the bars. The rain began. "Like tears from above," I told myself, giving voice to my feelings about my own fall from grace. I suppose I felt sorry for myself, but even that made me feel guilty because I knew what I was dragging Tammy and the kids through. At that moment, I thought about the offer from that asshole at AT-LAS GLOBAL, *$300 fucking million, and you said 'no' – you greedy asshole.*

I called David's cell phone. "Hello, David speaking."

"David, it's Steve. Can you stop by here for a minute?"

"Sure. What's going on?"

"Oh, I just wanted to see you for a few minutes in person. I need some information. That's all."

"I'll be right down as soon as the rain stops."

"Thank you. Goodbye."

Seldom did I summon David. I had a key to the vacant basement, so we didn't risk being seen together. Soon the rain slacked off to just a mist. A shadow of a man appeared at the front door with an umbrella. I opened the door.

"Hey, Steven, how are you?" he asked as he looked around the room, always seeming amazed that he stuck me in such a setting.

"Well, David, I'm nowhere. I can't just keep hanging out here. I need to get something going. Do you know an attorney I can trust to take care of our situation? I've got to get my family situated."

"Yes, I understand." He looked down at the ground, and I could almost see the disappointment as he realized his problems weren't going away anytime soon, that he wasn't going to realize his desire to bring me into his company. "There is an attorney I know of who has been able to help out some people that came to us wanting to relocate. He's a one-man firm. His name is Rodriguez Molina. His office is located beside the Holiday Inn."

"Can you call him for me?" I asked.

"I don't know him that well."

"Well, I'm going to go see him. Can you get me his number?"

"Sure."

David called his secretary to retrieve the number. "Steven, I'm sorry about all of this. It's just not possible to bring you on with your background and what's going on with our company. You don't know how much I want things to be different," David said.

"Yes, David, I can assure you I do. Look, I may drop by from time to time if that's okay."

"No problem. Call me and let me know when we can go out to dinner. I still want to stay in touch."

"Will do." I shook his hand. "David, thanks for your effort in trying to make things work. Some things are just simply out of our hands."

"Take care my friend. Goodbye."

Another door closing, I thought as he left — *how many more before they're all shut?*

I left the building and flagged down a cab. Luckily, the rain had dissipated. On my way back to the hotel, I made the call to Mr. Molina.

"*Buenos días, señor,* Molina's office."

"Yes, I need to make an appointment to see Mr. Molina."

"Today?"

"Yes, ma'am."

"Today at 2:00 is fine for you?" he asked in extremely broken English.

"Yes. I will be there," I replied without hesitation.

After stopping by the hotel for lunch with Tammy and the kids, I grabbed a cab and arrived at the Holiday Inn. The office building was attached to the hotel but had a completely different entranceway. I took an elevator to the second floor. I opened the large wooden doors and stood in a small reception area with the secretary I had spoken with earlier.

"I'm Mr. Keller, here to see Mr. Molina."

"Yes, sir, follow me." She took me back to what appeared to be the only conference room and offered me some water.

"Thank you."

"Mr. Molina will be here in a moment."

I scanned the room after the receptionist left. I noticed a picture of a Judge Molina. He must have been a father or some family relation. *Family connections, I thought – in Panama, that's currency, just like back home.*

The door burst open and this curly-headed Spanish man, who looked to be in his mid-forties with a short, plump build, came blasting into the conference room like he had just left a dog fight.

"Hola, Mr. Keller," he said in a strong Spanish accent.

"Hello, Mr. Molina," I said, shaking his hand.

"How may I help you?"

We sat down at the conference table, and I began to lay out the whole scenario. After I finished, he ended his last notes and smiled. "Well, Mr. Keller, that's very interesting. Let me think about everything. Can you come back in three days?"

"Yes, sir, I'll be here." I shook hands and left the office.

Three days, just wait three days, I reminded myself. In three days, I'll know if we have a chance or if we need to run again.

"How did it go?" Tammy asked when I returned.

"I'm not sure. I need to take you and the kids with me on Friday. I'm not sure if he was taking me seriously."

THE GRINGO AND THE PIT BULL

Friday at 10:00, my family assembled in the lone conference room. Rodriguez Molina came barreling through the door as he had done on my first visit. This time he stopped in his tracks at the sight of my entire family. He tilted back and his eyes became as wide as saucers. "Mr. Molina, this is my wife, Tammy, my son, Cole, and my daughter, Sydney."

He composed himself and melted away the facade of his business face. "It is very nice to meet you." He stuck out his hand to shake Tammy's.

"Do you have children, Mr. Molina?" I asked.

"Yes, I have a daughter, a little older than your son looks to be and a son about your daughter's age." Mr. Molina sat down at the table with his arms resting on the tabletop, leaning toward us. "So, Mr. Keller, your story is real."

"Mr. Molina, this situation is very real, and we need your help," Tammy pleaded.

Mr. Molina sat back in his chair and folded his hands on his well-fed stomach and began to smile. "You know, Mr. Keller, I thought this was some kind of set up. I thought you were an undercover agent who was wired trying to set me up. You never know in Panama. I can see that you are who you say you are. I'm curious; why me?"

"David Vonn with Rainforest LTD told me that you would be able to assist us. I was associated with his firm, but he is having some troubles now. He referred me to you."

"I can't remember what I did for him. It doesn't ring a bell."

"You want to call him? I have his number."

"No, no, it will not be necessary. What, exactly, do you want, Mr. Keller?"

"We need a Visa or some other documentation that will allow me to work and us to stop relocating constantly."

"We would like to move out of hotels and acquire transportation," Tammy added.

"Okay, okay, I will need to form a company. Tammy, you will be the President. Mr. Keller, your name cannot be anywhere. I will need three officers. They must be Panamanian."

"Where are we going to find those?" I asked.

"Leave it all to me. I will need to pick you up tomorrow night at seven. Would you like to go to dinner? I can bring my wife, and we can visit."

"That would be great," Tammy and I responded.

A company, I thought. Even as fugitives, we need corporate structure. The irony is beautiful.

The next night, Rodriguez arrived promptly. Tammy and I saw him pull up through the glass window of the tiny lobby. A woman stepped out of the green Range Rover. She was as tall as Rodriguez, with a powerful frame and high, wide cheekbones. Her jet-black hair was pulled back into a bun. As is customary of the Panamanians, she did not hold back on the makeup. Her face was striking, and she held a regal air about her. Rodriguez came around to greet us. "Hola, this is my wife, Maria."

After the introductions were out of the way, we loaded into the Range Rover. Rodriguez and I sat up front, and the ladies sat in the back so they could talk. Maria and Tammy hit it off. Both possessed similar personality traits: both ran the households; both were very fashionable; both seemed to have a knack for reading a situation.

As we drove to dinner, Rodriguez made a stop at a two-story duplex. A man was washing a car parked underneath a metal roof structure. As we pulled in the driveway, he turned to us and smiled. He was missing most of his upper and lower teeth. He placed the water hose on the ground and walked toward Rodriguez's door. Rodriguez asked him to sign a paper. "Gracias!" Rodriguez stated. The window rolled up, and we drove away.

"What was that?" I asked.

Rodriguez turned to me, laughing and stated, "That was one of Tammy's board members. He must be on a thousand corporation's boards, and the poor bastard doesn't have a clue that he's on one."

"Why does he do it?"

"He gets checks every month from these companies."

"Doesn't he wonder where this money is coming from?" I asked.

"All he cares about is seeing me come by with papers to sign. He knows if he signs, he gets paid. The man makes a great living," Rodriguez laughed.

"This is all he does?" I asked.

"Yes. I have others I use as well."

"I'm learning," I said.

Rodriguez laughed. "Relax, *gringo*. By Monday we'll have you situated in Panamá."

Every country has a system; I mused with fascination. You just have to learn the rules. Rodriguez knew his country's system well, and once he set himself to a task, he was like a pit bull with a bone that wouldn't let go. He had the corporation complete by Monday morning. Tuesday, he assisted us in opening a bank account, all under the corporation's name. Rodriguez's wife, we found out over dinner, was infatuated with Barbra Streisand, so we affectionately started referring to her as Barbara. It was "Barbara" who took us car shopping. By the end of the day, we drove off the lot in a four-year-old Lexus SUV with low miles. It was black with a light tan interior. The outskirts of the city contained bad roads. A smaller car would have a real short life here. The small SUV would give us enough room to haul the kids' cargo on trips.

A few more calls were made to some of Rodriguez's clients, and we rented an apartment in one of the many towers located near Rodriguez and Barbara's. They insisted we stay close in case any emergencies arose. The following week we moved from the hotel, which meant buying furniture and appliances for the apartment. Barbara brought us a baby crib for Sydney. We were setting up house from scratch.

The apartment was located on the 11th story and contained a large sliding window that slid completely open, exposing the view which overlooked several miles of terra cotta tiled roofs bordering the

Pacific Ocean. The apartment building contained a pool and a large concrete patio that wrapped completely around the second floor of the building. On the same floor there were large, private rooms for the kids to play in. We began to finally feel settled in.

I called Manuel, who immediately drove by to see where we had moved. He looked around the apartment and, to my surprise, left abruptly. "I'll be back in a few minutes."

"Where are you going?"

"To get you a house gift."

Within a half hour, the doorbell rang. I looked out the peephole, and a short, dark-complexioned woman with a thick ponytail and a pink nanny uniform, holding a suitcase, was at the door. I opened the door. "Hi, how are you?"

She handed me a note. It read, "Call Manuel."

I rang his number as she proceeded to enter the apartment.

He answered, "Hello, Manuel."

"Manuel, I got your note."

"Very good. She's your nanny, Cellíe."

"My what?"

"I've got three. I don't need her. She's great with kids, and she can cook. You're going to need her. She can go to the store for you."

"How much does she charge?"

"A hundred and sixty a month, plus room and board."

"Where does she stay?"

"That small room across from your laundry room is the maid's quarters. Every apartment has a maid's quarters. The maid service is the second biggest industry here besides construction. If you don't like her, just send her back – no problem."

"Okay, Manuel...thank you." I didn't know how to respond nor how I felt about having a live-in nanny. It felt a bit...colonial.

"Hey, I've got a job this weekend. I'll be back on Sunday night. I'll call you then. Goodbye."

I hung the phone up and turned around to find Tammy with a quizzical look on her face, staring at Cellíe and me.

"Hi, Tammy, say hello to Cellíe. She's our nanny."

"Our what?"

"Manuel dropped her off for us. She was our housewarming gift."

She reacted with predictable compassion. "Hi, I'm Tammy. Do you understand English?"

Cellíe shook her head.

"Hola, me llamo Tammy."

Cellíe smiled and replied, "Hola, mucho gusto. Me llamo Cellíe."

The kids ran in, and Sydney ran to Cellíe. Cellíe reached down and gave her a hug. She quite obviously had a magnetism.

Cellíe quickly became a part of the family. She was invaluable for navigating, housekeeping, childcare, grocery shopping, and other necessities. We toted a Spanish-English dictionary, and we quickly learned to trust and depend on her. She seemed to embrace our family, and she adored the children.

A new life, I thought that night as I watched Cellíe teaching Sydney Spanish words, *complete with "corporate structure," household help, and a view of the ocean. If you didn't know better, you'd think we'd made it. However, every paradise is temporary when you're running.*

REINVENTING MY LIFE

Somewhere during the whirlwind of setting up our new life, I began to work for Rodriguez. I would handle mostly Europeans who wanted to set up a company in Panama. We processed visas for people acquiring second citizenships. Often times, Rodriguez was approached by businessmen who wanted him to represent them in establishing bank accounts and corporations. Rodriguez included me in the meetings and would often recess, dragging me off to his private office to get my read in determining if a particular business concept was real or some kind of sham. Frequently, they were frauds, and I would advise Rodriguez to steer clear. I was grateful for the work, and it felt in my wheelhouse.

I employed a team of outside computer consultants to install a network in the office. I was getting ready to put together deals. Rodriguez knew the incoming President of Panama, Martin Torrijos. This meant we would be able to venture into road contracts as well as a variety of opportunities that surrounded the Canal. The new year was looking robust.

Christmas time in Panama was just as commercial, if not more so, than the United States. We enjoyed the many lights and Christmas programs. It was the easiest time ever for us to buy for the kids because they had no toys at the time. Tammy and I stored a multitude of toys for them in David Vonn's old building that I had once used. We also included presents for Cellíe this year under the tree. We showered the kids with toys, and I believe it was the most memorable Christmas they ever had. Cole got a Green Machine, which was a dragster version of a big wheel. He rode it around the pool area for hours. Sydney dressed up in her plastic high heels, wore plastic beads and heart-shaped sunglasses. I thought Cellíe was going to pass out from laughter.

Tammy and I had agreed to refrain from buying each other gifts this year. However, we both secretly had purchased some clothes for each other. Cellíe prepared a large meal, and we all sat down and gave thanks for the day. It was a special time, but there was something other than the snow that was missing. Like a gathering at a wake, we could feel the void. Nothing needed to be said; we realized we would have to deal with this void, knowing our families were back home, celebrating without us. My parents, Tammy's parents, wondering where we were, if we were safe. The thought that we would someday see them again brought us hope. Hope brought us peace of mind, and we hoped this void in our families would be short-lived.

We enjoyed our celebration, just as we had in the United States before all the turmoil had hit us. We pushed all worries away for a day and focused on our family. We felt content, safe, and thankful. This very moment I realized why I had left. This was living. Robert was right; this was my heartbeat.

AN IMPERFECT FUTURE

New Year's turned out to be a special event too. Rodriguez and Barbara decided to take both families, including their nanny and ours, to the Coronado Resort. It was a perfect getaway for the families. The kids played and swam all day. At night, the adults attended a party after a delicious seafood dinner. In between dinner and the resort's private party for guests and locals, Rodriguez and I had a chance to reflect on the past year and our future. We sat at a small table in a room that would soon be packed with people. As we smoked Cuban cigars and drank some local favorites, Rodriguez tilted back in his chair. "You know, gringo, I'm the luckiest man in all of Panamá. You know why?" Rodriguez asked, blowing out the smoke.

"Why, Rodriguez?"

"Because out of all the attorneys you could have gone to, you walked into my office. You are going to make me a fortune." He let out a deep laugh, forcefully blowing smoke out.

"Well, I couldn't do it by myself; I couldn't do anything if not for you." I held up my glass. "Here's to a really successful year ahead and a bright future."

He seems delusional, I thought as our glasses clinked. *Of all people, he should know that any day, any moment, it could all end, that I'm not a golden goose but a ticking time bomb.*

Our glasses met, and we both finished off the toast.

Tammy and I danced the night away and brought in the New Year no differently than we had numerous times in the United States. For a few hours, we forgot about being fugitives. We were just Steve and Tammy, dancing like we had at a hundred corporate events, innumerable celebrations. For a few hours, the past didn't exist.

COLD CALLS

The first of the year started off with a strange request.

My phone rang. "Steve speaking."

"Hello Steve, David Vonn here."

"David, how are you?"

"I'm okay, but I have a problem."

"What's going on?"

"I have a client in town from Europe. He owns the largest real estate company in Monte Carlo. He wants to look at some property in Bocas Del Toro. It's beside Costa Rica."

"Okay. So, what's the problem?"

"Well, since Robert left, I really don't have anyone I believe can field this guy. Could you tag along with me and help close this deal?"

Back in the game, I thought. "How long will I be gone?"

"We'll leave on Friday and be back on Sunday."

"How are we getting there?"

"Private plane."

"If Tammy is okay with it, I'm in."

"Okay. Call me back. I really need you."

Tammy could see the opportunity. If I was part of the deal, then I would have to be compensated accordingly.

I met David and the French businessman for dinner. The next morning, they came to my apartment, and we traveled to the airport. The plane was a twin engine. David had four of his executives and me, which left me sitting beside the pilot.

"*Hola, amigo*. My name is Juan," the pilot said with a smile.

I lied, "Hi, I'm Max. Nice to meet you. You do know how to fly this plane, don't you?"

Juan laughed. "Amigo, I was Noriega's pilot."

As if that was reassuring, I lied again, "That's good enough for me."

This flight was an hour and a half. Juan flew some low altitudes just so he could show me some key spots he wanted to point out. When we got close to Bocas Del Toro, Juan circled an island where remote tribes of people lived. I could see them scrambling, securing shelter, perhaps worried they were under some kind of attack. The dugout canoes and grass roofs resembled photos I had only seen in *National Geographic*. The people's skin color was the same as Cellíe's. *I wonder if she's a descendant.* Juan told me they were called *Bri Bri* and that there were still quite a few groups of indigenous people in Panamá. He said they maintain their indigenous languages and many of their original cultural practices. He also explained that they have a degree of autonomy in the *comarcas* designated for them. It felt extraordinary to witness this. Juan knew I would be blown away, and he was right.

Bocas Del Toro was a vibrant little town. It reminded me of Key West, perhaps fifty years ago. It contained a couple of nice restaurants and small hotels. From the air, the beaches outran the eye in what appeared to be an uninhibited landscape. It was truly a spectacular place. On the bay side, the water was so calm that numerous houses and some private hotels were built out on the water, elevated on stilts. The Caribbean side of Bocas featured large waves, challenged by some of the best surfers in the world. We toured the properties in a runabout. I wasn't sure about the Frenchman, but I was certainly sold on the locale. The place was magnificent.

Fortunately, the trip was successful, and we landed the deal. Frankly, I'm not convinced my influence was even a factor; the place sold itself. After a brief celebration, we again boarded the small aircraft. If the Bocas airport had one plane a day, that was a busy day. I had envisioned a remote airport, just a field and maybe a tanker for gas. However, there was a small building we had to pass through. Awaiting our departure were two customs agents dressed in military uniforms. A local driver dropped us off at the airport. He had been calling me Max all day. I was uncomfortable using my real name down here. I handed my fake passport to the officer. The man who drove us to the airport shook my hand. "Well, Max, have a safe trip back."

The officer looked at the paper and looked at the guy. "It says Steve Keller here. This man is not Max."

"Yes, this is Max. Everybody calls him Max," he said to the officer.

The officers looked at me with a stare of apprehension, as if getting ready to take action. My heart started pounding. "My nickname is Max. That's what I go by. My name is Steve Keller."

The driver looked confused, and the officer stamped the paper and slowly handed the birth certificate to me. I grabbed the paper and tried to walk off cool, though I reckon my pace was quicker than normal. The plane's engines were revved up as the plane was receiving turning directions on the ground. I ran to the door of the plane and leaped in, pulling the door closed and hitting the latch. "Let's go!" I said with a hint of panic. As I took in my audience, all of whom were staring at me with a shocked look, I tried to regain my composure. "We are ready, aren't we?" I tried to recover.

"Oh yes, yes, let's go!" they exclaimed.

I climbed up to the cabin with Juan. He asked, "Where you been, amigo?"

"Oh, just saying goodbye." The sweat was rolling down my face. It wasn't from the heat. Damn, that was scary. I didn't see that coming. Too close, I thought, *way too close.*

When we landed, no customs agents were present. I found that very strange.

That evening we arrived in Panama City without incident. I called Tammy on my cell phone.

"Are you back?"

"Yes, in one piece surprisingly."

"Did something happen?"

"No, no, everything is fine. The meeting went well, and David wants us to join him for dinner with the French guy."

"Okay, I'm in," Tammy replied.

At 8:00 pm on the nose, David, his girlfriend, Cecill, and the Frenchman pulled up in front of our apartment building.

Tammy and I recognized the restaurant that had been selected. It wouldn't have been our first choice but not our last either. We were seated in a private room located in the back of the restaurant. Now I realized why this restaurant was chosen. David knew the management and was given VIP treatment. To my surprise, a couple of gentlemen in suits showed up, which invoked David to rush around the large table to greet the two. I leaned over to Cecillia, "Who are the two guys?"

"The short, heavy-set one is the head of Immigration, and the other is in charge of Economic Development for Panama."

"Has David lost his mind?" I pleaded in a yelling whisper.

"He thought it would be appropriate for you to meet the Immigration guy. Maybe we can get something worked out."

"Please call me Max. Do not use my real name," I directed.

"I'll tell David."

The meeting was less risky than I thought. The two Government guys were enthralled with the money bags from France, which took the spotlight off me. I was introduced as Max, and no last names were given for either Tammy or me. I was sitting across the table from two Cabinet members of the Government. *Sometimes the best hiding place is right in front of their faces.*

However, as I sat there, watching these government officials fawn over money, I couldn't shake the feeling that the walls were closing in – the close call at the airport, now this, too many people knowing my face, even if they didn't know my name. In business, I'd learned that when you start feeling uncomfortable, it's usually for a reason, and I was feeling very uncomfortable.

THE LAST STOP

Date: February 12, 2004

Like any father, I had to keep grinding; I couldn't let my premonitions rule the day. I had a family to protect, people to move, bills to pay, and my suspicion that the law dogs might be closing in on me was just one more concern I had to carry around.

My day started off normal at least, as normal as it could for someone who had dragged his family off to a Central American country to live in exile. It had been six months since we'd fled to Panama and tried to reestablish ourselves in a land completely foreign to us. I was proud of how we had acclimated, making friends, making a living, learning a new language, finding ways to get off the ground, seeing the jungle from above the treetops. As I daydreamed of the view from the Ferris wheel and the Gamboa Resort and Juan's prop plane, I suppose I smiled.

"What are you smiling at?" Rodriguez, at that point, my closest companion and confidant, asked from behind the wheel.

"Oh, just thinking about your country, *compadre*, feeling grateful."

He gave me a quizzical look.

I tried to clarify. "These recent weeks, though I cannot shake my fugitive feelings, I have felt enriched, like I'm living the way I should have forever, spending every day with Tammy and the kids, learning something almost constantly, flying into new territory all the time, making companions like you."

Rodriguez smiled. "I appreciate your company too, señor."

My cell phone rang. It was Tammy. "Hi babe, how are ya'?"

Her voice came over, strained. "I feel awful. I can barely move from the couch. Can you please come home?"

"Of course. Do you need to go to the hospital?" I asked, secretly hoping the answer was no. Settled or not, I still wasn't comfortable with our names splattered all over the documents of any organized institution.

"No," she sighed, "I just need some rest, but you can do one thing for me. Are you with Rodriguez?"

"Yep," I replied. "Why?"

"I'll tell you when you get home," she said. "Just get here."

I hung up and looked over at Rodriguez. "My wife is sick. I have to get back and take care of the kids. Can we wait on this?"

We had several meetings we'd scheduled – meetings that would determine whether I could build any kind of financial stability for my family in Panama. Our future relied on it. However, in situations like this, family came first – at least it did now. Back in my high-powered CEO days, that had rarely been the case. Those days are gone; I reminded myself. Everything was gone, except my family, and I intended to hang onto them, come hell or high water.

Rodriguez nodded. "I'll take you home. We can reschedule." He turned around and drove me back to our gated apartment complex. I waved at the guard and made my way to our little Panamanian oasis. The kids greeted me like they hadn't seen me in years and hugged me *aggressively. As long as I don't lose these little rug rats, I thought, nothing else matters.*

Tammy came into the room, holding her head and looking pale, wearing a robe. She looked like she was taking her first stroll in a hospital ward, recovering from surgery.

"You don't look so great," I said, stating the obvious.

She gave me a half-smile. "You sure know how to charm a woman."

I hugged her. "What do you need?"

"Can you take Cole to his karate class?" she replied.

On the surface, it was a simple request that any dutiful husband would do for his sick wife. However, on a deeper level, the truth was that nothing in my life was simple anymore. Over the past six months, I lived with constant paranoia that my every move was being watched, that even the tiniest infraction, like being pulled over for a busted taillight, could expose my identity and result in my extradition back to the United States.

"You know how I feel about driving," I told her. "We've talked about this. You know what could happen. Besides, the way I am with directions, I might end up in the Panama Canal."

"Please, honey?" she pleaded. "Just this once? He's already dressed, and I can barely walk."

I sighed as I looked at her pale face, shaded with a hint of green. There was no way out of it. "Okay," I relented. "Anything else for your fugitive chauffeur?" I joked.

She smiled apologetically. "I also said he could get a video."

A wave of paranoia crested over my head – all that driving, all that opportunity for something to go wrong. I let it crash over me then refocused my brain on the odds. I knew the Panamanian police were lax on speeding and keeping to your own lane because not a single driver in all of Panama seemed to understand or care about traffic regulations, including the police. Therefore, I was confident the odds were in my favor...but I was obviously just pumping myself up for the task, combating the completely reasonable apprehension I struggled to shake.

The minute we got into the first real bit of traffic, I started to shake. A panic attack was quickly approaching. I'd become somewhat ac-customed to them in the past few years: the racing heartbeat, the sweat seeping from my pores, the constricted feeling in my throat. They were agonizing and brutal. I had to get off the main road – now. I glanced in my rearview mirror at my five-year-old son, suited up in his little karate outfit, unaware that the man who was still his hero was about three breaths away from completely losing his shit. He was calm and unconcerned, his mind focused on five-year-old boy's stuff, which I assumed was visions of himself as some kind of su-per-ninja.

I turned off the main road and, taking discreet deep breaths, drove into the back streets. It took a while, but my heartbeat slowly evened out, and I found my way to Cole's school. I relaxed a little. *First leg down, I thought. Jesus, is it always going to be like this? Will the fear of being caught send me into a panic attack every time I have to take my kids to school or my wife to the store? How long can this last?*

I felt calm enough as I walked Cole into the karate school. I pulled out my phone and made him give me his fiercest karate pose. I snapped the picture and said, "Go get 'em, buddy." As he ran to join his classmates, I realized I hadn't said one word to him the entire trip over. I'd been too focused on not getting arrested. A pang of guilt hit me, yet I knew I had good reason to be distracted. In fact, I had the best reason – the loss of my family – the only thing that mattered to me anymore. If I was taken away, who would take care of them? How would they get back home? Where would they go if they did? Who would Tammy turn to?

My troubled thoughts were broken by the kids' screams as they clumsily thrust and parried their way across the mat. My son's enthusiasm made me laugh, and I took more pictures. No matter how it all played out, I knew one thing for sure – I had fantastic children. They had become the center of my universe, and I wasn't going to allow anything to break my connection to them. I hadn't always felt that way, but there's something about the threat of losing everything that brings a person clarity on what's important in life. I had my family, and I was grasping what it really meant to live in the moment. Jesus once said, "Don't worry about tomorrow because it will bring its own troubles." How right He was.

After the class, I was so busy making the extra effort to communicate with Cole that I took a wrong turn on the back road. Muttering under my breath, I tried to navigate my way up to Calle 50, the main road through town. I didn't have a choice. Without a reference point, my feeble sense of direction would have landed us hopelessly lost in the back alleys for hours. As I got back onto the main drag, I noticed that the rush hour traffic had thinned. I didn't notice the motorcycle that pulled up next to me.

The hairs on the back of my neck involuntarily stood up. I knew I was being watched. I glanced over. Outside my window, a Panamanian police officer stared back at me, motioning to roll down my window. In broken English, he said, "Sir, over to side, over to side."

"No problem," I said, nonchalantly, even though my adrenaline had just surged one thousand percent.

"Daddy, why are you being pulled over?" Cole asked from the back.

"Oh, I must have a broken taillight or something," I lied. "Don't worry." Of course, I was worried. I looked at the AK-47 strapped to the officer's back. All the police in Panama carry AK's, I told myself. If I just stayed calm, I would probably only need to pay the fine on the spot, and we could go on our way – or so I hoped. I fished in my pockets but only came up with six dollars. It was nowhere near enough to pay the fine...or the bribe. I suppose could always go to the bank. A cop once took Rodriguez all the way to the ATM so he could pay his fine. I just hoped my fake ID, which I had required after the airport incident in Bocas, would hold up to scrutiny.

The policeman motioned me toward a large asphalt parking lot that, surprisingly, seemed abandoned. I obediently followed his motorcycle through traffic, and, as I turned into the lot, I spotted other cars racing in from all directions, closing off any exit points. My first instinct was to gun it, crank the wheel and get the hell out of there. There was one opening on my right, but it was entirely blocked by traffic. Even if it hadn't been, I knew I wouldn't have taken the chance, not with Cole in the back seat. I looked back at him. He was smiling, oblivious, humming a song I didn't recognize.

More cars zoomed into the parking lot, and I sat there, feeling my hope fade away. *Jesus, they really pulled out all the stops. This is serious.* I found myself singularly focused, thinking only of keeping Cole safe through this. I silently prayed for his safety as Panamanian police officers added to the swarm surrounding us. I didn't want him to die because of me.

Suddenly, the doors of a dozen cars flew open, and at least thirty plain-clothes police officers spilled out and sank to their knees with guns drawn. From somewhere in the crowd, I heard, "Sir, keep your hands on the steering wheel, and don't move."

That wasn't going to be a problem.

One of the plain-clothes officers, gun still drawn, cautiously approached our truck. In his hand, I saw a piece of paper with my mugshot.

"Is this you?" he asked.

I looked at the picture. *Who is that guy?* I didn't recognize him at all; I didn't look anything like him. He was a clean-shaven CEO in a power suit and designer glasses; I was a goateed foreigner in a wrinkled shirt and contact lenses. However, that was just the surface stuff. The real difference between that guy and I lay much deeper. I could see it in his eyes, the thing he still had that I no longer did: bravado, optimism, hope. It made him a complete stranger to me.

"It doesn't look like me," I said truthfully. "What do you think?"

The officer looked at the picture and then back at me. He did it three times, in fact, before abandoning the effort. "I'm going to ask you again. Is this you?" he uttered authoritatively.

I shook my head. "No, sir, it's not. I don't recognize that man." That, at least, was true.

He frowned and pulled out another picture. I swallowed hard as I saw my wife staring back at me from the photo.

"Is this your wife, sir?" The way he said "wife" unnerved me, as if she was considered my accomplice. At that point, I knew I needed to call in reinforcements.

"Look," I replied, feigning indignation, "I don't know what is going on here. I need to see my attorney." It was the wrong thing to say, I realized, but I was no longer thinking straight. I was terrified.

The police officer had had enough. "Are these pictures of you and your wife?" he shouted.

I looked back to see Cole staring at both of us, wide-eyed, tears beginning to form. I felt angry and utterly helpless. All I could manage was, "Please stop shouting. You're scaring my son."

Just then, an arm shot through the window. I flinched. Somehow, an agent had snuck up on our truck. In a flash, he grabbed my car keys and held them up in the air, like a hockey player holding the Stanley Cup. A roar went up among the agents. It was absurd. What did they think I was, some kind of international terrorist?

"Daddy, what's going on?" Cole asked, frightened and confused. Tears streamed down his face. I glanced at the cops with their guns still drawn, then back to Cole. I couldn't lie this time to make him feel better.

"It's not good, son. Listen, Mommy is going to come get you, okay, so don't worry. She'll explain everything when you get home. But I need you to do something for me until then, okay? Don't leave my side, understand? Whatever happens, even if someone asks you, you tell them, 'I want to stay with my daddy,' okay?"

He nodded, and as he climbed into the front seat with me, two men in dark sunglasses approached my window. The one on the right said in an American accent, "Mr. Keller, we both know why I'm here. If you come quietly, this doesn't have to get crazy, and your son won't be hurt. Get out slowly so I can put these cuffs on you."

"Who are you?" I asked.

"We're with the FBI, with the United States Embassy, and we've come to take you back to the States. Time's up, sir."

END OF THE LINE

A tall, heavy-set man, dressed in black stepped in between the newspaper photographer and the truck. "Mr. Keller, we both know who you are. The United States Embassy will be here in a few minutes. I need for you to sit tight. Young man, do you want to sit in this car over here? It's much cooler," the man asked Cole.

"No, thank you, I'm fine where I am at," Cole replied.

My boy, I thought, loyal to the end.

We felt like we were waiting in a convection oven, sitting in our black truck on that lonely asphalt. The sweat beads were rolling down both of us. A car came whizzing onto the scene. The rogue crowd parted, making way for the two suits walking toward us.

"Mr. Keller, I'm Agent McCormick with the U.S. Embassy. We both know why I'm here. I need you to come with us."

"Okay." I opened the door and assisted Cole down to the ground. I held Cole's hand, and we were escorted to a beat-up Toyota Corolla. The crowd encircled us.

McCormick said, "Mr. Keller, I need to put these cuffs on you."

I held my hands out in front of me, and a guy placed handcuffs on me loosely. I still managed to pick Cole up and place him in my lap in the back seat of the Toyota. We began the ride to the police station.

Cole's head was tilted down. His mouth was opened; he looked perplexed. He raised his head to meet me eye to eye. "Daddy, I thought the police only locked up bad guys."

The words hit me like a punch in the larynx. In all my planning, all my maneuvering, I'd never prepared for this moment, never prepared to explain to my son why his father was in handcuffs. I felt ashamed.

"Cole, sometimes the police make mistakes. Your Mother will have to explain all this to you. We'll work it out. Don't worry."

The caravan, including my SUV, pulled into a building I had seen many times in passing. To the left side of the building was where the government food rations were given out to the poor. I remember seeing hordes of people waiting at the other end from where we were pulling in. Panama City may have been reaching for North American standards, but this place was nothing short of a third world jail. The large officer in black took us through a wooden door located on the backside of the building that looked as dirty as any door found in a grease monkey mechanic shop. I stepped inside and noticed all the ancient office desks and wooden chairs. Disorganized stacks of papers were scattered everywhere. The phones were all rotary dials. They took Cole and me to a room that contained a large two-way glass located on a side wall.

The large officer and another special agent came in to talk to me. "Mr. Keller, we just want you to know that...well, we're sorry for this. We've been watching you for several weeks, and we do not object to your undertakings in Panamá. You have not broken any laws in Panamá. We don't want to do this. It's your Embassy that is doing this – not us."

Even our captors feel sorry for us, I thought. When did I become the kind of man that inspires pity?

"I appreciate that guys. Believe me, I do. Can I use a phone? I need to call my wife and let her know what's happened. She needs to come and get Cole."

"Is there anything else we can do?"

"Well, if you don't mind, in the back of my truck there are some toys and books. Do you mind bringing them to me for Cole?"

"Sure, Mr. Keller."

Moments later the guy brought me a couple of toys for Cole and a book. "What's the number Mr. Keller?" I gave him the phone number for Tammy, and he made the call. "Here you go," he said as he handed the cell phone to me.

"Hello, Tammy."

"Where are you guys?"

"Tammy, something bad has happened."

"Oh my God, were you in a wreck?"

"No. It's over, Tammy. They found me. I'm at the police station with

Cole. I need you to get Rodriguez and come down here."

"I'll be right there!" click, the phone went dead.

Numerous people kept parading by our room. Some would stop in. They all wanted to see the *dangerous criminal* but acted sorely disappointed once they saw me. They quit after a while. Cole and I sat in the room together, alone.

"Your Mom is on her way to pick you up."

Cole was looking all around. He started to look up at the ceiling from one end of the room to the other, slowly. "Okay, Daddy. How are we going to get out of here?"

"No, son." Children have a way of breaking the tension in a tense situation. I smiled. "We don't have to break out. I have to deal with this another way. We'll work it out. In the meanwhile, I need for you to help your mom. No matter what happens Cole, I love you – to everywhere and back again. Come over here, and let's read this book."

I was on page two of *The Little Train That Could* when the door swung open and Tammy paused before running into my arms. *The little train that couldn't,* I thought bitterly.

"Oh, Tammy, I am so sorry."

"I know honey. Rodriguez is outside trying to do something."

"Go ahead and get Cole out of here. See if you guys can get an attorney here tomorrow."

"This place is so horrible. I don't want to leave you here."

"I know, Tammy, but I'll manage." We hugged each other and gave one another a departing kiss.

"I love you, sweetheart."

"I love you too." Tears rolled down her cheeks.

I grabbed Cole and hugged and kissed him. "Be a good boy. I love you, Cole."

"I love you, Daddy."

"Hey, Tammy."

"Yes, dear."

"I've got your Valentine's Day card in the back of the truck."

Tammy interrupted her crying with a small outburst of laughter at the absurdity of the thought. *Even now, I thought, even at the end, I can still make her laugh.*

"I'll see you tomorrow," Tammy stated.

I was left in the room all alone.

I guessed I was going to stay there for the night. I poked my head out the wooden door.

"Excuse me, sir." I summoned one of the plain-clothes guys sitting at a desk.

"Yes?"

"Can I please go to the bathroom?"

"Yes, it's around here, down the steps, to your left."

I walked around the three desks in the room adjacent to mine and descended the steps. As I stopped on the ground floor, I looked to my right and saw several iron bar cells with dirt floors. It was the stuff right out of a western movie. The bathroom was a trough made of concrete. It was the nastiest setup I had ever experienced. However, compared to the poor souls I saw laying on the dirt floors, shoeless, I had prime real estate in my observation room. I walked back to my room passing the plain-clothes guys.

"Thank you."

"No problem, Mr. Keller. There is a mattress in that room if you want to use it."

"Okay, thank you." This meant I would stay in the observation room for the night. That was comforting. Of course, the light wasn't going to go off. The room was being used to store tables and some chairs. I placed the nasty, soiled mattress under a wooden table to block the light. I laid down on my back and attempted to sleep off the wait.

I thought, *From king-sized beds to a stained mattress on a concrete floor – the American Dream in reverse.*

At about three o'clock in the morning a man came into the room. "Mr. Keller, excuse me, Mr. Keller," he stated in a muffled voice.

"Yes...yes, sir." I rose up to see what was going on.

"I'm going to have to put a leg iron on you."

"Okay."

The man fastened an ankle bracelet with a chain attached to my right leg. He then fastened the other end to a wooden chair located beside my leg. "There – that should do it."

"Okay. Goodnight," I replied. *Do these guys want me to escape? Is this wooden chair, the open door an invitation?* Here in Panama, you could pay your way out of almost anything. The problem was, I had no money, and I had nowhere to go. There was only one thing to do: sleep.

The next morning a man came in at seven o'clock. He unlocked the leg iron and handed me a small Styrofoam box. "Here you go, Mr. Keller."

"What's this?" I asked.

"We don't serve food here, but I brought you something from the kitchen next door."

"Thank you very much."

The man left, and I opened the box. I tried to discern what was between the two pieces of bread, but I just couldn't get there. It looked beyond disgusting. I hadn't grown that hungry yet.

At eight o'clock I asked one of the guys if I could use his phone. Since it was a local call, he had no problem with my request.

"Hello, Tammy Keller," she answered the phone on the first ring.

"Tammy, what is going on?"

"I'm with Rodriguez, and we have secured an attorney to come down and handle this."

"Did you pay him?"

"Yes, I gave him a thousand dollars. I'm going to meet him at his office, then I'll see you later. Did you sleep last night at all?"

"A little. I slept in that same room you were in."

"That's horrible."

"It's better than the alternative; trust me."

"Stay strong, honey. I'll see you later. Goodbye. I love you."

"I love you too."

THE SHELL GAME

At nine o'clock, another guy came to the room. "Señor Keller, you have a Mr. Rodriguez and some others out front. I will get you soon."

"Thank you." I had a strong feeling of hope, a sense of rejuvenation, knowing something was moving. I no longer felt lonely and vulnerable. I sat in one of the wooden chairs and patiently waited. I began to hear a lot of commotion in the office beside my room. A group of guys had entered the room and were walking toward me. When the group entered the room, I realized it was not the welcoming party and not my attorney. Instead, five guys with AK-47s and machine guns stormed into my room.

"Mr. Keller, let's go!"

I got to my feet, thinking I was being escorted to the front of the jail. I wasn't really sure, and no one was talking. The group escorted me out back where I was instructed to sit in the back seat of a large SUV. I had a guy on each side of me. Three guys rode up front. We drove out of the gates of the jail and looped around the city on a bypass. The guy on my right side pulled out a small newspaper. I looked at the picture on the pages and there I stood with my son, Cole, dressed in his karate outfit. The caption was in Spanish, but I understood enough to make it out. It referred to me as the most dangerous, escaped criminal from the U.S. *Was my government trying to have me killed? Maybe that explains the need for all the guns.*

The man to my right looked at the picture and stated, "There goes our cover. Who the hell leaked this shit out is what I want to know. Roberto, we're through," the man angrily protested.

"I've been making calls. I can't locate the source," a man up front stated.

About twenty minutes had passed and I became more frantic by the minute. I still had no idea where we were going. I felt like I was being taken for a ride. *The old gangster movies, I thought, take them for a ride. Is this how it ends?*

Feeling resigned, I thought I would at least try to get some information. I turned my head to the guy sitting to my right who held the paper. "So where are we going?" I asked, afraid of the answer.

The man turned from the window, "Airport!" He quickly turned back.

I was perplexed as to why we would be going to the airport. In another five minutes I saw a chain-link fence and airport signs. Before I had time to think about why, we pulled up to the airport, and I was surrounded by the five men, who escorted me into the airport.

"Why am I being taken to the airport?" I demanded.

The lead guy said, "Because we want to know how you got in here without a passport."

"I could have told you that back at the jail," I stated.

"Let's go!" the man abruptly instructed.

In the middle of the airport, across from a row of ticket agents, was an art deco designed structure. I had seen it before and thought nothing of it. I always thought all this plywood was to simply hide dead space. One of the agents pushed on a section of the wall, opening the concealed door. Two soldiers dressed in ecru, brown, red-trimmed military uniforms decorated with a plethora of ribbons were waiting behind the door. I was escorted up a staircase constructed with unpainted wood and shown to a cramped room containing a small wooden desk and chair. The room resembled a closet. An old light hung down over the desk with a metal shade exposing a single light bulb. It reminded me of a torture scene from a movie I had seen where a guy was asked repeated questions about his whereabouts until the torture broke him. One of the military guys came in carrying two pieces of paper. He laid them on the desk and slid them toward me. "Your Embassy wants you to sign these papers."

I picked the papers up. They appeared to be some sort of legal contract written in Spanish. "I'm not going to sign these contracts. I can't even read them. Can you translate them for me?" I asked.

"No, sir, that's not my job!" He looked at me with an air of power. "Suit yourself." He turned and walked away.

I waited under the light, sitting at the desk for forty-five minutes. *The waiting game, I thought, I've played it before – in business, in court, in life. The one who waits longest usually loses.*

Two more men appeared in suits with badges hanging from strings around their necks. A conversation commenced between the military guys and the two suits. The two suits turned and walked toward me.

"Mr. Keller, I'm FBI Agent Allen. This is Special Agent Gifford. We're with the United States Embassy."

"Good to meet you guys. What's with these papers?"

"Mr. Keller, you have to sign these papers."

"I can't read Spanish. What do they say?"

"Look pal. You can sign these papers, or you can continue to sit here. It's up to you."

"I'm not signing them."

"Very well then." The two men walked out of the room.

I sat under the light for another hour. *These guys are not kidding at this point.* They returned to my room. "Well, Mr. Keller, any consideration?"

"I want to use your phone and call my wife. Is that possible?"

"Yeah." He pulled out his phone.

She quickly picked up. "Tammy Keller."

"Tammy, it's Steve."

"Oh my God! Where are you? We waited an hour for you at the jail with the attorney."

"Listen, I'm at the airport with a couple of agents from the Embassy. They want me to sign some papers that I can't read; they are written in Spanish."

"What happens if you sign the papers?"

"Good question. Hold on." I turned to Agent Allen. "What happens if I sign?"

He looked at his watch and stated, "In forty-five minutes we'll be flying to the United States."

"They will fly me back to the U.S., Tammy."

"Well, that may be better than going back to that horrible jail you just came from."

"You got that right! I wish I could have seen that attorney."

"So do I."

"Are you okay?" I asked.

"Yeah, Rodriguez is really stomping out fires on this end. There was an article in the paper that really made everybody wig out."

"I saw it. It was incredible. I don't know what to do, Tammy."

"Just sign the papers so you don't have to go back to that horrible place."

"You guys get back to the U.S. I'll call you when I can."

"I love you."

"I love you too, Tammy. Tell Rodriguez that I'm sorry for all of this."

"I will honey. Goodbye."

"Give me the papers." I signed the papers, and we immediately began walking to a Delta gate. We were the only ones boarding.

"All the way in the back," Agent Allen stated as we began walking down the aisle of the large Delta jet.

"What, no first class?" I asked. *Even now, at the end, I can't help myself.*

I sat beside the window and the two agents sat beside me. "So, Mr. Allen, where are we going?"

"To Miami."

"And then to Kentucky?" I asked.

"No. You're going to the Miami holdover. You'll go to court there."

"Can I use your phone? My wife thinks I'm going to Kentucky."

"No, you can't make calls on the plane."

I knew better than this. I owned a plane. The FAA is only concerned about using a phone in the air because it may interfere with the plane's instruments.

"That's only in flight."

"No, that's anytime."

"May I get you all something to drink?" the stewardess asked.

"Ma'am, do you have a problem with me making a call from a cell phone while we're sitting here?"

"No, you can make calls while we're on the ground."

I turned smiling to Agent Allen, "Okay. I guess it's okay to use your phone then."

Agent Allen rolled his eyes and blew out a breath, reluctantly handing over the phone.

"Thank you. I'll have a Bud Light," I conveyed to the stewardess.

"Bring him a Coke. I'll have a Sprite," Agent Allen quickly countered.

I rang the number. "Tammy Keller."

"Tammy, it's me. I'm on a plane."

"You signed the papers?"

"Yeah. Listen, I'm not going to Kentucky. I'm going to Miami."

"For how long?"

"I don't know. I may have to go to court there. Will you call my family and let them know what's going on?"

"Yes, I'll call them in a minute."

"Listen; we'll get through this. You be careful and stay strong. I love you," I said.

"I love you too. We'll make it. I've got Rodriguez."

"What about Cellíe?"

"We had a cry fest. She is leaving tomorrow."

"Tell her that I'm sorry, and I will miss her. Tell her to keep studying her English."

"I will."

"Take care of those babies. Kiss them for me. Get home safely. I've got to go. I love you."

"I love you. Goodbye."

I hung the phone up, not knowing when I would ever be able to talk to her again. I had gone from CEO, a position that brought the illusion of control, to realizing, at that moment, that once the man gets a hold of you, you no longer possess any control. He flies the plane. I could only pray that my family made it home safely. I had faith in Rodriguez. He would fly back with Tammy if he had to. Thank God for that man.

I experienced an array of emotions on that flight, replaying so many precious moments that I had, thankfully, learned to value. I cherished these moments and wished I could have stopped time and remained frozen in one of my selected memories. In the scenes, people wouldn't age, and the circumstances needed no embellishing. It could have been a moment when I was a kid at Christmas or when I got married or the birth of my kids or the Christmas in Panama.

Nonetheless, I had to confront reality in that moment. I looked around the plane at all the passengers. I was certain no one else was sitting with handcuffs. *God only knows what awaits me when we land. These people are worried about going to the baggage claim; I'm worried about going to the cage.* I wasn't sure of the life expectancy of a white-collar in prison, but I feared it was short.

However, for some reason beyond my finite comprehension, my heart rate was not racing. As I stared out the window, looking down at the vast clouds, I somehow felt at home; my head had always been in the clouds. My dreams and visions soared high. I always reached for the stars. To me, this was normal. For a moment in life, I had realized my dreams. Like many other entrepreneurs, I dreamed big. I may have been imprisoned for it, but my dream couldn't be confined.

I reflected on my errors, evaluating all my decisions and, particularly, my hubris. I believe entrepreneurship inherently requires a minimum amount of courage and, perhaps, arrogance, so I was not too hard on myself for it. However, it was hard not to regret turning down that $300 million. Perhaps, if Jerry Wendorf hadn't been such a pretentious asshole, I might have been like that Frenchman in Bocas, touring the world, considering if I should buy a remote island. Nonetheless, I couldn't waste time blaming Jerry; it felt childish and unmanly. I was, unfortunately, still bitter, gripped with resentment that the insurance companies, that fundamentally exploitative outfit of crooks and, frankly, parasites, had won. Their lobbying, their bribery had landed Kelco in court and had wrestled me down from the clouds. They had their grip on power, tragically, and it obviously did not matter that we were Americans, earnestly attempting to follow the law. It was obvious that our purported protections, our rights as Americans, did not hold up in the face of their economic power.

Facing my fate, one thought outweighed all others, one statement kept playing over in my head: if you want to play, you gotta pay. But what was the price? Had I missed something along the way? Where had I failed to fill that void? What was the price for dreaming?

Then it hit me like I had just fallen through the hull of the plane and was free-falling to my death. A cold sweat came over me, and I became anxious. I looked down at the handcuffs and realized the price. This action against me was insignificant, perhaps negligible in the scheme of things. The price of such an overzealous, corruptible Justice Department that allowed itself to be purchased by private entities would mean the disillusionment of the creators of commerce in this country. The price was the very fiber that separated this country from other oppressed third world countries. This inflated price, if left unchecked, would sell for cheap the very heart of America. It was a defeating feeling, that we were *for sale.*

If we fail to be the land of opportunity, the land to dream, the land to innovate, then what have we become? If justice becomes something other than what the Constitution prescribes, then what is the purpose of our government? The price? It was not just my freedom but the collective failure of our highest ideals. This was not just an attack on Kelco; it was an attack on the American way of life, the American dream. If it can happen to me, it can happen to you.

The price...is all of us.

EPILOGUE
DAYS, MONTHS AND YEARS

I remember vividly having been met by U.S. Marshals at the Miami Airport when I landed from Panama, quickly shackled in leg and wrist irons attached to a chain wrapped around my waist. The Marshals escorted me through the airport. My clanking chains drew attention, and people looked at me like I had the plague, steering clear of the spectacle I had become. I entered the basement of the Miami Federal Correction Facility and was ordered to strip naked as I awaited a green jumpsuit and a bedroll. I joked to the intake officer as he processed me for intake into the prison system and asked what his job entailed.

He responded, "My job is to keep you alive."

Being a new inmate, his words were a rude awakening to my new reality. To survive would also be my job for the next nine years.

While incarcerated, I gravitated to religious groups and learned about seemingly every culture that existed, sharing cells with people from all walks of life. With all our worldly belongings stripped away, it became apparent how equal we all are in creation. It was then that I began to appreciate humankind truly and how the different circumstances of all races and cultures could bring us together. I learned something of the struggles marginalized populations and races bear, experiencing personally what oppression felt like and looked like.

My family used to say that they were locked up with me. There's a lot of truth to that. I was housed in Lexington, Kentucky, at the Federal Medical Center. My family was able to visit me, usually once a week, and my kids visited once a month, over a weekend. The visits were stoic encounters. We sat in a designated area with plastic chairs and a tiny knee-high table. The visitors' process to pass security checks at the barbed wire prison gates was often inhumane, leaving the visitors out in the rain or frigid, snowy conditions for extended periods until they were processed into the building by the guards. My mother became depressed after realizing that no appeal was going to be heard to reduce my sentence and that every motion we filed in the Federal Court system seemed to result in no relief. Her health suffered, and she had severe complications later in life that resulted in her demise. My children endured the long trips from Michigan, where they lived with their mom, and trudged through the long waits outside the visiting room to see me. This went on for nearly nine years. Despite feeling guilt for dragging them through that demoralizing process, I was deeply thankful for the opportunity to see them. If it wasn't for those visits, they would never have known their father during childhood. I learned that we could get acclimated to just about any conditions thrown at us. Humankind are adaptable creatures.

I tried to surround myself with other guys in for white-collar crimes and some smart folks from different backgrounds. I tried to use my time to educate myself in studies that I never had time for while running Kelco. I studied Spanish and got my paralegal certificate. The Federal prison system offered little in the form of education beyond a GED. I did tutor other inmates and taught some financial literacy classes from time to time. I involved myself in religious studies as well. We had a great group of sharp guys, and we encouraged one another daily. It's hard to get discouraged when your buddies are making you look up.

The impact the case against Kelco has had on me now serves as a constant reinforcement of the idea that there are no second chances in life. Credit card companies suddenly cancel cards. Stock brokerages close my accounts without notice. Banks have closed my accounts, stating that I am a threat to the bank; Chase, your whole lot strikes me as cowards. Such treatment is undoubtedly due to the money laundering charge associated with the "mail fraud" leveled against Kelco. The impact of being a convicted felon in America haunts me every day. Every day I wake up not knowing if something beyond my control will dramatically shift my finances.

Tammy divorced me two years into my sentence. Shortly after, I learned she was pregnant. This was a very painful pill to swallow in the joint. It wasn't like you could run down to the local pub and have a beer to get your mind off it. I had to see it through completely sober eyes. However, getting to see my kids overshadowed any other emotions at that time. I never chastised Tammy because it was a situation that none of us should have experienced. I wasn't in her shoes, and she wasn't in mine. As long as she brought the kids to see me, I was grateful.

Thankfully, since my time in prison, I have been able to get back on my feet somewhat, and I still have that entrepreneurial fire. I currently consult for corporations in the Life Settlement industry who were once my competitors or allies during the Kelco years. My life beyond prison with the kids has been so rewarding. I was able to take them on a few once-in-a-lifetime trips to Alaska and Florida, where we made memories that I will always cherish. It didn't make up for the time that I was gone, but any time we can share means the world to me. The kids turned out amazing. I am so proud and so thankful for them.

Surprisingly, my family and I grew closer than ever through the hardship we shared. It was a bond stronger than we ever had before. They championed my freedom and tried everything imaginable to free me from that hellhole. Nothing worked. However, they rallied and were there for me, and for that, I am eternally grateful. I got to see the kids through high school and see them both graduate. I am thankful every day I wake up and so thankful for all I have. I can honestly say that I am not in the least bothered by people who have more than me; instead, I often worry for them, thinking of the price they might be paying. As I get older, simpler is better for me.

My mom used to say the bright side of my incarceration is that it might have saved my life. In prison, I got in the best shape of my entire life. The lifestyle there was the antithesis of my prior lifestyle, and I still carry those lessons today, conscious of my diet and exercise. I am now remarried to a girl from my hometown of West Liberty. She was a freshman cheerleader when I was a senior in high school, and she often reminds me that I would not give her the time of day, didn't even acknowledge her existence, never knowing she had a serious crush on me. Now, I'm the one with the crush. Before we married, dating someone who knew me from years back, knew my family, and was not judgmental of my incarceration was helpful. With such a background, not only is it hard to maintain financial accounts, but it's often detrimental to relationships. Sharing life with Norma Keller has been a Godsend.

I must also admit that the toll of this whole experience has challenged my mental health. I am an advocate of serving one's mental health, and I have been in therapy for quite some time. I was diagnosed as suffering from PTSD and other symptoms from this experience, and the road to recovery has been long. Every day has its ups and downs, and still, my world seems far from normal. However, in today's world of uncertainty, oddly, I seem to fit in better.

I originally wrote this book some ten years ago so that my children would one day know the truth. I wrote it so that the sacrifice we all made might somehow make a difference in this crazy, ever-shifting world. I wrote it seeking reform in D.C., hoping that transparency and honesty would someday prevail and the underhanded practices of Corporate America pimping out our politicians might become a thing of the past. As of this writing – not much has changed. I wrote it to advocate to business professionals to maintain balance and embrace what's most important in their lives. It's so easy to lose oneself with the allure of power and money and corporate titles. I have learned that nothing is more important than family. If we fail to grasp that and don't hold onto that treasure, we are personally bankrupt.

There's not a day that goes by that I don't think of my surrogate family at Kelco. We all were affected by this travesty. It will forever be a part of us. We move on, but we never forget. Our group had invested their lives in our shared dream and their personal dreams that were shattered. I love them all, and they were one of the most essential parts of my life. I am proud of all of them to this day. We achieved something that very few people will ever know. We might have scars, but we raise our heads high because we know what we accomplished. We know how special this group was. I am also grateful for many of these folks that supported me while I was going through the worst experience in my life. If I could have free rein and my core group back at the helm, we would lead the whole industry once again. There is no doubt in my mind. This was absolutely the dream team in Corporate America.

I remain in contact with Keith Drach, who successfully fought off COVID-19. His wife Susan recently had a heart transplant, and both are healthy and well. They continue to face challenges and courageously persevere. Though I, at times, feel a guilt for the ways Keith suffered from this ordeal, I choose to focus on how grateful I am to still have him as a friend. Keith continues to be an inspiration. I have not kept in contact with Grant. However, I hold no animosity to any actions he felt led to take to free himself from this injustice. None of us should have had to go through this to begin with. Grant Sutherlin took over his father's flight school and aircraft sales business in 2003. He has been successful with some 30 specialized employees. Grant still resides in Lexington, Kentucky.

I hold no animosity or hate for anyone portrayed adversely in the book. Many government folks were merely played by large corporate powers and didn't really understand all the elements involved. The system is broken, and without proper accountability, there can be no fixing a system with a design flaw. Playing by rules that hurt people and devastate lives doesn't seem right, but it's the people setting the rules that are the real problem. I believe we must address the fundamental source of the problem – the limitless money polluting Capitol Hill. We must place term limits on lifelong, career politicians, and we must reform the lobbying system. We also cannot continue to incentivize the prosecution of Americans; we cannot support a system that rewards law enforcement for so many speeding tickets per month, so many arrests per year, so many forfeitures, and so on. I can assure you that our forefathers never set up the judicial system with a profit motive in mind. We the people are not a commodity. Our worth is inherent, and united by a shared vision of genuine equality for all, we are powerful.

THANK YOU

I wrote this book with my children in mind so they may someday know the absolute truth. They were my drive to get through this and kept me enduring these long years, and somehow, they had a way of giving me the strength to keep going. I love you, Cole and Sydney Keller. What beautiful souls you are and what blessings you have been.

To the many employees who devoted their lives to Kelco, I can't imagine having gone through this ordeal without feeling pride in our endeavors and without the liberty of conscience I feel, knowing the truth of our intentions. There's not a day that goes by that I don't think about you and what could have been.

A special thanks to the many people who tirelessly worked on this case and supported me throughout the years. Along the way, I witnessed many who have since passed. I want to give special recognition to my father, John E. Keller (1925–2013), and my mother, Betty J. Keller (1930–2018). They never missed a ball game throughout my childhood, nor a visit during my incarceration. They are the best parents ever, heroes in my world, and I love and miss them dearly.

I also thank an unlikely ally, Gloria Grening Wolk (1933–2012), the consumer advocate and watchdog for the industry who championed my case and innocence for many years and became a good friend and pen pal. She was a brilliant woman and carried a thoughtful heart.

To my brother, Tim Keller, thank you for converting the original handwritten pages into a word processor and for your generosity in helping so many others connected to this case. To my sister, Liz Woods, who spent untold hours working with Gloria and traveling many miles to interview people and uncover the truth. Your relentless pursuit of my freedom is a blessing. To my niece, Kristin Keller Allen, who assisted me with legal documents, the manuscript, and anything that needed to be done. Thank you.

I would also like to thank my other immediate family for their many prayers and visits over the years: Rich and Nicole Woods, Justin and Erica Perry, Richard L. Woods, and John and Jenny Wells. I feel blessed beyond what I deserve to have such a wonderful family.

To my friend Wade Larson you're like a brother to me, and a true friend.

A heartfelt thank you to Senator Tom Buford (1949–2021), who not only offered his support but also friendship, and to Governor John Y. Brown (1933–2022) for his support, visits, and efforts on my behalf.

To my good friend Rick Rader, thank you for all the support you've given me and my kids. To Erin Johnson, for your friendship and constant support of the family. To Mitchell Cain, who has walked many roads with me – we're on a better one now. To Bob and Kathy Allen, who found time to visit and offer support – you're the best. To others who visited and encouraged me, including Kara Carpenter, Deanna Hill, and Jan Hatfield, thank you sincerely. If I've left anyone out, it's not intentional but no less heartfelt.

A special thank you to Tammy Keller, for enduring a six-hour trip one way to keep my relationship with my kids alive over eight and a half years. That is an irreplaceable gift, and I am forever grateful.

I also have deep appreciation for my editor and publisher, Charles "Chas" Allen. He is the one who inspired me to write this book. Through countless hours walking the track, thousands of conversations, and multiple drafts, Pay to Play was shaped. Chas is not only my editor and publisher, but also a great friend and business associate. Likewise, the edits made by David Buchanan significantly improved this manuscript. Thank you, David, for your attention to detail and for honoring my intended expression.

To all the people who wrote to me, visited, and helped where they could each of you was a beacon of hope in a very dark place. Thank you.

Finally, to my wife, Norma Keller. She entered my life during a season of deep brokenness and walked with me through some of its most difficult chapters. While our journey has not been without struggle, I remain grateful for the support and encouragement she gave me as I pursued this book and worked to rebuild my life after incarceration.